CW01190845

SAFARI CUISINE

ANDRES BIFANI

Published by Location Africa Films Ltd
P O Box 76677 – 00508 Nairobi, Kenya
Telephone: +254 Ø20 434 8280 – Fax: + 254 Ø20 434 8892
E-mail: africafilms@africaonline.co.ke
Websites: www.locationafricafilms.com & www.locationafricasafaris.com

Design & Layout: Andres Bifani
Photographs: © Andres Bifani
Food Styling & Recipes: Kiran Jethwa
Copy Editing/Proof-reading: Gordon Boy

Production Team: Andres Bifani & Lorraine Karuku
Photographic Coordination & Props: Lorraine Karuku
Layout & Design: Gerald Wanjala, Charles Lenjo, Lamodius Mutuku
Food Styling Assistant: Ken Kalunje
Additional photography (Chapter 2): Courtesy Matias Bifani, Lorraine Karuku, Bjorn Forslind

ISBN 978-9966-1528-0-0

Copyrights © 2011 Andres Bifani
Copyrights © Design, photographs and text Andres Bifani. All rights reserved.
No part of this publication may be reproduced, stored in a retrieval system
or transmitted in any form or by any means, electronic, mechanical,
photocopying, recording or otherwise, without the prior written permission
of the author and/or the publisher.

Printed by:
Gold Printing Group
www.goldprinting.cc

Contents

SIMEX LEWA
RHINO CHARGE 1
SAFARICOM MARATHON
ABERDARES
SAMBURU
SHOMPOLE
TROUT TREE
LOISIJO
RHINO CHARGE 2
MASAI MARA
SOUTH COAST
LAMU

SAFARI CUISINE
Menus

CHAPTER 1 – SIMEX LEWA

Tartlet of tea-smoked kole kole with crab and chive mayonnaise
Honey-roasted duck with cabbage and smoked bacon and maple gravy
Malt whisky semi-fredo with figs and espresso syrup and toasted pistachios

Carpaccio of seared ostrich with caramelised button mushrooms, roasted black pepper and minted horseradish cream
Honey-braised pork belly served on a bed of parsnip and spud mash with an apple calvados sauce
Kiwi and vanilla panacotta with lightly poached lime syrup

CHAPTER 2 – RHINO CHARGE 1

Terrine of ham hock with mustard butter, pickled cabbage and toasted brioche
Herb-crusted rack of slow-cooked Molo lamb, with crushed minted garden peas and rosemary jus
Steamed vanilla sponge with sticky macadamia and date syrup

CHAPTER 3 – SAFARICOM MARATHON

Set Menu

CHAPTER 4 – ABERDARES

Home-cured trout with onion and thyme confit and pancetta
Poikje-braised lamb shanks with lemon and parsley gremolata, borlotti beans, roasted garlic and thyme
Vanilla cheesecake with dark chocolate base and strawberry coulis

Roast butternut soup with nutmeg and hazelnut essence
Whole roast loin of pork on the bone with pan-roasted tomatoes, tomato fondue and creamed spinach
Double chocolate tarts with frozen muscavado and nutmeg cream

CHAPTER 5 – SAMBURU

Duet of rabbit pie with fennel mash, spring onions and rich orange jus
Pot-roast chicken with sausage stuffing and caramelised parsnips and sautéed kale
Lemon tart with caramelised goat cheese and crème anglaise

CHAPTER 6 – SHOMPOLE

Poached salt beef with potato croutons, rocket and mustard butter
Tandoori-baked quail with onion strings and cucumber and yoghurt salsa with roasted cumin
Triple chocolate mousse

CHAPTER 7 – TROUT TREE

Set Menu

CHAPTER 8 – LOISIIJO

Seared chicken liver with horseradish, port cream and crisp belly of pork
Poached loin of gammon with cauliflower gratin au gruyère with citrus braised pok choi
Berry-crowned pudding with port syrup

CHAPTER 9 – RHINO CHARGE 2

Black forest ham with grilled asparagus, quail eggs and paprika hollandaise
Slow-roasted rib of beef with roast onion and garlic purée
Pineapple upside-down cake with vanilla ice-cream

CHAPTER 10 – MASAI MARA

Fresh beetroot and asparagus salad with cumin-crusted haloumi and balsamic syrup
Fillet of beef with bubble and squeak, fine beans and gorgonzola cream jus
Gooseberry crumble with oat and cinnamon crust and ginger custard

CHAPTER 11 – SOUTH COAST

Artichoke vol au vent with smoked aubergine lemon and parsley
Swahili seafood curry with roasted coconut and cumin-steamed jasmine rice
English trifle with amarula cream and raspberry cointreau jelly and candied cashew nuts

CHAPTER 12 – LAMU

Chana-stuffed sweet peppers with a fresh tomato and coriander chutney
BBQ'd lobster with a smoked sweet pepper and chili marinade, a lemon and basil beurre blanc and polenta chips
Pear and frangipane tart with clotted cream

14 Tarlet of tea-smoked kole kole with crab and chive mayonnaise

83 Roast butternut soup with nutmeg and hazelnut essence

27 Carpaccio of seared ostrich with caramelised button mushrooms, roasted black pepper and minted horseradish cream

97 Duet of rabbit pie with fennel mash, spring onions and rich orange jus

41 Terrine of ham hock with mustard butter, pickled cabbage and toasted brioche

110 Poached salt beef with potato croutons, rocket and mustard butter

69 Home-cured trout with onion and thyme confit and pancetta

127 Seared chicken liver with horse-radish, port cream and crisp belly of pork

STARTERS

143

Black forest ham with grilled asparagus, quail eggs and paprika hollandaise

159

Fresh beetroot and asparagus salad with cumin-crusted haloumi and balsamic syrup

179

Artichoke vol au vent with smoked aubergine lemon and parsley

195

Chana-stuffed sweet peppers with a fresh tomato and coriander chutney

19 Honey-roasted duck with cabbage and smoked bacon and maple gravy

85 Whole roast loin of pork on the bone with pan-roasted tomatoes, tomato fondue and creamed spinach

31 Honey-braised pork belly served on a bed of parsnip and spud mash with an apple calvados sauce

101 Pot-roast chicken with sausage stuffing and caramelised parsnips and sautéed kale

45 Herb-crusted rack of slow-cooked Molo lamb, with crushed minted garden peas and rosemary jus

115 Tandoori-baked quail with onion strings and cucumber and yoghurt salsa with roasted cumin

73 Poikje-braised lamb shanks with lemon and parsley gremolata, borlotti beans, roasted garlic and thyme

131 Poached loin of gammon with cauliflower gratin au gruyère with citrus-braised pok choi

MAIN COURSES

147

Slow-roasted rib of beef with roast onion and garlic purée

167

Fillet of beef with bubble and squeak, fine beans and gorgonzola cream jus

183

Swahili seafood curry with roasted coconut and cumin-steamed jasmine rice

199

BBQ'd lobster with a smoked sweet pepper and chili marinade, a lemon and basil beurre blanc and polenta chips

23 Malt whisky semi-fredo with figs and espresso syrup and toasted pistachios

35 Kiwi and vanilla panacotta with lightly poached lime syrup

51 Steamed vanilla sponge with sticky macadamia and date syrup

79 Vanilla cheesecake with dark chocolate base and strawberry coulis

89 Double chocolate tarts with frozen muscavado and nutmeg cream

105 Lemon tart with caramelised goat cheese and crème anglaise

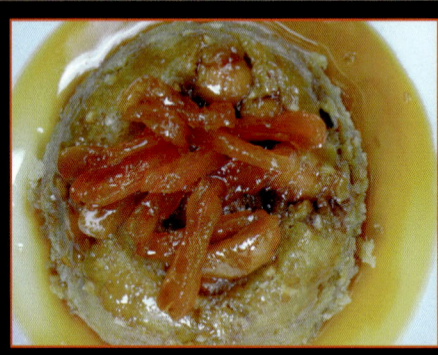

117 Triple chocolate mousse

135 Berry-crowned pudding with port syrup

DESSERTS

151

Pineapple upside-down cake with vanilla ice-cream

171

Gooseberry crumble with oat and cinnamon crust and ginger custard

187

English trifle with amarula cream and raspberry cointreau jelly and candied cashew nuts

203

Pear and frangipane tart with clotted cream

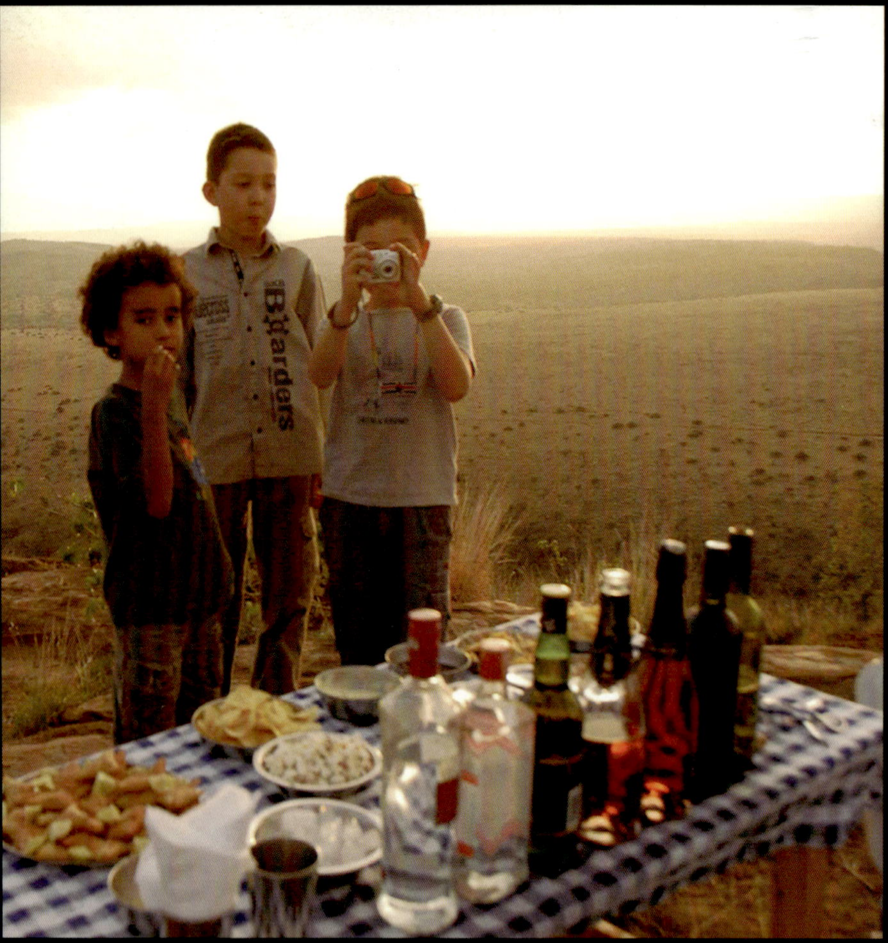

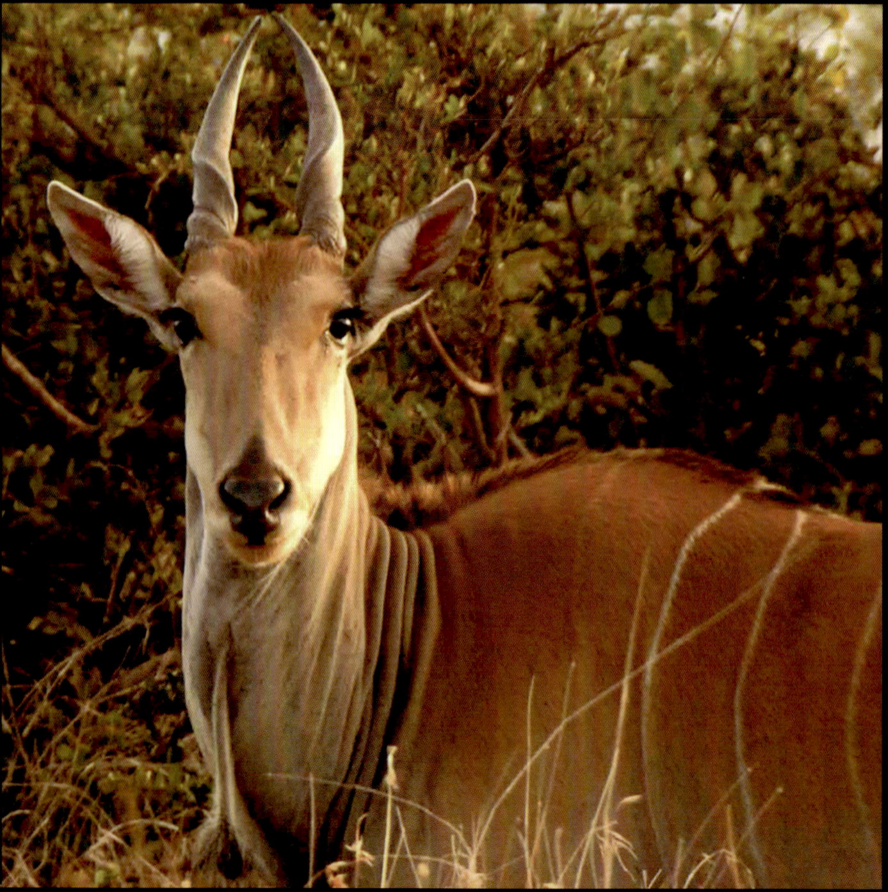

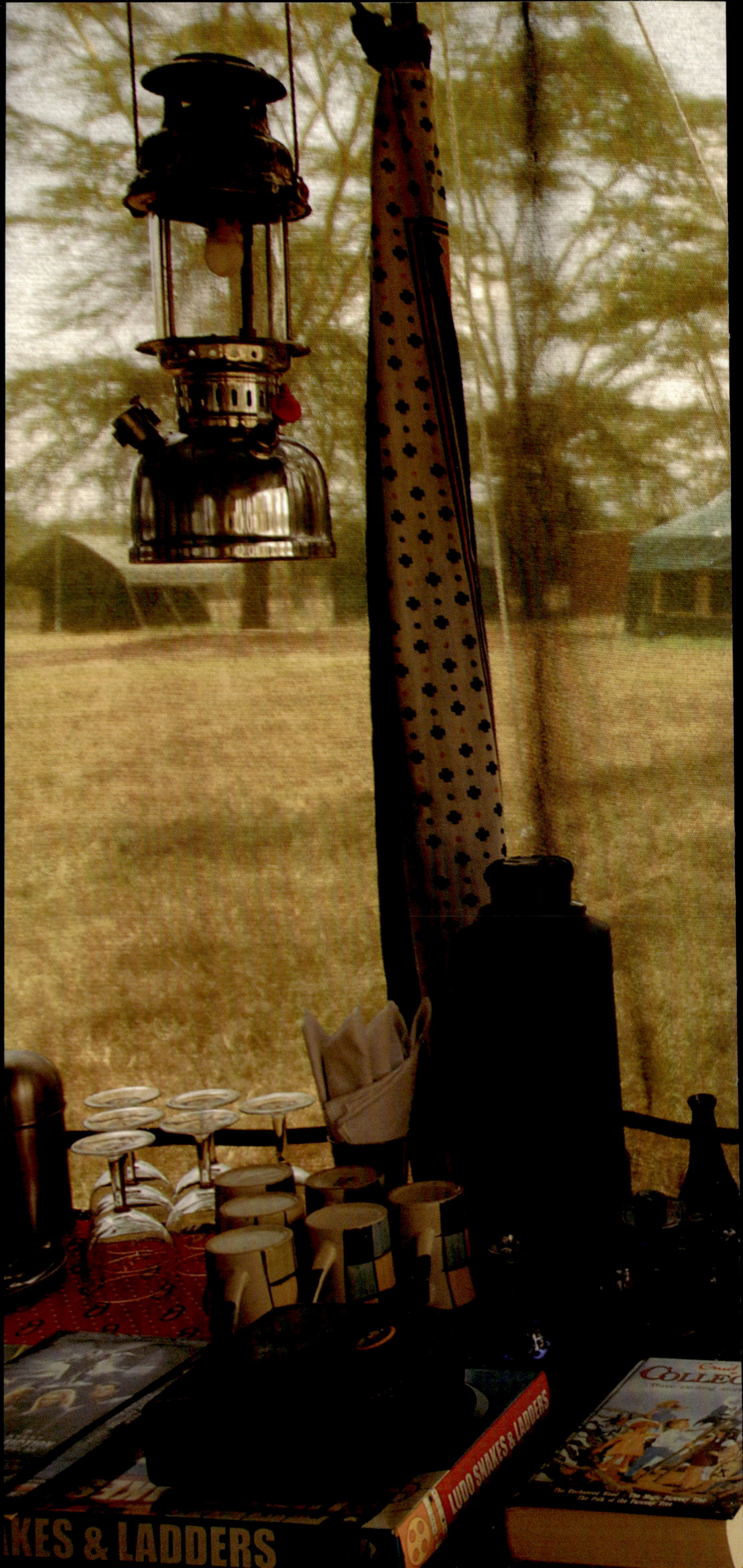

LUDO SNAKES & LADDERS
AKES & LADDERS

WILD EARTH AFRICA
LEWA WILDLIFE CONSERVANCY SIMEX 3D

Tartlet of tea-smoked kole kole with crab and chive mayonnaise

RECIPE

Serves 6 people

Bush Equipment
Basic smoker

Pre-prep
Tart cases, chive mayonnaise

Ingredients
for 1 fish:

- 2 tbsp tea leaves
- 5 tbsp plain rice
- 1 tbsp brown sugar

Method

1. Mix tea leaves, sugar and rice and place on a double layer of foil in a dry, clean wok.
2. Lightly oil a grilling rack and place over wok.
3. Place fish directly on to the rack and cover tightly with a lid, or seal with another layer of foil, winding a length of towel around the lid for extra insulation.
4. Turn heat to medium and 'smoke' for half an hour or until fish is done and smells aromatic. The fish can be prepared in advance, an hour or so before serving.

Ingredients
for the tartlet:

- 12 short-crust tart cases
- Chive mayonnaise
- Sliced smoked kole kole
- 200 g picked crab meat
- 20 ml olive oil
- Juice of 2 lemons

Method

1. Mix crab meat with olive oil and lemon, and season with salt and freshly ground pepper.
2. Spoon a healthy portion of mayonnaise into the tart cases
3. Spoon crab mixture on to this
4. Wrap the sliced fish around the crab
5. Garnish and serve

14 Safari Cuisine

SUBSIDIARY RECIPES

Short crust pastry tarts

Ingredients

- 1 mug plain flour
- Pinch of salt
- 2 tbsp cubed butter
- 2–3 tbsp cold water

Method

1. Put the flour and salt in a large bowl and add the cubes of butter.
2. With your fingertips rub the butter into the flour until you have a mixture resembling coarse bread crumbs.
3. Using a knife, stir in just enough cold water to bind the dough together.
4. Wrap the dough in cling film and chill for 10–15 minutes before using.

Chive mayonnaise

Ingredients

- 4 free-range egg yolks
- 2 tsp ready-prepared English mutard
- 1 tbsp white wine vinegar
- 570 ml/1 pint vegetable oil
- Sea salt

Method

1. Place the egg yolks in a large, clean bowl.
2. Add the mustard and vinegar. Whisk with a balloon whisk to blend.
3. Add a very small amount of oil and whisk until blended in. Add a bit more oil and whisk again.
4. Continue adding oil, whisking thoroughly between each addition, until the sauce emulsifies and thickens after a few minutes. Stop adding oil when the mayonnaise is of the desired consistency (you may not need to use all the oil). If the mayonnaise is too thick, thin with a little warm water.

Tips/Pointers

Kole Kole is a member of the Jack family and is a commonly eaten fish in East Africa. This recipe will work well with most oily fish such as Mackerel, Yellow Tail and Rock Cod. When preparing this dish, it is important to use freshly made mayonnaise. Adding chives to bought mayonnaise is a poor substitute for the fresh mayonnaise.

Wild Earth Africa

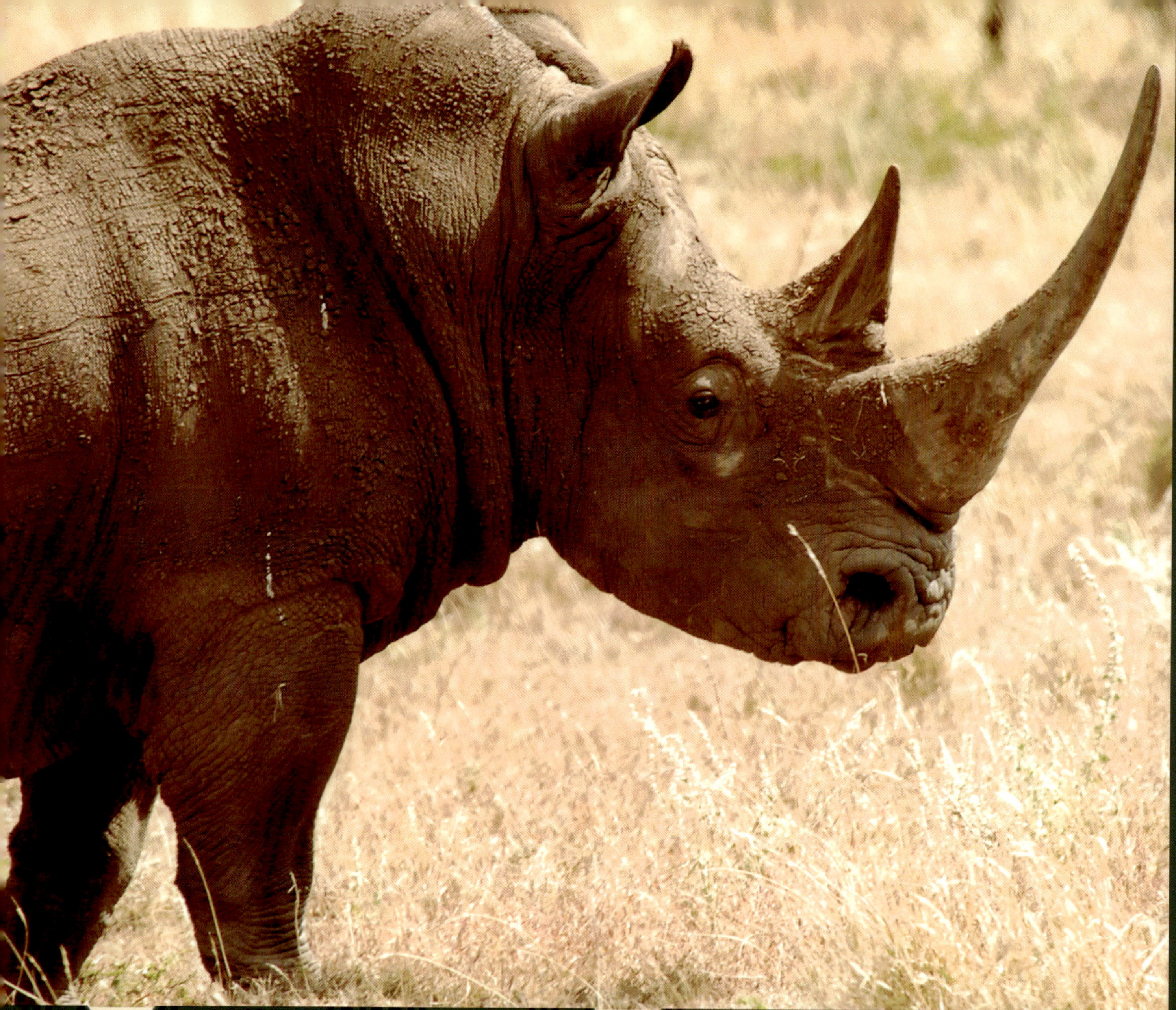

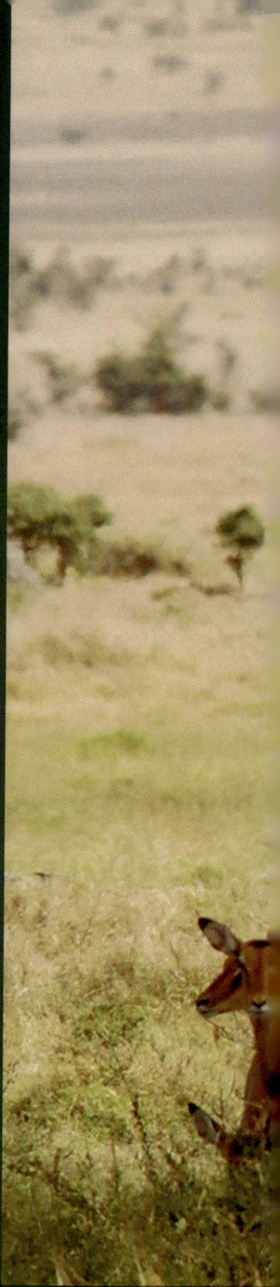

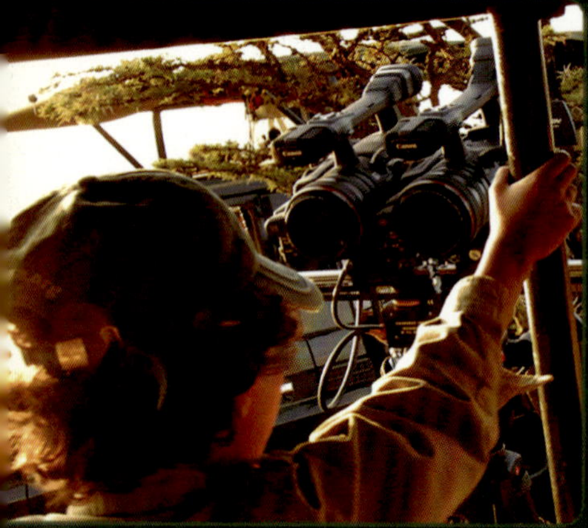

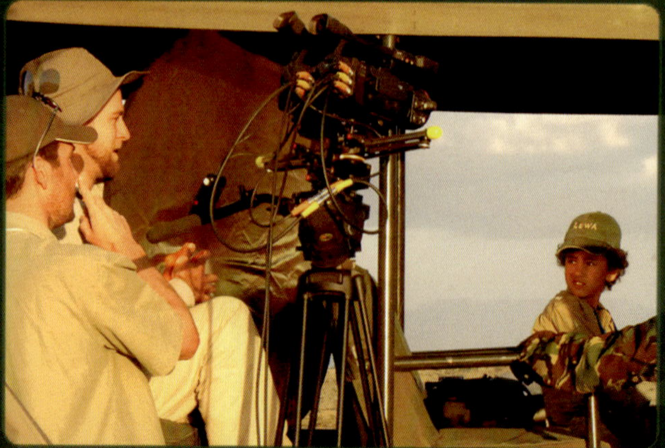

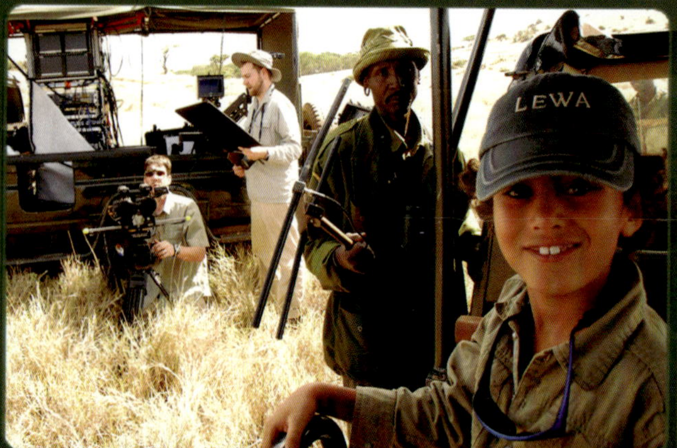
LEWA

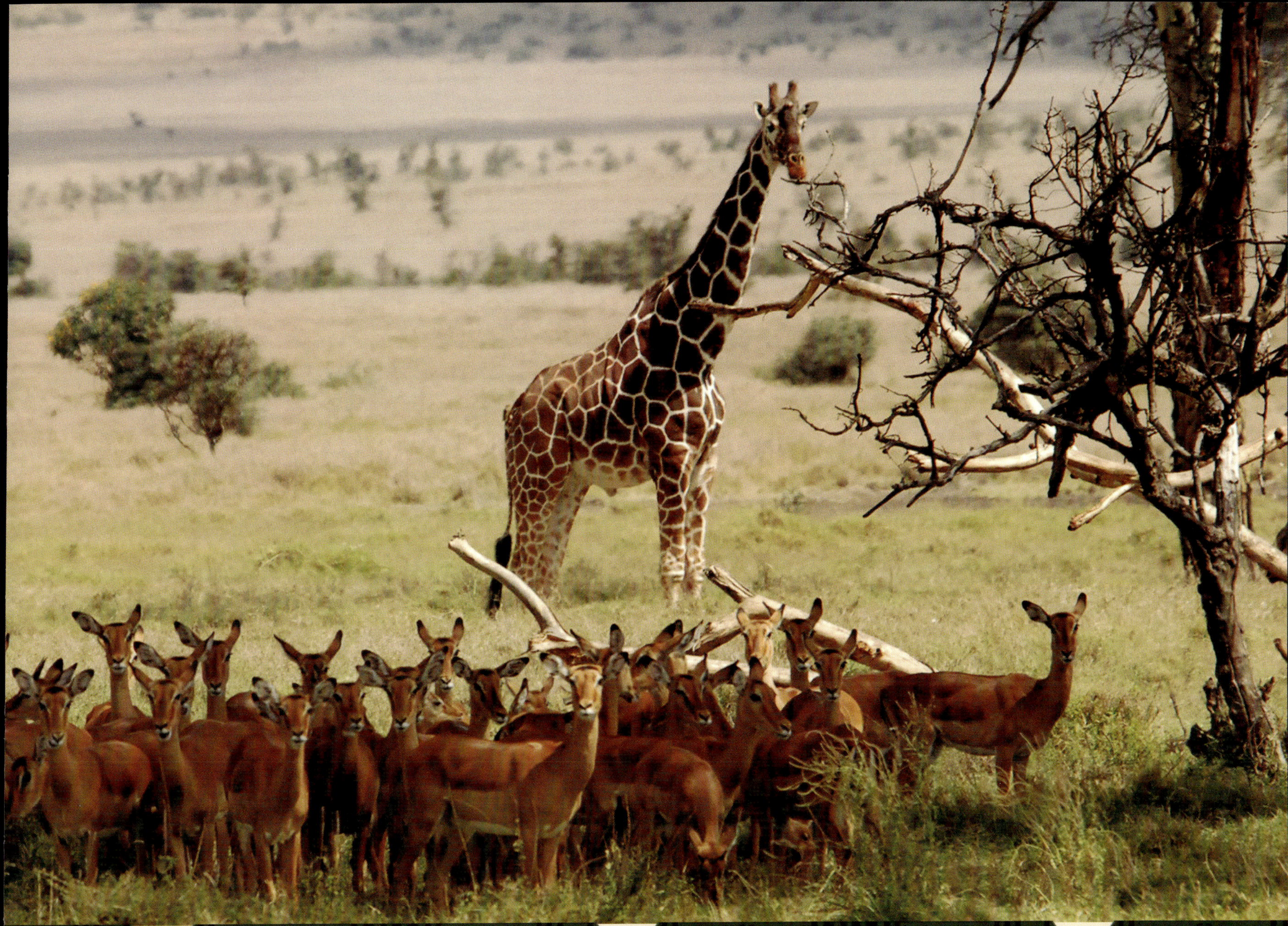

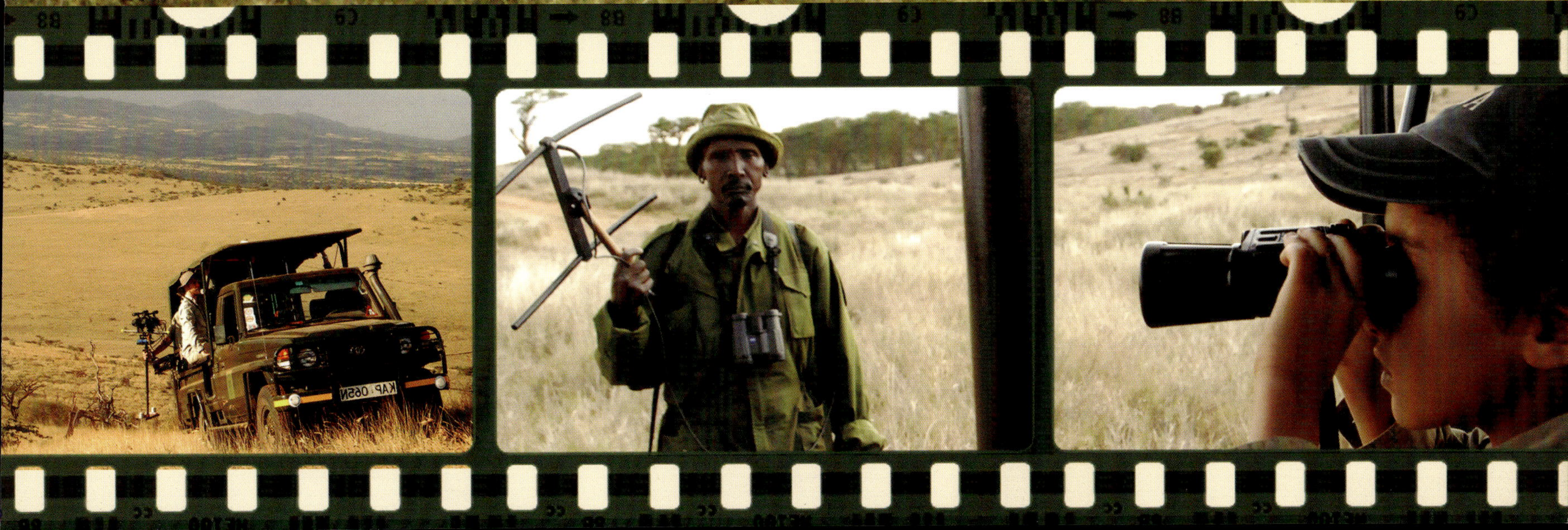

Safari Cuisine

Honey-roasted duck with cabbage and smoked bacon and maple gravy

RECIPE

Serves 4 people

Ingredients

- 4 large duck breasts
- 1 red cabbage shredded
- 1 handful of raisins
- 1 handful chopped apricots
- 1 tbsp white wine vinegar
- ½ a cup of orange juice
- 200 g smoked bacon
- 2 tbsp maple syrup
- Gravy *(see recipe)*

Method

1. Shred the red cabbage, discarding the hard stalk. Blanch in hot water until tender. Remove and drain.
2. In a saucepan, add the vinegar, orange juice, raisins and apricots. Boil and reduce the liquid by half.
3. Add the butter. Allow this to melt, and whisk gently to combine.
4. To this add the cabbage and set aside.
5. Score the duck breast fat in a criss-cross manner, being careful not to cut all the way through.
6. Place the duck, skin-side down, in a very hot frying pan, and cook until crispy and golden brown.
7. Turn the duck over. Deglaze with a splash of port, and place in the oven.
8. Cook the duck as desired (medium rare is recommended) and allow to rest for 5 minutes before serving. Do not discard juices from the pan, as these will be used for making the gravy.

Simple 'bush' gravy

Method

1. Keep all the juices and fat from the duck.
2. Place on the heat and begin to fry the diced bacon in this. De-glaze with red wine or port.
3. To this add 1 cup of water with a stock cube dissolved in it.
4. In a separate cup dissolve 1 tsp of corn flour in about 100 ml of milk. Whisk this into the boiling gravy until the desired thickness is achieved.
5. Stir in the maple syrup and test for seasoning.
6. Serve with duck and cabbage.

Tips/Pointers

Making gravy, or jus, in a professional kitchen is usually a 2–3 day process, undertaken on a large scale. The above recipe will, for any kind of meat, produce delicious gravy quickly and easily.

WILD EARTH AFRICA
LEWA WILDLIFE CONSERVANCY
SIMEX 3D

Tartlet of tea-smoked kole kole with crab and chive mayonnaise

Honey-roasted duck with cabbage, smoked bacon and maple gravy

Malt whisky semi-fredo with figs and espresso syrup and toasted pistachios

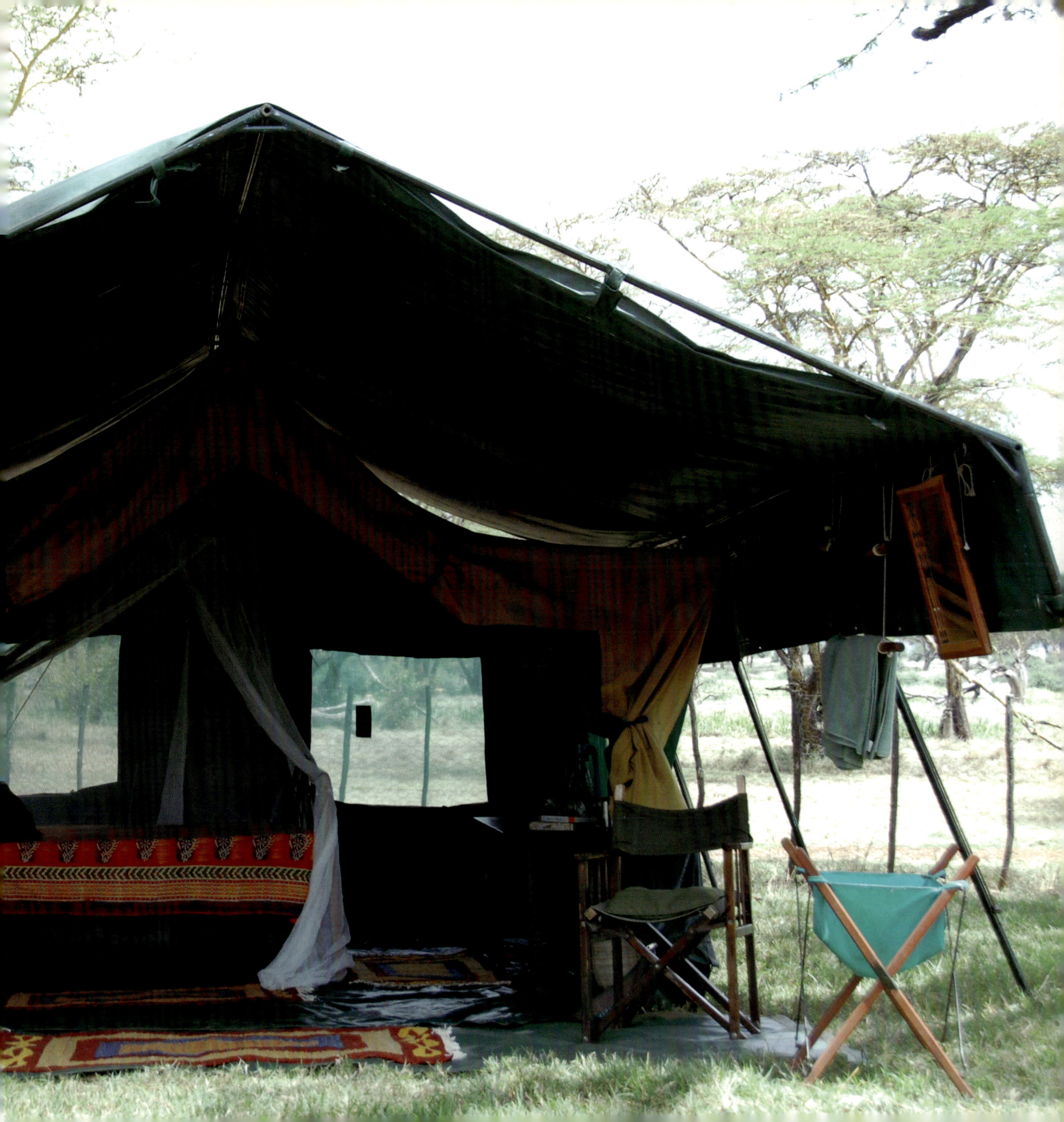

Malt whisky semi-fredo with figs and espresso syrup and toasted pistachios

RECIPE

Serves 6 people

Ingredients

- 5 cups cream
- 2 cups sugar
- 12 egg yolks
- 1 tsp vanilla extract
- 1 cup roughly chopped, toasted pistachios
- 2 tbsp malt whisky
- 4 shots espresso
- 1 tbsp muscavado syrup
- ½ cup of figs

Method

1. In a large bowl whisk the cream into medium peaks.
2. Add 1 cup of the sugar to the cream and continue to whisk until stiff peaks form. Turn the cream out into a large bowl.
3. Whisk the egg yolks and the remaining 1 cup of sugar. Whisk until the yolks are pale yellow and have tripled in volume.
4. Add the yolks to the whipped cream. Add the vanilla extract and begin to fold the yolks into the cream. Add the pistachios and the whisky, and turn the mixture out into a glass serving dish. Freeze overnight.
5. For the figs and espresso syrup, place the espresso and muscavado sugar in a saucepan and heat. Add the chopped figs and reduce the liquid until it is syrupy in texture.

To serve

Cut the semi-fredo into pieces of the desired size. Place individual pieces in a serving bowl and top with berries and chocolate sauce. Garnish with powdered sugar and a sprig of mint.

Tips/Pointers

Be sure to serve this dish immediately after slicing it, as it tends to melt quite quickly. Always use a knife dipped in hot water that will slice through easily without crushing the dessert.

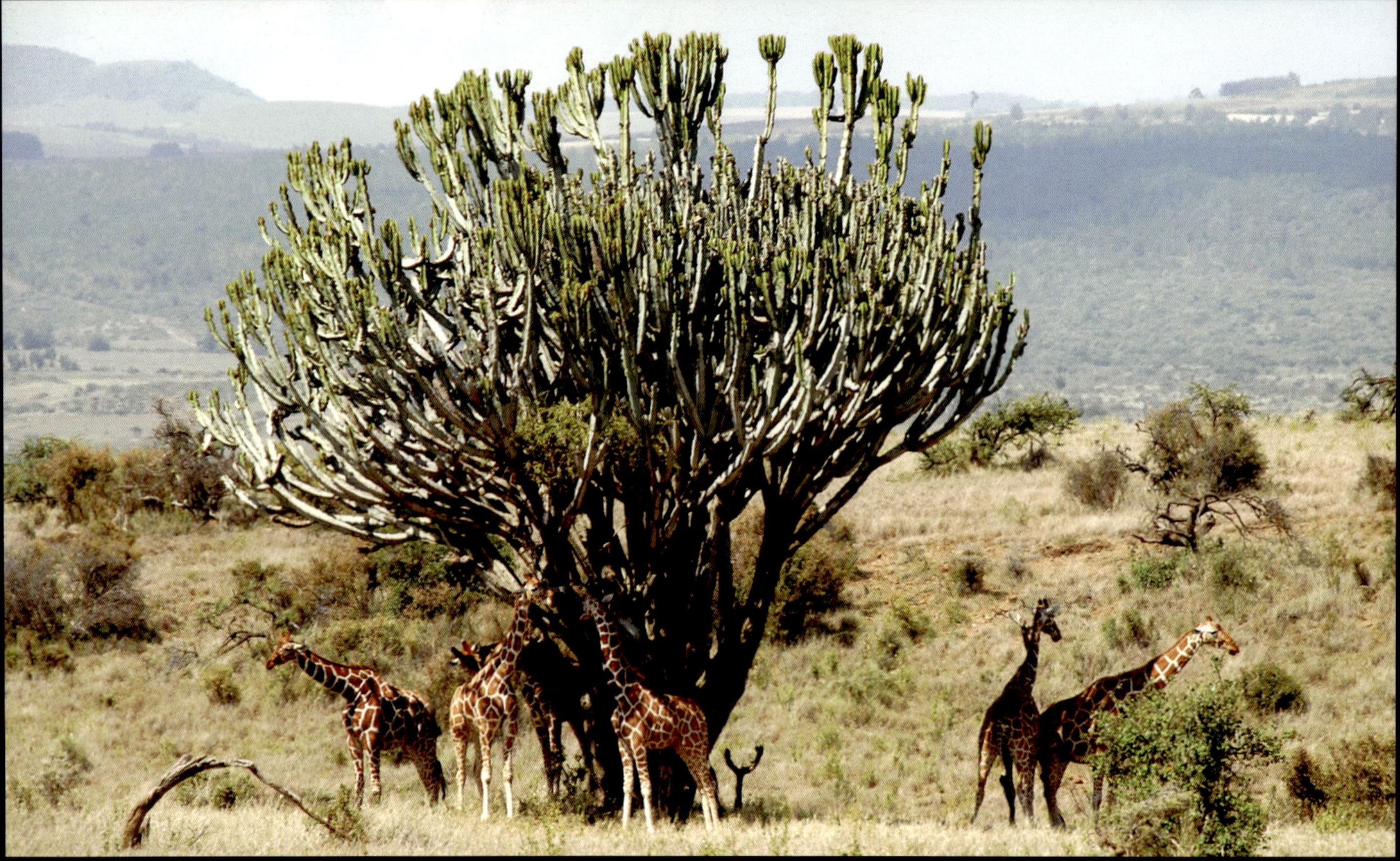
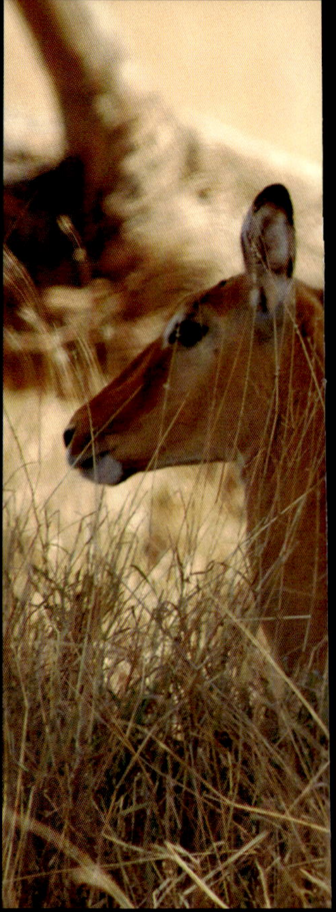
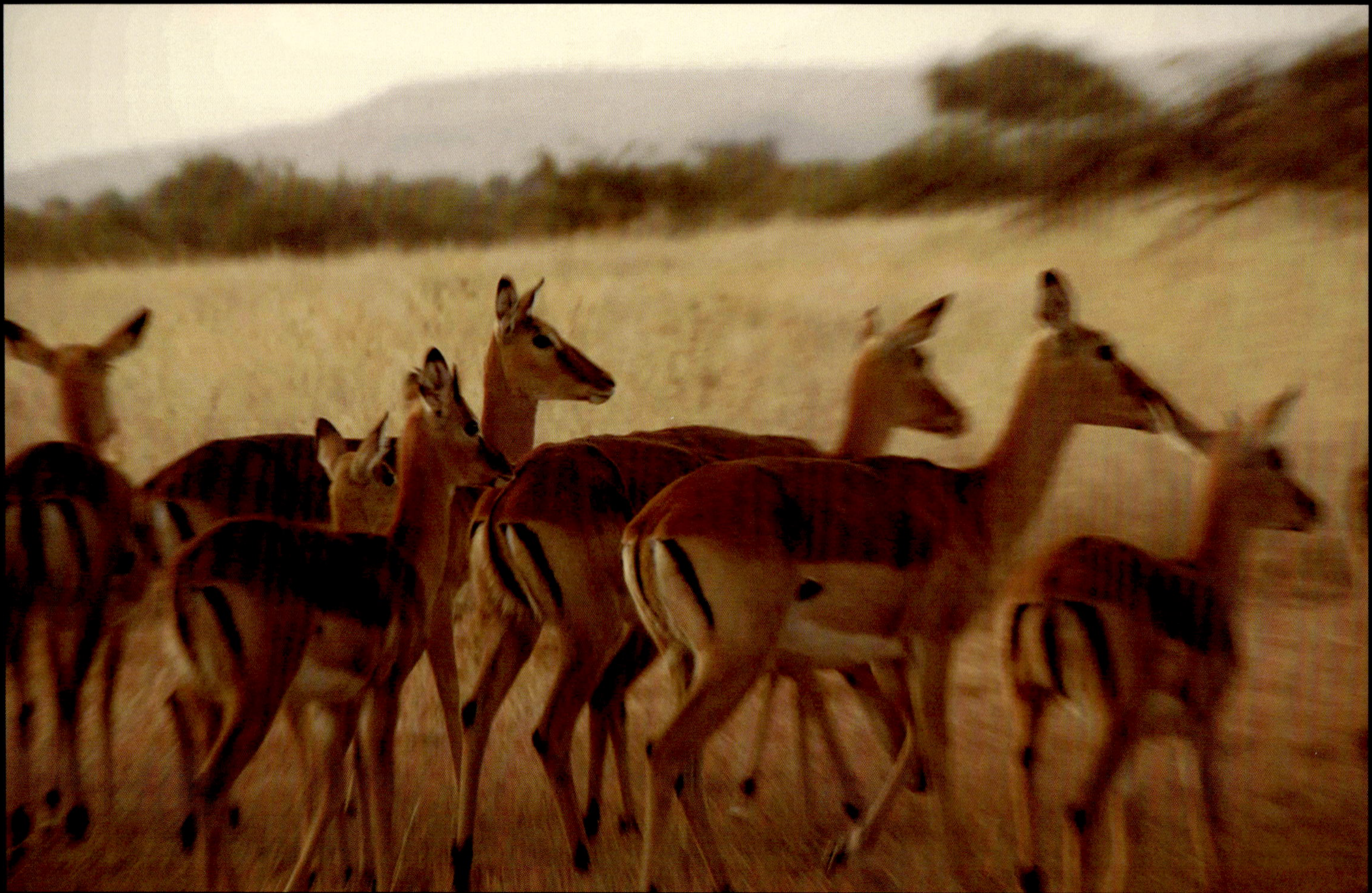
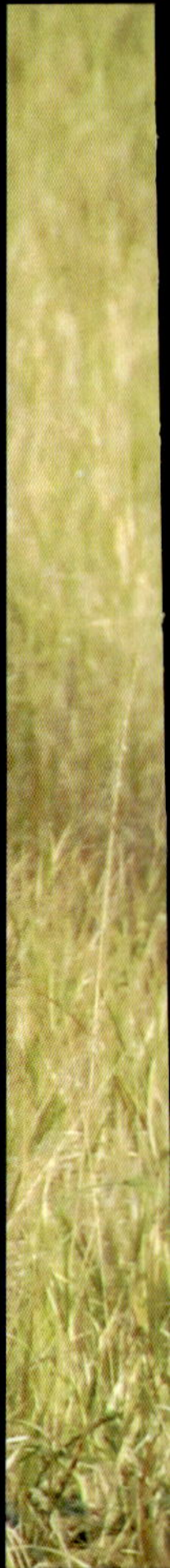

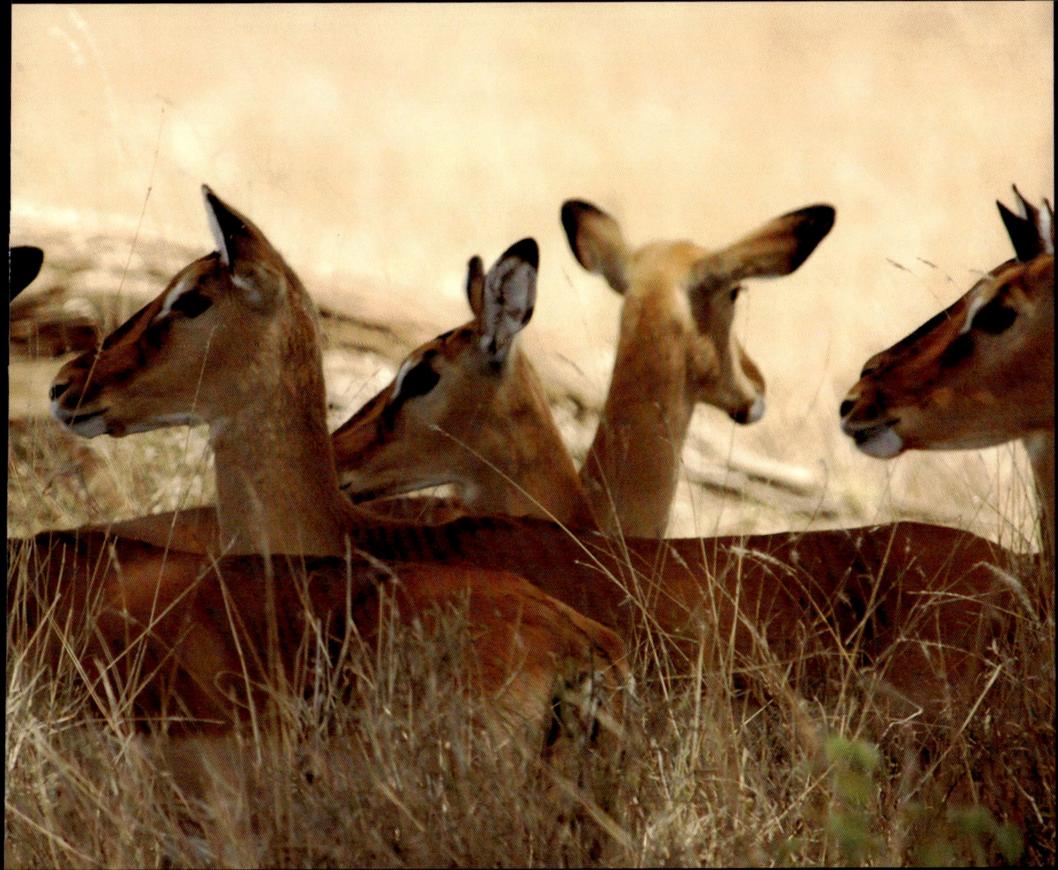
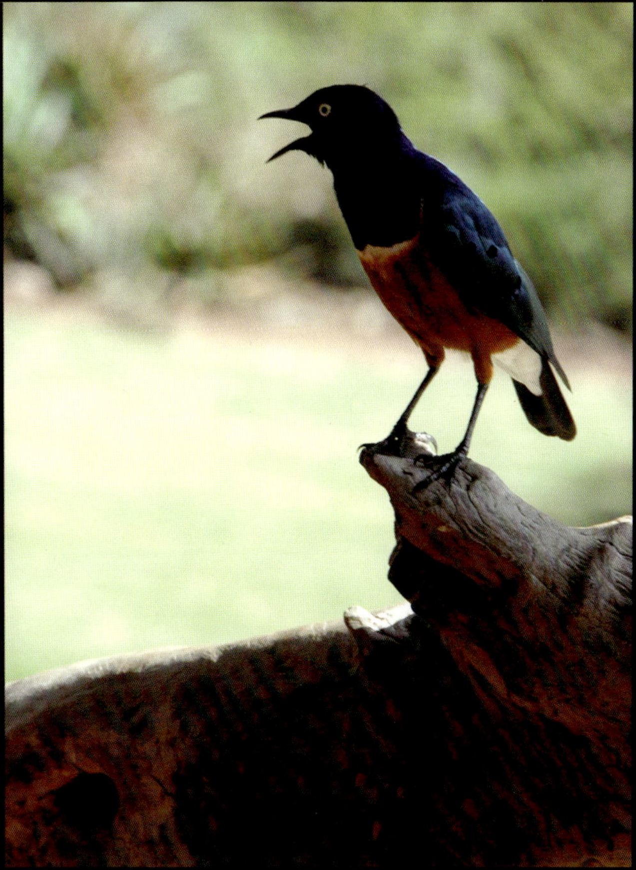
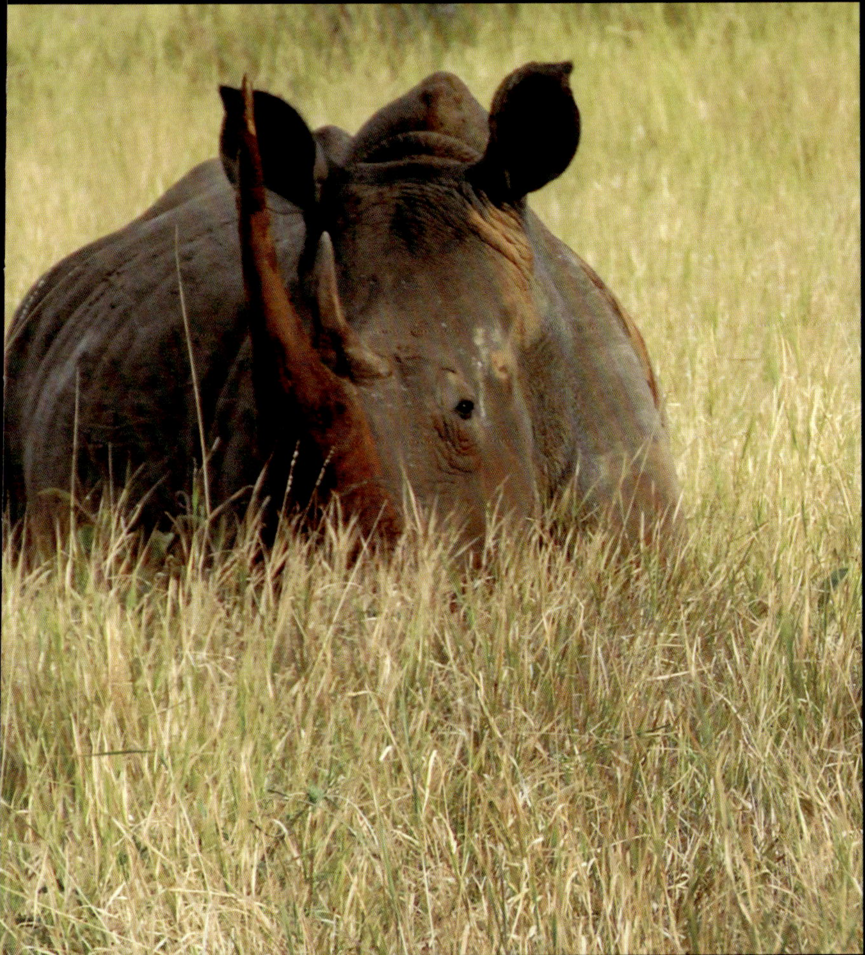
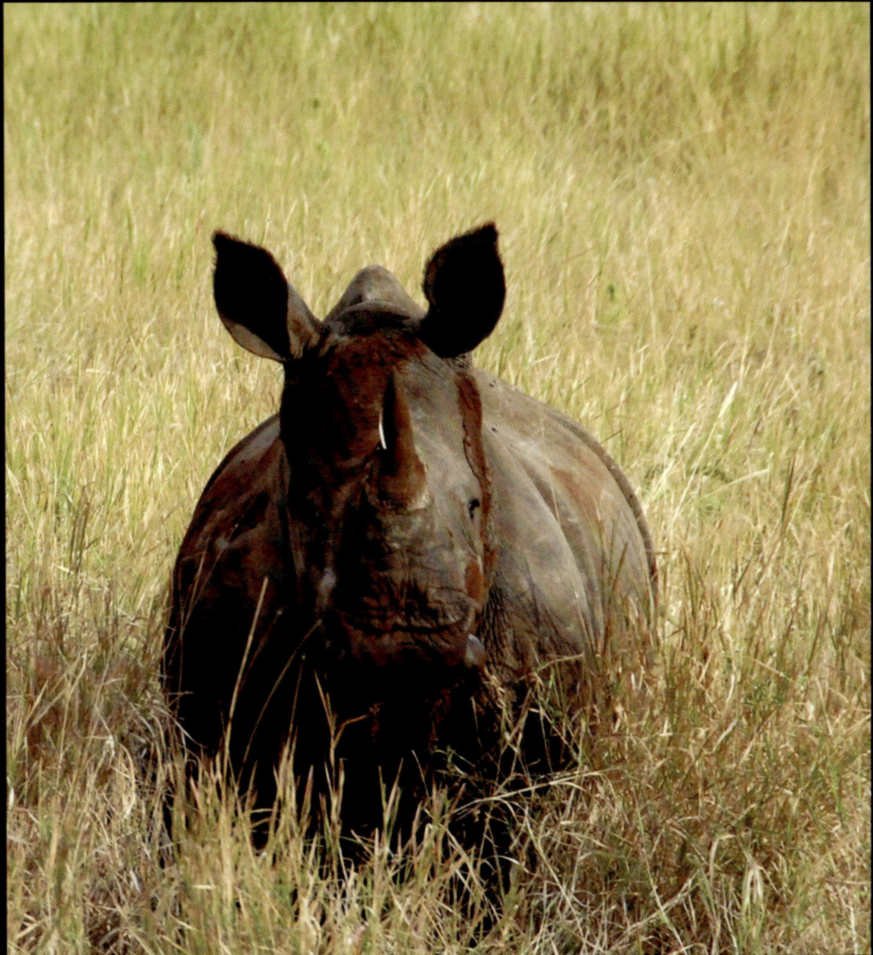

Carpaccio of seared ostrich with caramelised button mushrooms, roasted black peppe and minted horseradish cream

RECIPE

Serves 12 people

Ingredients

- 2 ostrich fillets
- 1 handful crushed black pepper
- 2 punets mushrooms
- 4 tbsp unrefined sugar
- 4 tbsp white wine vinegar
- 1 jar horseradish cream
- 1 bunch chopped mint
- 1 packet rocket or rucola
- A good drizzle of olive oil
- Sea salt

Method

1. Season ostrich fillets with salt. Then roll and cover completely with crushed black pepper.
2. In a hot pan, sear fillets on all sides for no more than 1 minute, so they are evenly caramelised on the outside, but reman rare in the middle.
3. Pour the vinegar into another hot pan. Add sugar and dissolve. Boil this mixture until the sugar begins to caramelise.
4. When the sugar is golden brown, throw in the cleaned mushrooms. Stir until all the mushrooms are covered in caramel, and set aside.
5. Wrap the ostrich fillet in cling film, in a tight roll. Then put in the freezer and allow to go hard.
6. With a very sharp knife slice the ostrich fillets into thin slices and arrange on a plate.
7. Season the ostrich with sea salt, and dress in a drizzle of olive oil.
8. Spoon the mushrooms over the meat, and add the rocket.
9. Add all the chopped mint to the creamed horseradish, and serve.

Tips/Pointers

Be sure to add the mint to the creamed horseradish just prior to serving. This will give you the full impact of this refreshing herb.

Wild Earth Africa

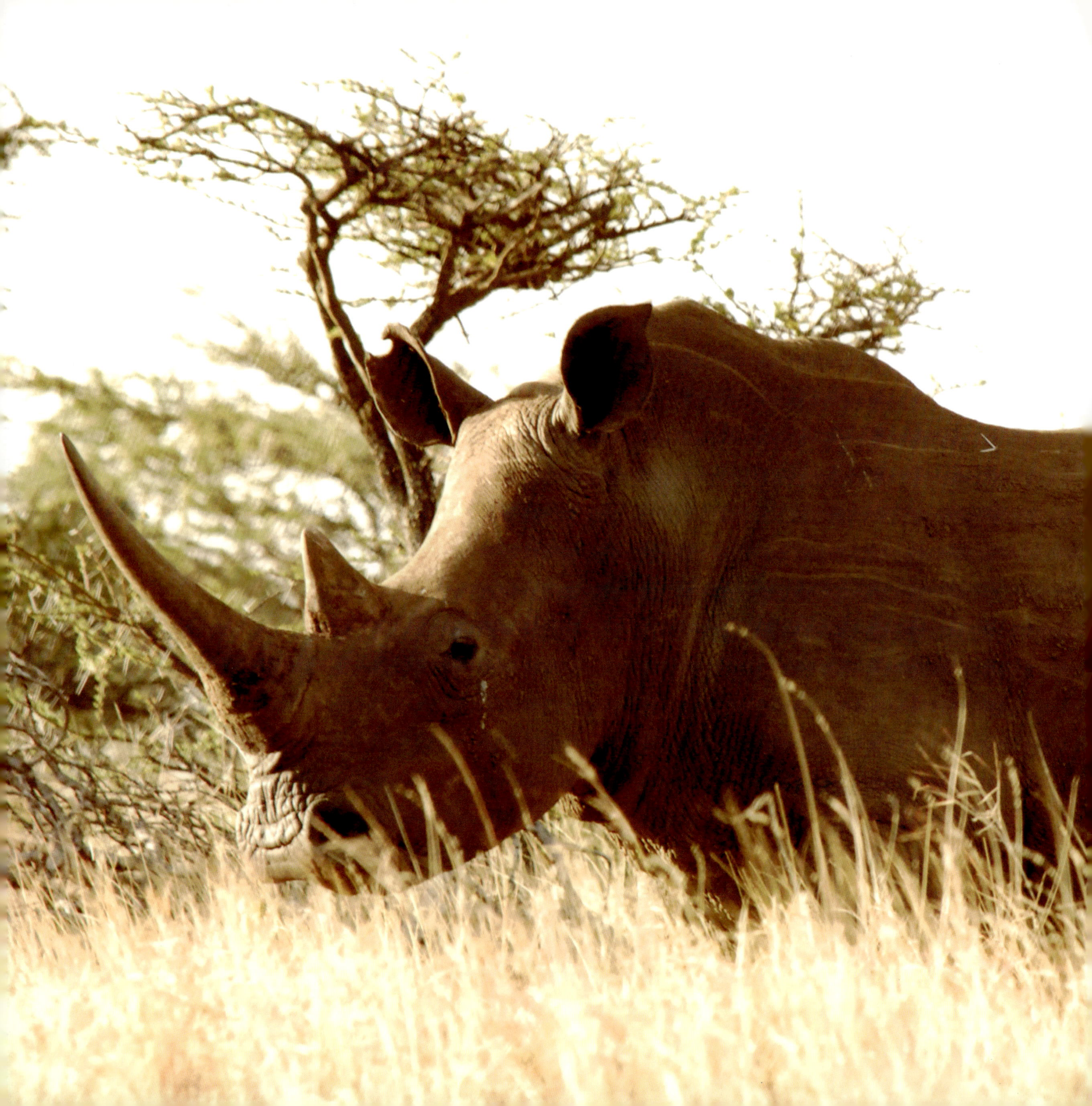

WILD EARTH AFRICA

LEWA WILDLIFE CONSERVANCY

SIMEX 3D

Carpaccio of seared ostrich with caramelised button mushrooms, roasted black pepper and minted horseradish cream

Honey-braised pork belly served on a bed of parsnip and spud mash with an apple calvados sauce

Kiwi and vanilla panacotta with lightly poached lime syrup

Honey-braised pork belly served on a bed of parsnip and spud mash with an apple calvados sauce

RECIPE

Serves 10 people

Ingredients

- 4 kg side of pork belly
- 2 tsp fennel seeds
- 4 tbsp honey
- 1 kg parsnips
- 2 tbsp butter
- 1 tsp fresh sage
- 1 cup double cream
- 2 cloves crushed garlic
- 2 tsp freshly cracked black pepper
- 1 kg baby potatoes
- 1 kg cooking apples cubed
- 100 ml calvados
- Gravy *(see recipe)*

Method

1. Score the pork belly, then rub with salt and pepper. Massage the honey into the skin, and sprinkle the fennel seeds on to this. Place in a very hot oven.
2. Roast for about half an hour until the skin of the pork puffs up and begins to turn into crackling. Turn the heat down to 180°C and roast for another hour.
3. Meanwhile, peel and chop the parsnips, and place in boiling water. Cook until tender.
4. Take the pork out of the oven, and baste with the fat from the bottom of the tray. Keep the juices and fat as gravy for making the sauce.
5. Take the whole new potatoes (unskinned) and cook.
6. In a saucepan, melt the butter. In this, fry the cracked black pepper, sage and garlic until the butter starts to brown.
7. Deglaze with the cream and reduce by a quarter.
8. Place the cooked parsnips and spuds into a bowl and begin to mash, keeping the skins of the spuds in the mash.
9. Add the cream and mix thoroughly. Keep warm.

Calvados sauce

Method

1. In the juices and fat from the pork, begin to fry the cubed apple. Deglaze with calvados.
2. Add 1 cup of water with a stock cube dissolved in it.
3. In a separate cup, dissolve 1 tsp of corn flour in about 100 ml of milk. Whisk this into the boiling gravy until the desired thickness is achieved.
4. Stir in 2 tbsp of butter and test for seasoning.

Tips/Pointers

If using a 'dutch oven' to cook the pork, be sure to have plenty of charcoal on top to begin with, so the crackling cooks properly. After about one hour, you can reduce the amount of charcoal, lowering the intensity of the heat and making sure the meat within cooks thoroughly without burning.

Wild Earth Africa 31

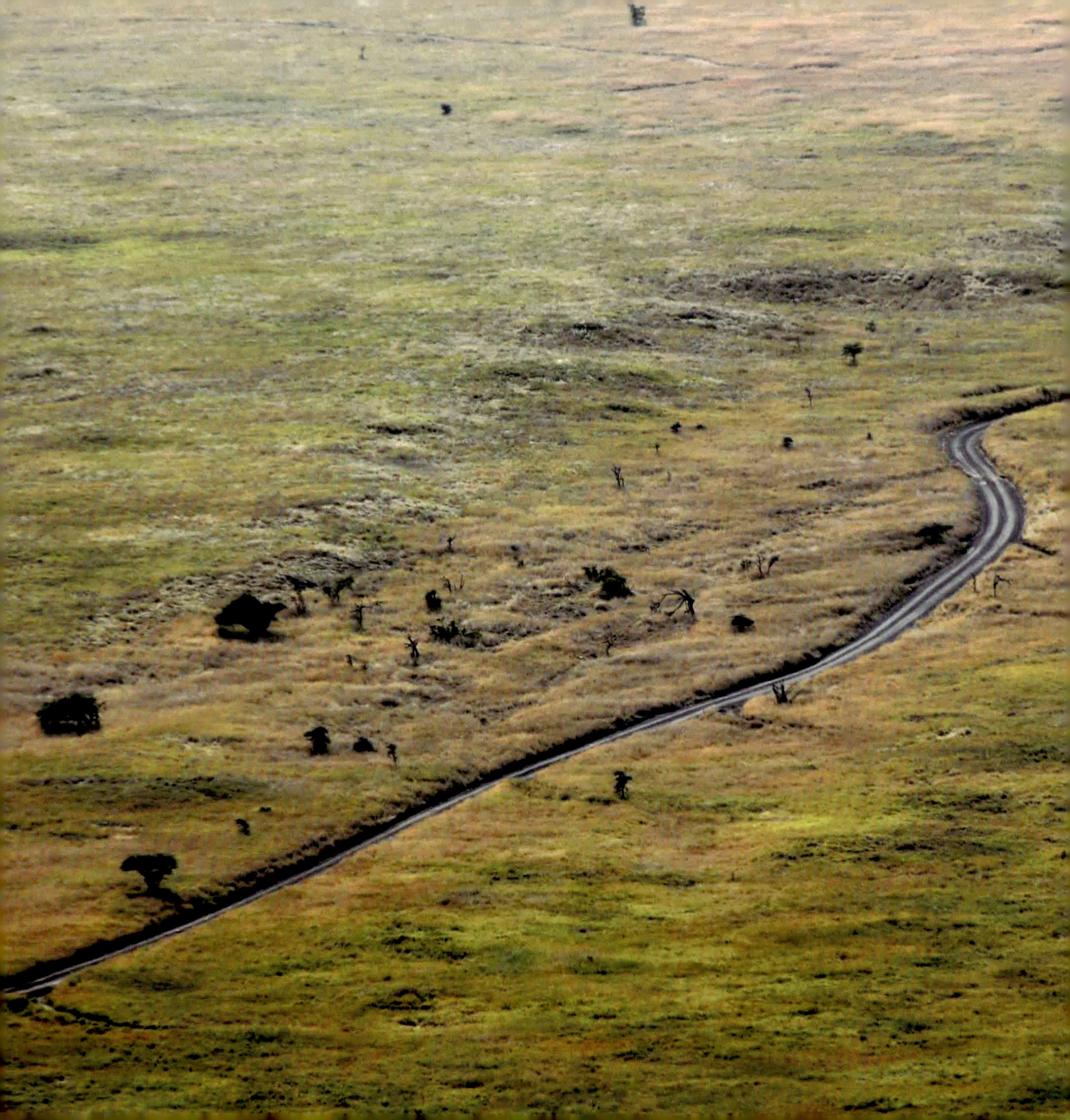

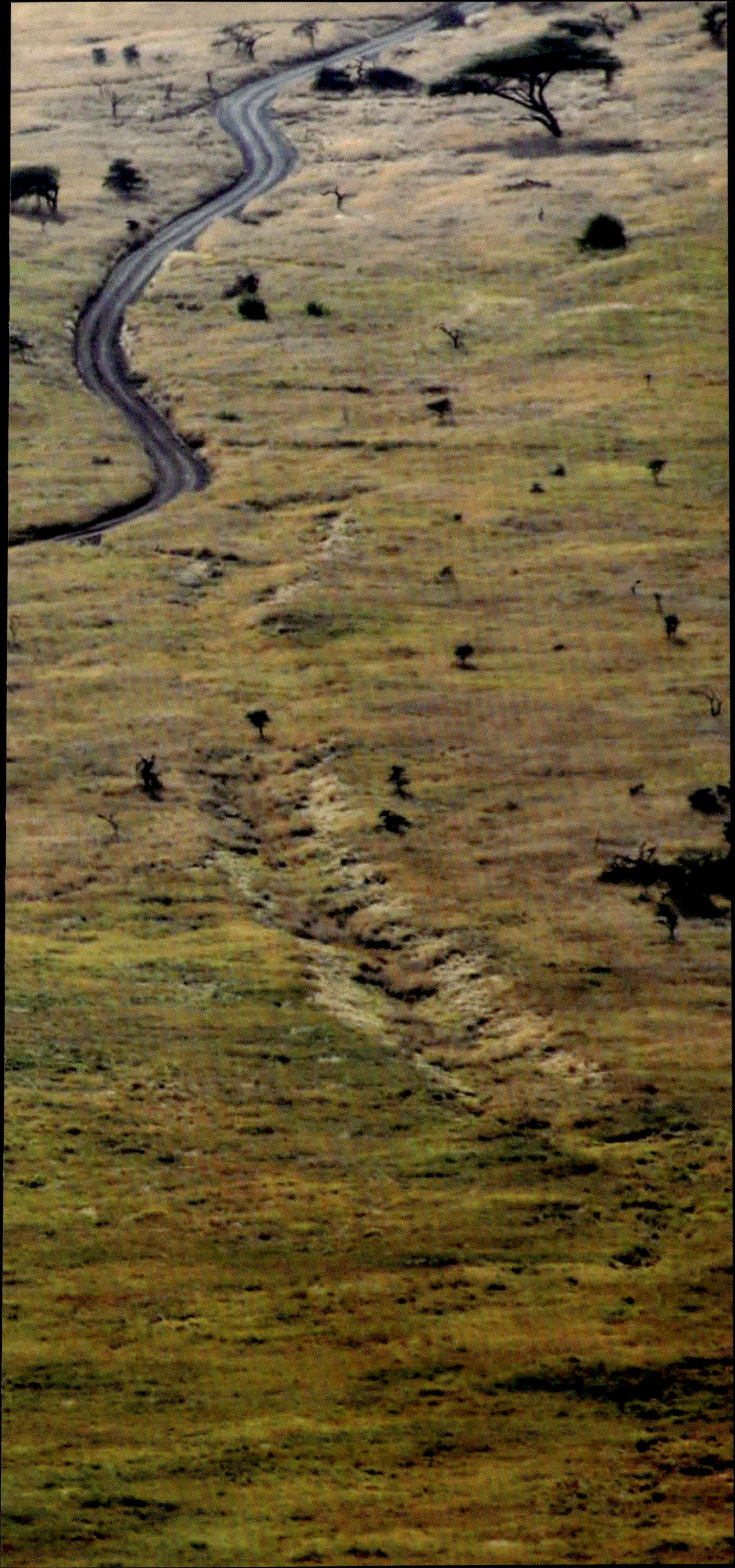
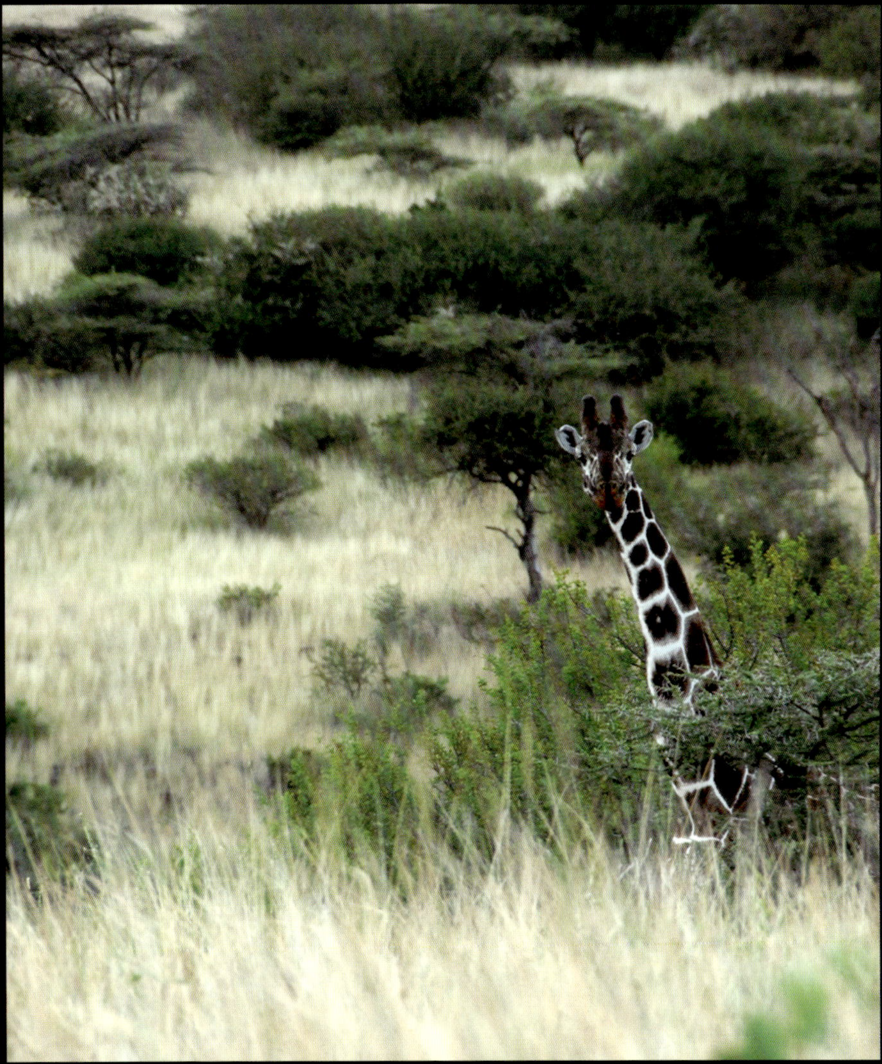
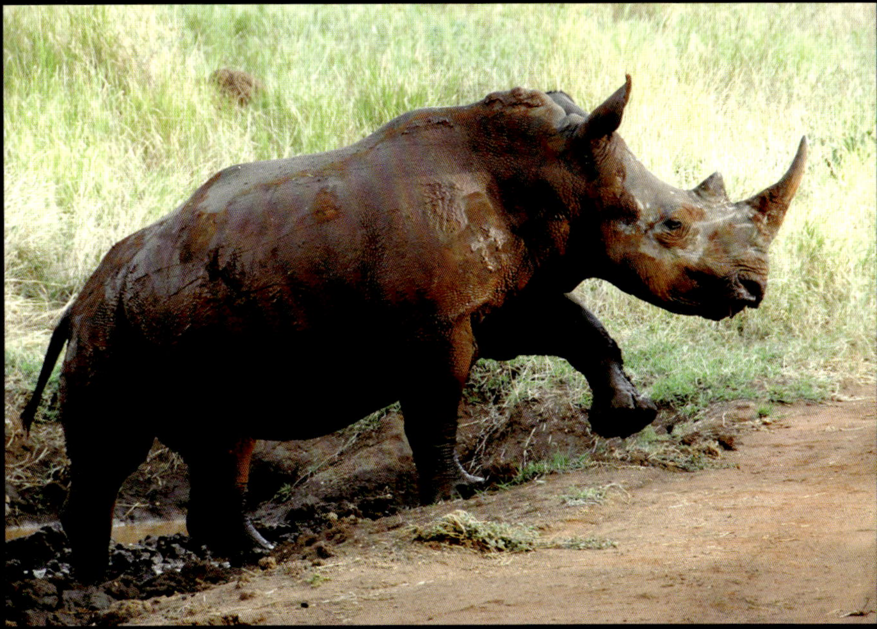

Kiwi and vanilla panacotta with lightly poached lime syrup

RECIPE

Serves 4 people

Ingredients

- 240 ml cream
- Zest of 2 limes
- 1 vanilla pod
- ½ cup of milk
- 2 tsp gelatin *(dissolved in 20 ml warm water)*
- 2 tbsp icing sugar
- 1 sliced kiwi fruit
- 3 tbsp unrefined sugar

Method

1. In a saucepan, simmer the cream and vanilla bean (after having first split this down the middle and scraped out the seeds)
2. Add the milk and icing sugar, and stir in gently.
3. Dissolve the gelatin into the cream mixture and allow to cool.
4. Take 4 metal pudding moulds. Place one slice of kiwi in the bottom of each mould. Pour 1 tsp of the cream mixture over each piece of kiwi and place in the fridge to set.
5. After 20 minutes, remove from the fridge and fill the moulds with what is left of the mixture.
6. Put the moulds in the fridge for 2 hours.
7. Meanwhile, dissolve the unrefined sugar in a saucepan with 4 tbsp of water. Add the lime zest and boil until you have a syrupy texture.
8. Turn out the Panacottas on to a plate, after first heating the mould slightly in hot water. Serve with the lime syrup.

Tips/Pointers

It is important to set the kiwi slices into the bottom of their moulds before pouring in the mixture. If you do not to this, the kiwi may float to the top of the mixture, becoming lost when turned out, so making the dish look less attractive.

Wild Earth Africa

WILD EARTH AFRICA
LEWA WILDLIFE CONSERVANCY
SIMEX 3D

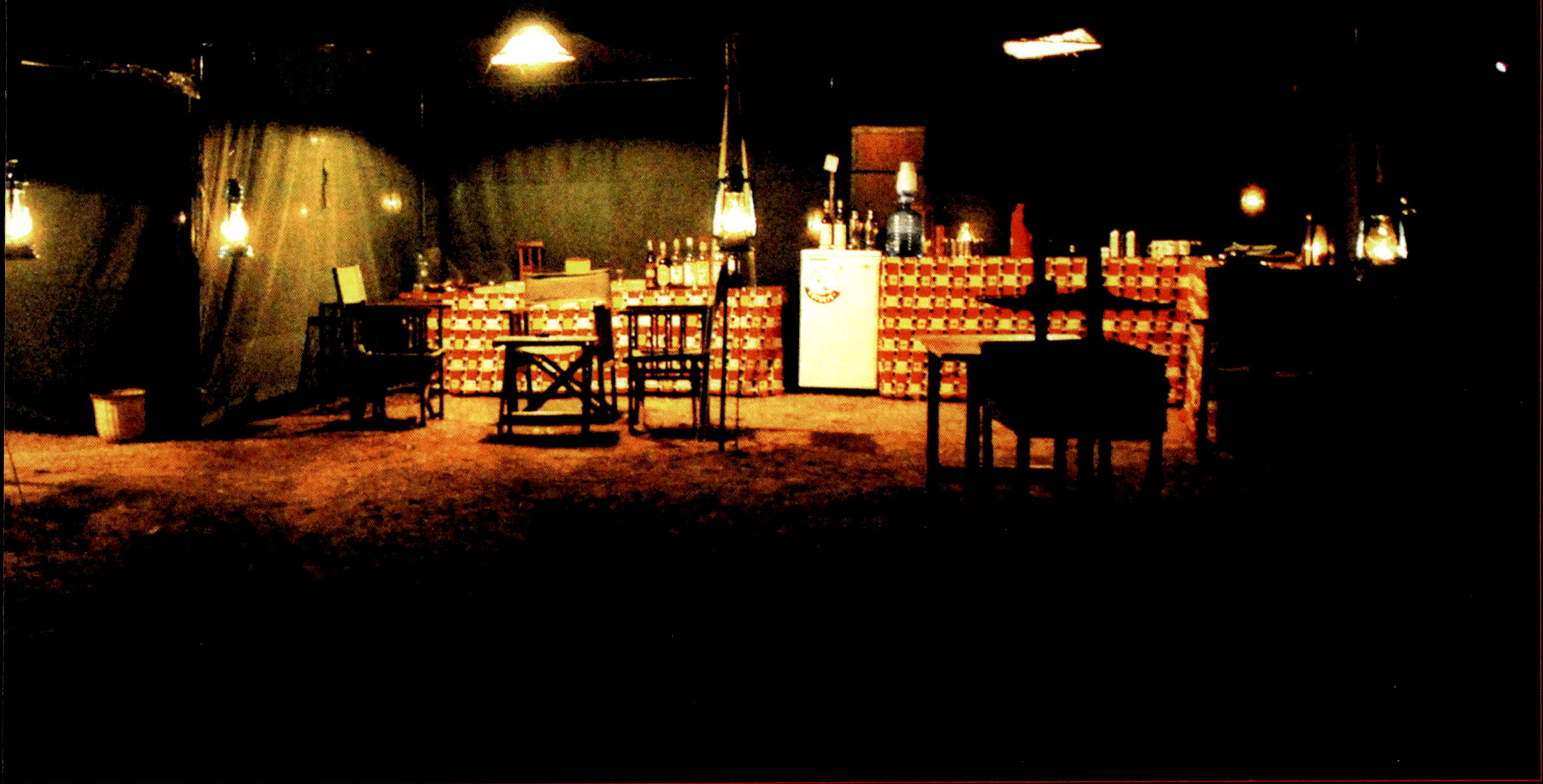

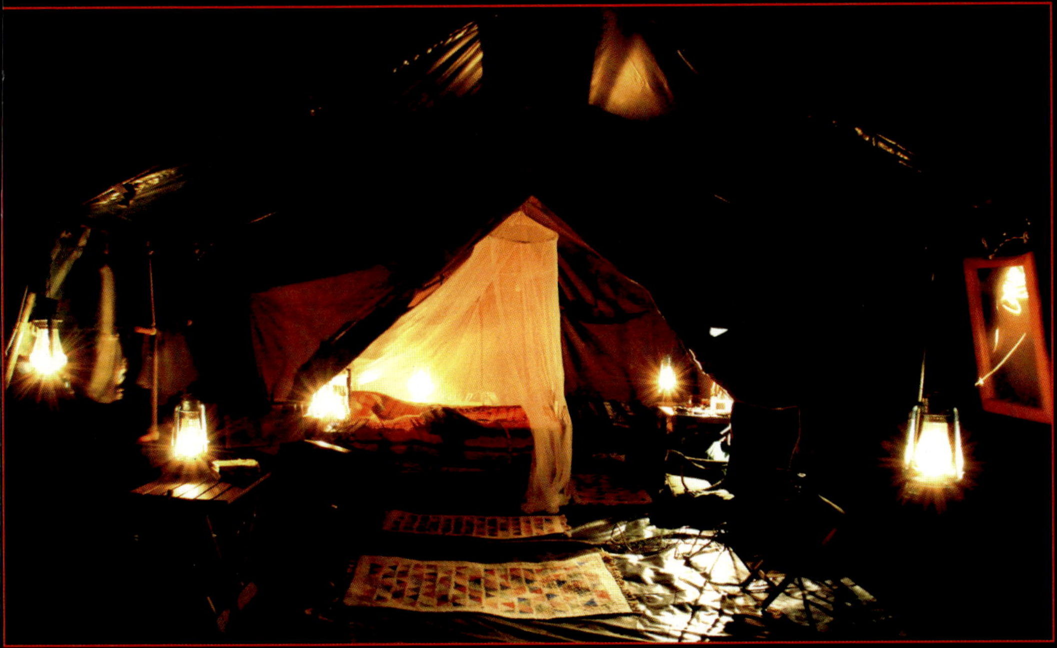

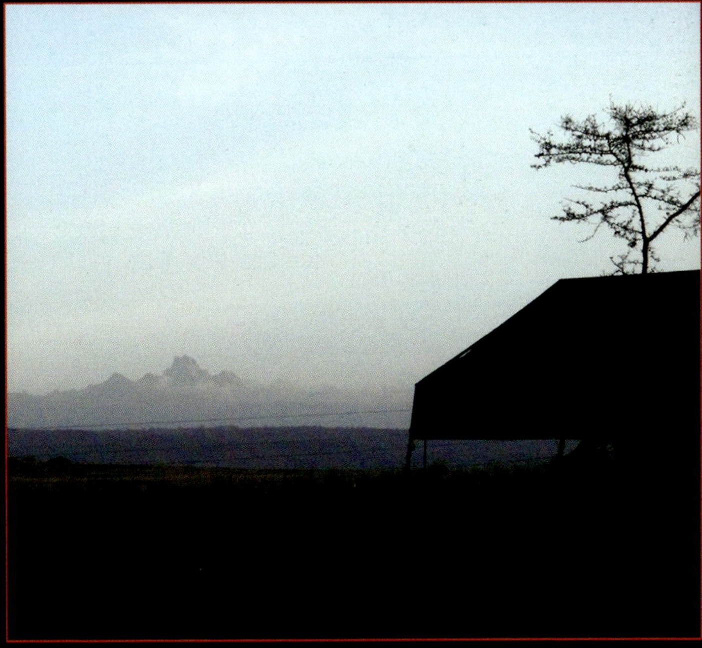

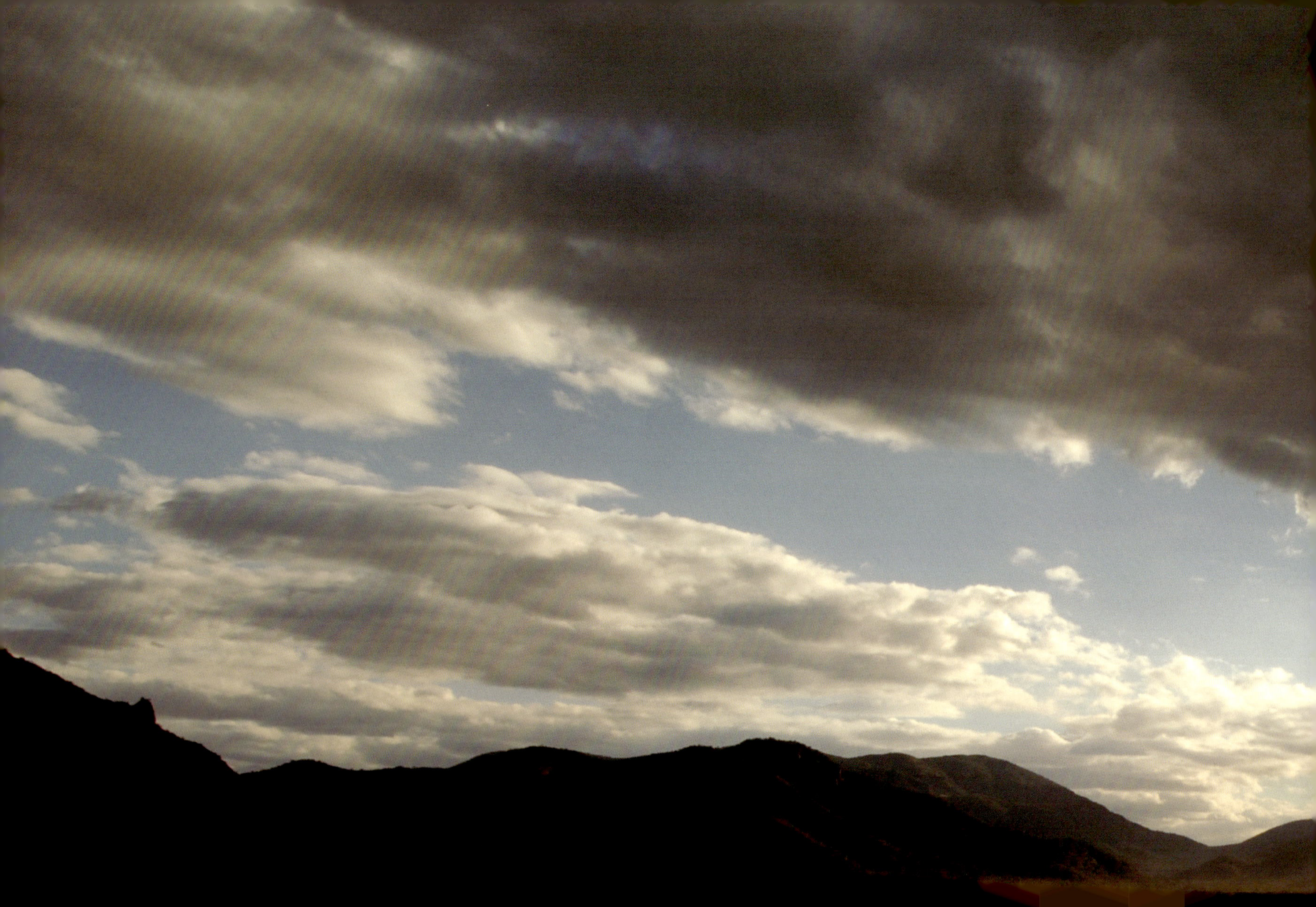

CHARGE 2008

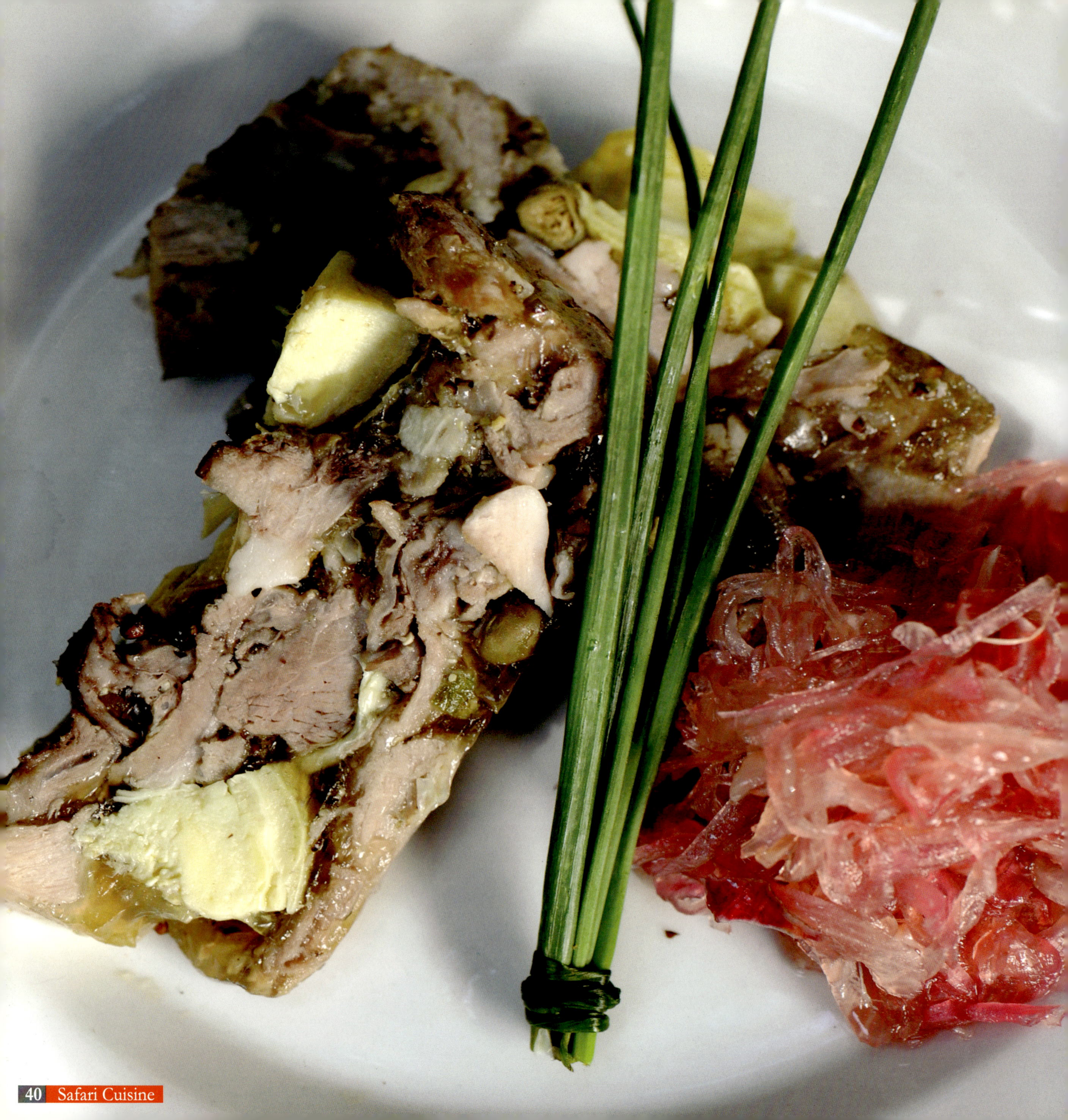

Terrine of ham hock with mustard butter, pickled cabbage and toasted brioche

RECIPE

Serves 10 people

Ingredients

For the terrine

- 3 unsmoked ham hocks, on the bone
- 2 pig's trotters, split lengthways
- 1 tsp caraway seeds
- 1 tsp fennel seeds
- 2 red onions, chopped
- 1 bottle (75cl) dry white wine
- 4 tbsp white wine vinegar
- 2 tbsp small capers, rinsed and drained
- 10 gherkins, rinsed and chopped
- 1 jar pickled artichoke hearts
- Handful of parsley, finely chopped
- Salt and freshly ground black pepper

Method

1. Put the ham hocks and the pig's trotters in a large stockpot and cover with cold water. Bring to the boil, and go on boiling steadily for 10 minutes, skimming off any scum.
2. Remove the hocks and trotters, and discard the water.
3. Return the hocks and trotters to the cleaned pan. Add the fennel, caraway seeds and red onions. Pour in the wine and vinegar, and add enough cold water just to cover the ingredients.
4. Bring to the boil, then simmer very gently for a minimum of two hours, or until the hocks are tender and the meat flakes easily.
5. Leave the hocks and trotters to cool in the liquid for about one hour. Remove the hocks, cover with cling film and set aside. Discard the trotters.
6. Strain the cooking liquid through a muslin-lined sieve into a clean pan.
7. Add the white of 2 eggs and stir in gently. This will help purify the liquid, as the egg white will trap all impurities, rising to the surface as it does so. Skim all the egg white from the surface.
8. Place the pan on a high heat and bring the liquid to a rapid boil. Boil until the liquid has reduced to 650 ml/1 pint, then pass it once again through a lined sieve. Wrap each 1.5-litre terrine in a double layer of cling film, leaving some cling film draped over the sides.
9. Peel the skin off the hocks, then shred the meat into nuggets. Place in a large bowl with the capers, gherkins and parsley. Mix well. Taste and season with pepper (adding salt only if deemed absolutely necessary). Pile the mixture into the lined terrine and press down firmly. Slowly pour in the reduced liquid, adding just enough to cover the meat. As you pour, tap the terrine dish on a hard surface to make sure the liquid spreads through the terrine. Cover with the overhanging cling film and chill overnight in the fridge.

Ingredients

For the English mustard butter

- 50 g very soft unsalted butter
- 1 heaped tsp wholegrain mustard
- Salt
- Freshly ground black pepper

Serve the terrine with the mustard butter, and with some pickled cabbage (or sauerkraut) and toasted brioche

Tips/Pointers

It is important to purify your stock. This stock acts essentially as natural gelatin in setting the terrine, and is full of flavour. The clearer it is, the more attractive your terrine will be.

Rhino Charge 2008

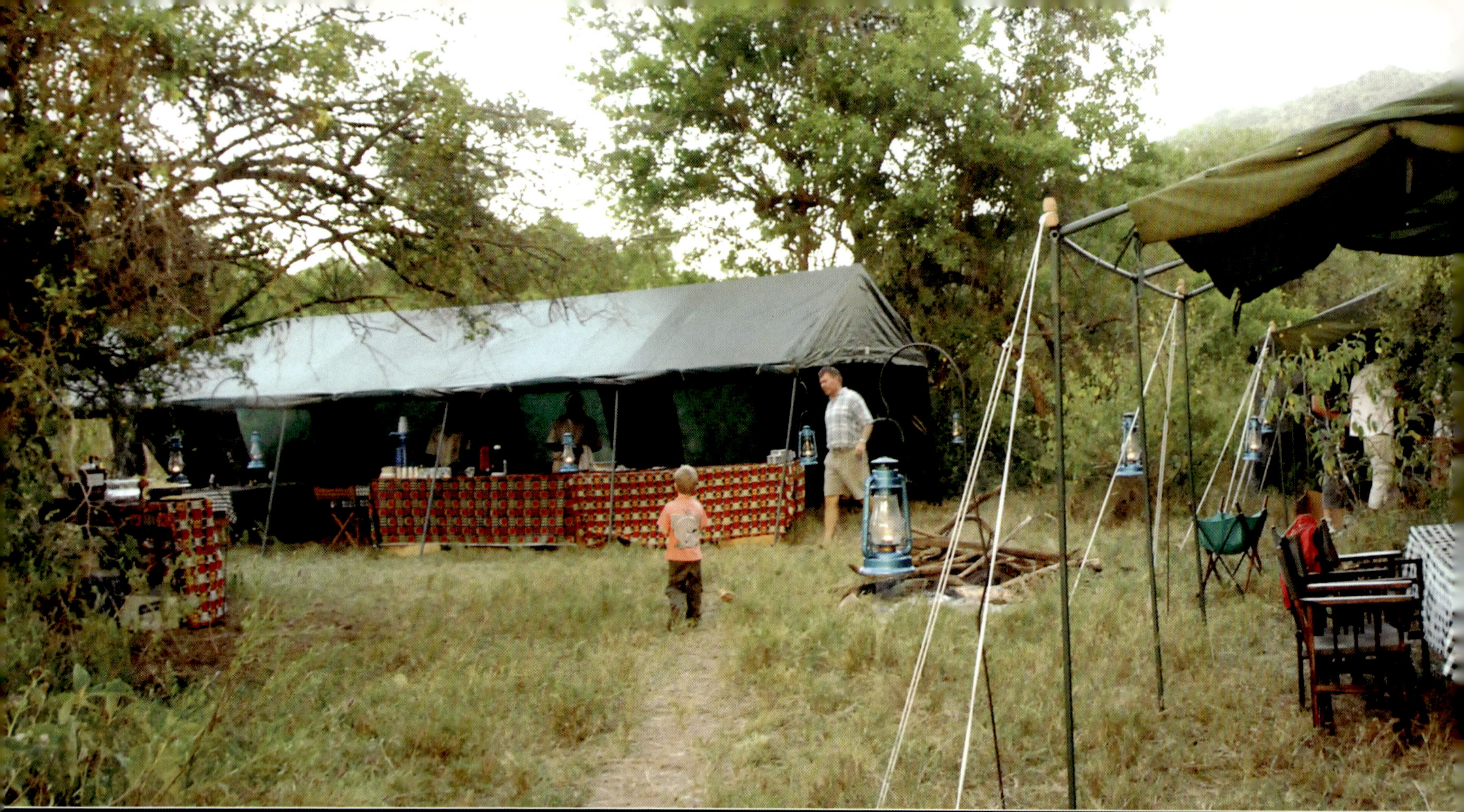

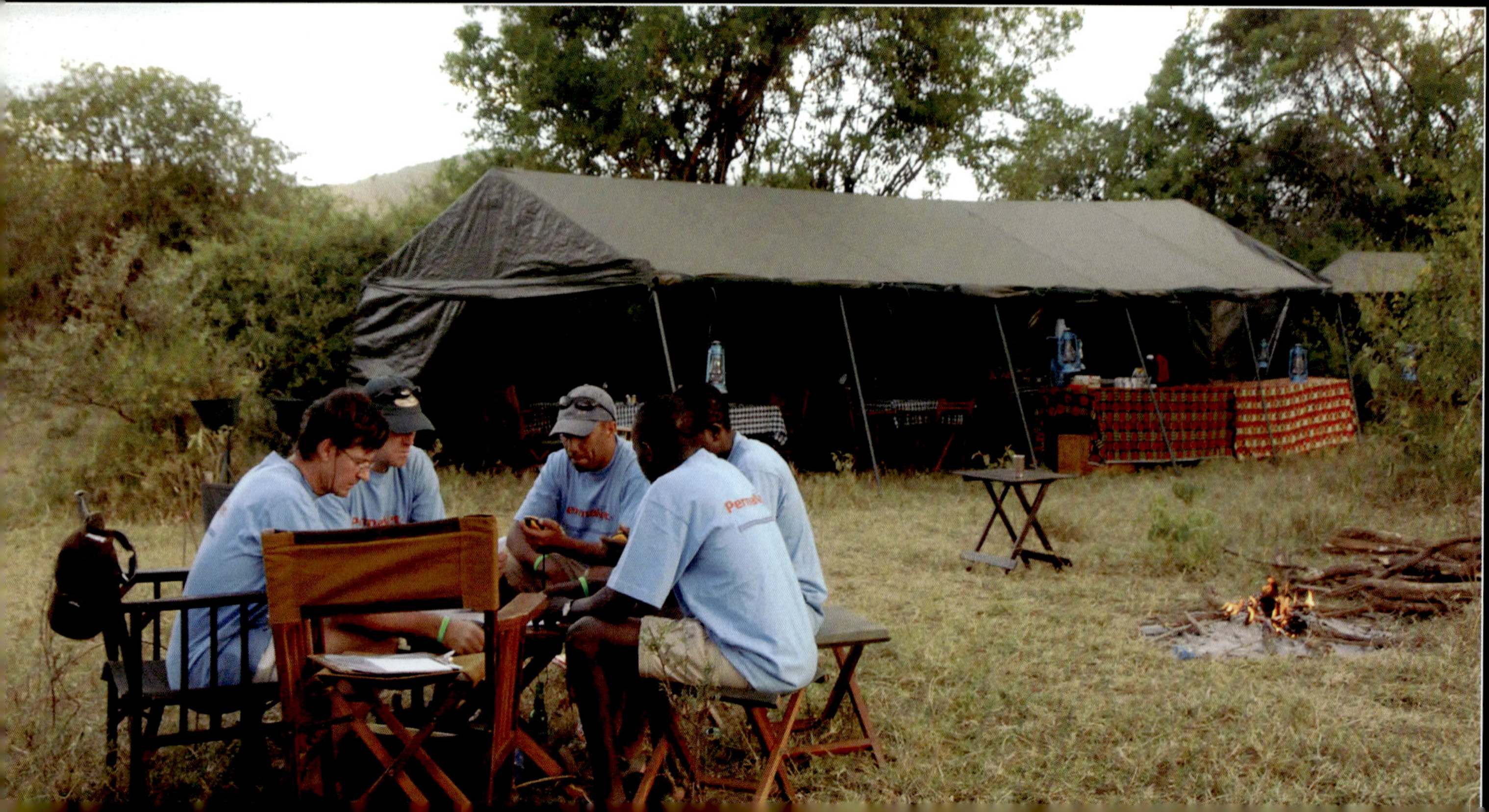

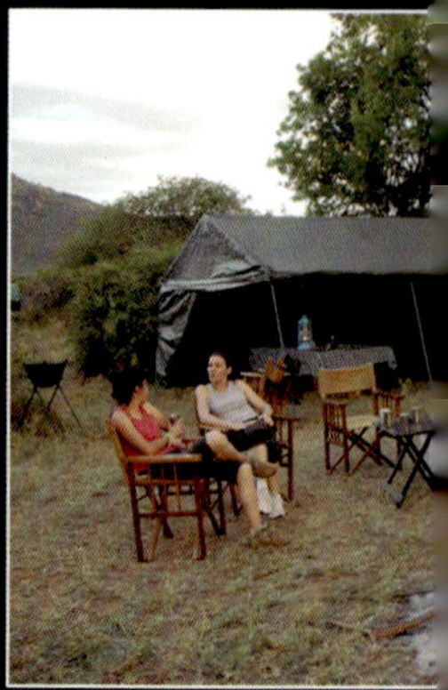

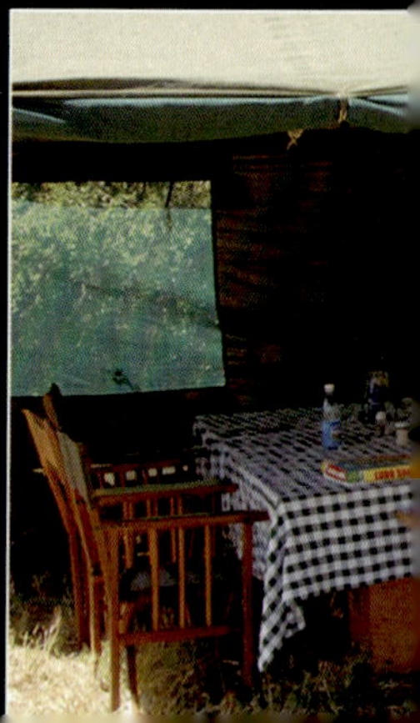

RHINO CHARGE 2008

CREWS CARS 3, 13, & 46

MENU

Terrine of ham hock with mustard butter, pickled cabbage and toasted brioche

Herb-crusted rack of slow-cooked Molo lamb, with crushed minted garden peas and rosemary jus

Steamed vanilla sponge with sticky macadamia and date syrup

Herb-crusted rack of slow-cooked Molo lamb, with crushed minted garden peas and rosemary jus

RECIPE

Serves 4 people

Ingredients

- 1 kg rack of lamb (cleaned and dressed by your butcher if possible)
- 2 tbsp Dijon mustard
- 100 g bread crumbs
- 1 handful parsley, chopped
- 1 handful basil, chopped
- 1 handful fresh marjoram, chopped
- Zest of 1 lemon
- Juice of 1 lemon
- 2 tbsp olive oil
- 200 g fresh sweet peas
- 1 bunch chopped mint
- 2 tsp chopped rosemary
- 200 ml gravy *(see recipe)*
- 2 tots cognac or brandy

Method

1. Heat your oven to about 150°C.
2. Into the breadcrumbs, mix the chopped parsley, basil, marjoram and lemon zest.
3. Coat the fat side of the lamb with a healthy spreading of Dijon mustard and then dip this into the breadcrumbs so they stick, covering the mustard completely.
4. Place the lamb in the oven and cook for about 3 hours.
5. Meanwhile, take your raw peas and crush gently with a pestle and mortar. Do not crush too finely, as the peas should allowed to retain some of their texture.
6. Blanch the peas in hot water, and strain properly.
7. Toss through the olive oil and lemon juice, then add the mint and seasoning.
8. Remove the lamb from the oven and allow to rest for 10 minutes, keeping the juices for the gravy.

The rosemary jus

Method

1. Keeping in the juices and the fat from the lamb, fry the chopped rosemary. Deglaze with cognac.
2. Add 2 cups of water into which a stock cube has been dissolved.
3. In a separate cup, dissolve 1 tsp of corn flour in about 100 ml of milk. Whisk this into the boiling gravy until the desired thickness is achieved.
4. Stir in 2 tbsp of butter and test for seasoning.

Tips/Pointers

If you are using a charcoal oven to cook your lamb, it is important to get the temperature right. In an oven that is too hot, the lamb may cook too quickly, or burn. One good test is to lay one hand, with a tea towel draped over it, gently against the side of the oven. You should be able to keep your hand there for 2 seconds before the heat becomes uncomfortable. Be careful not to burn yourself!

Rhino Charge 2008

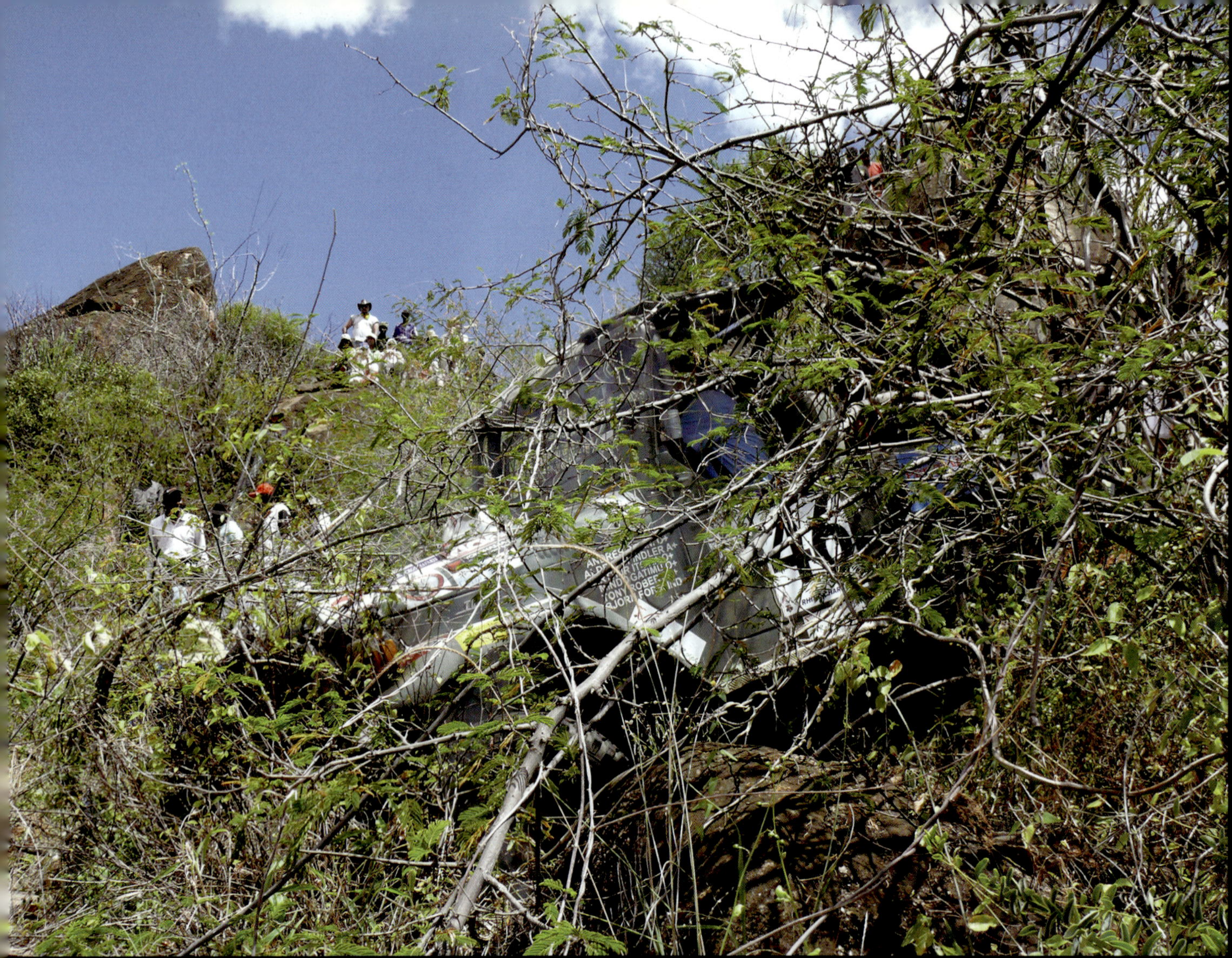

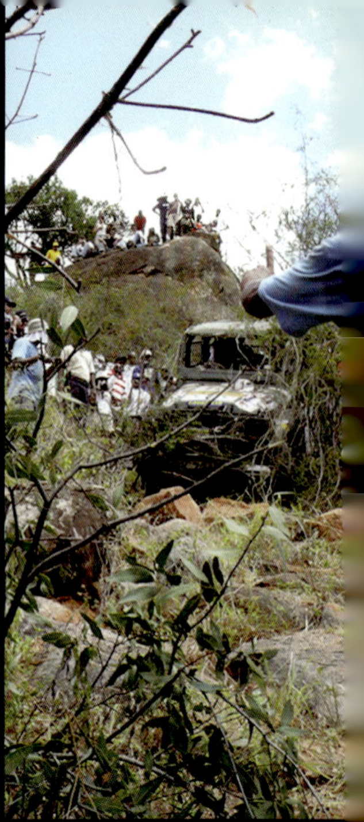

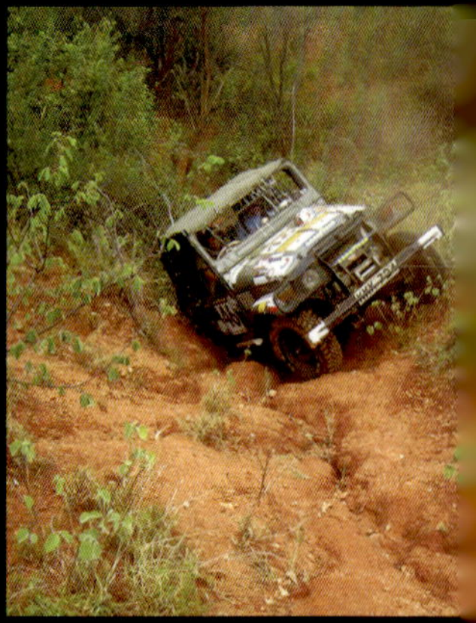

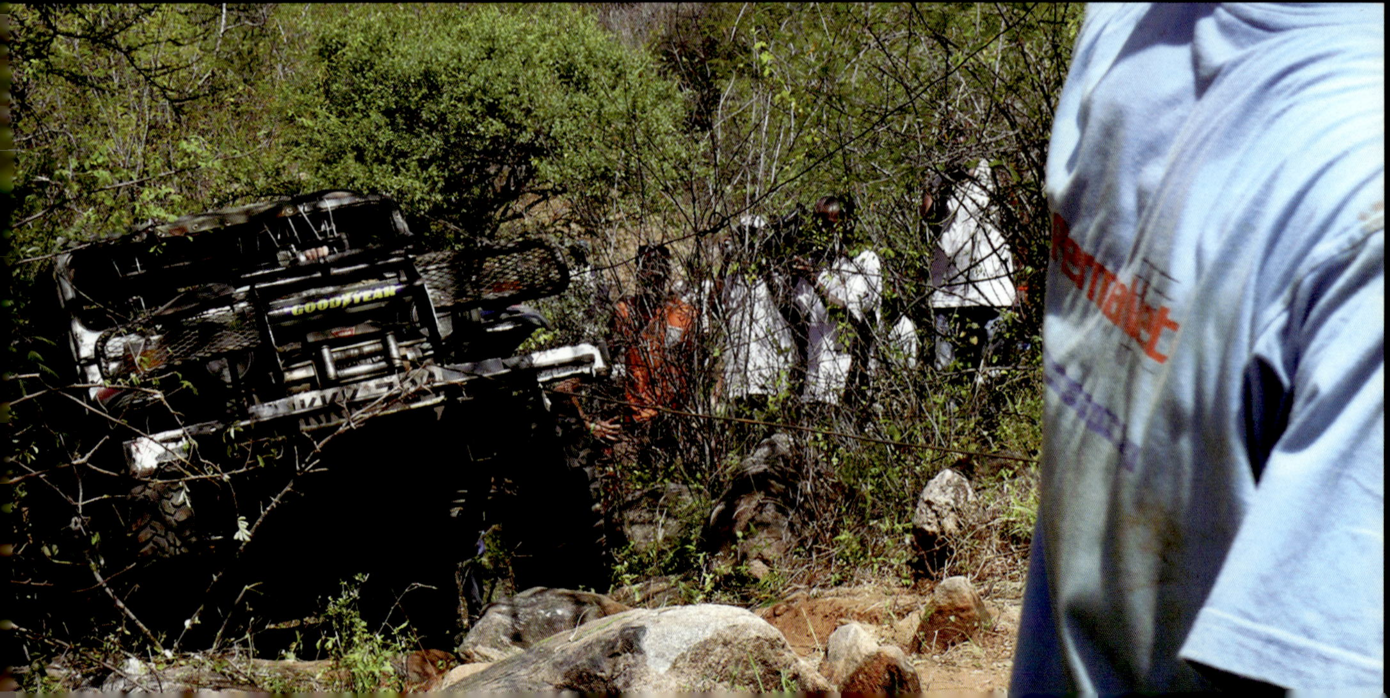
GOODYEAR

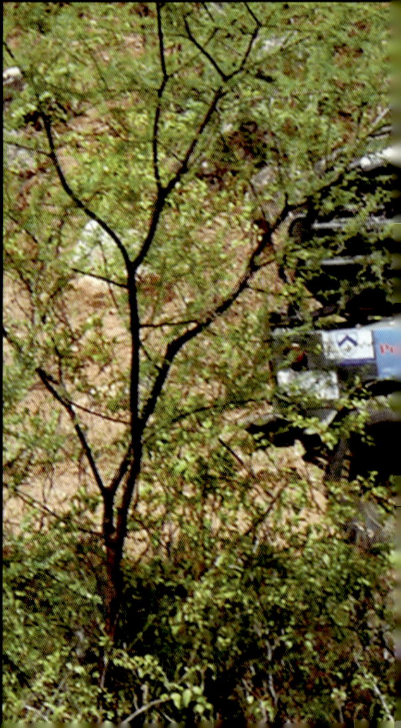

46

KKK
724
46

46

GOODYEAR
46
RHINO CHARGE
ANDRES BIFANI O+
ALDRIC SPINDLER A+
ARTHUR ITOTIA O+
MINDO GATIMU O+
TONY ROBERT A+
BJORN FORSLIND
Tvende
Red Lands Roses

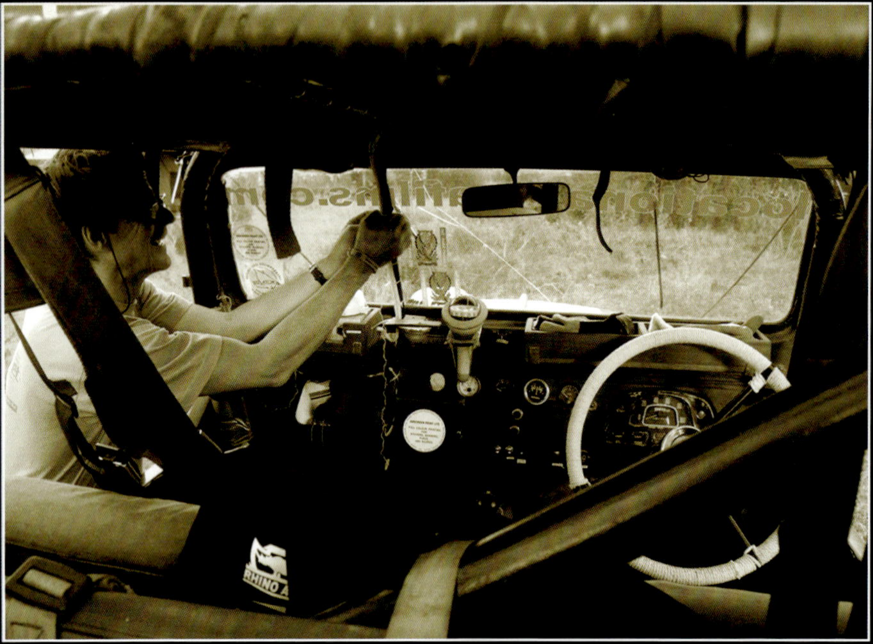

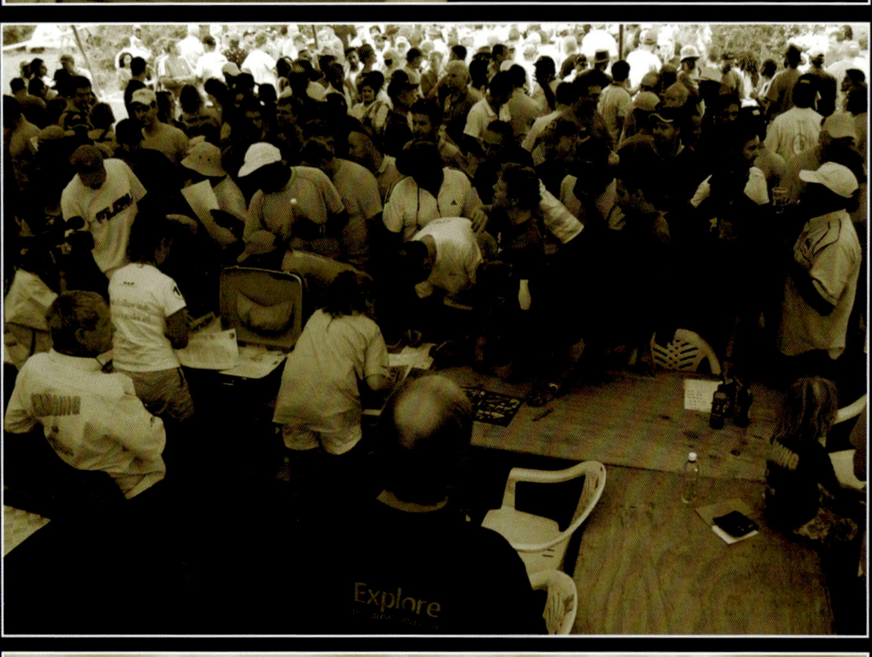
Explore

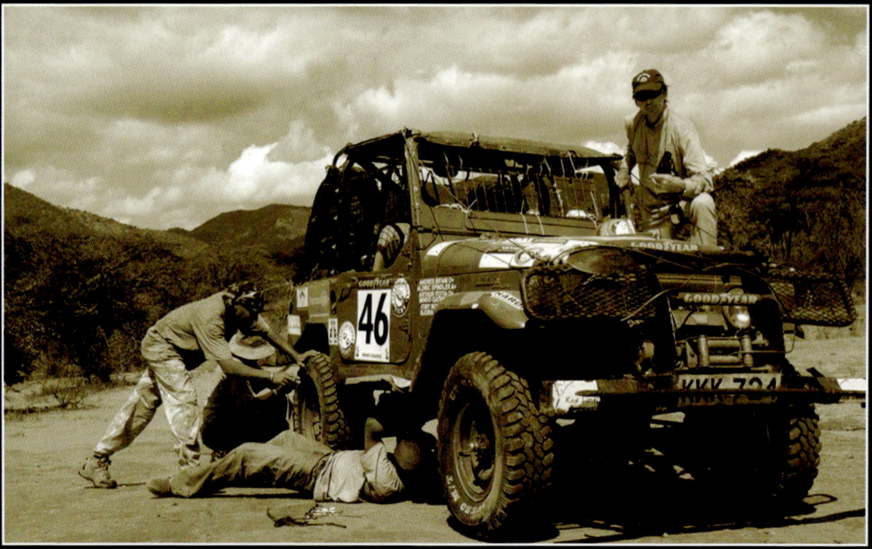
46
GOODYEAR

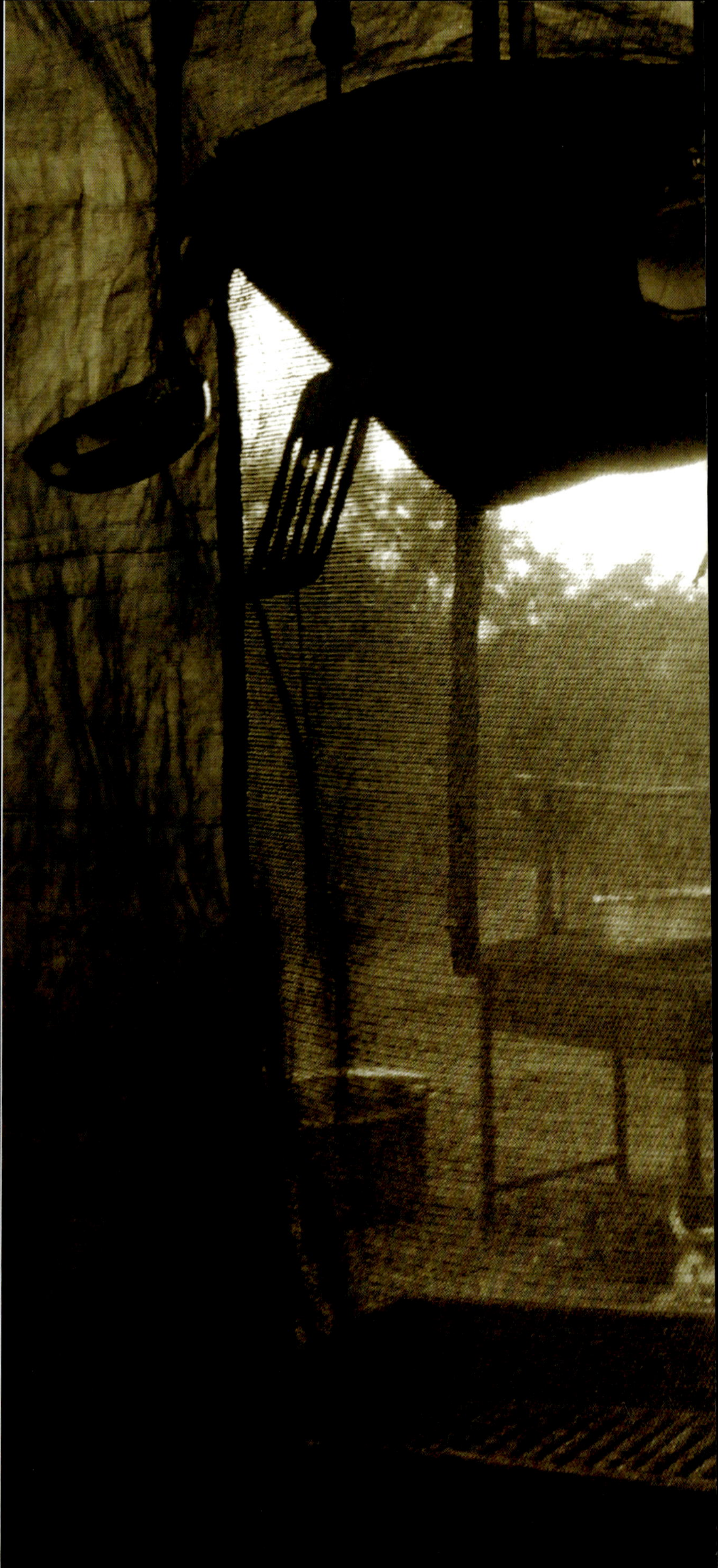

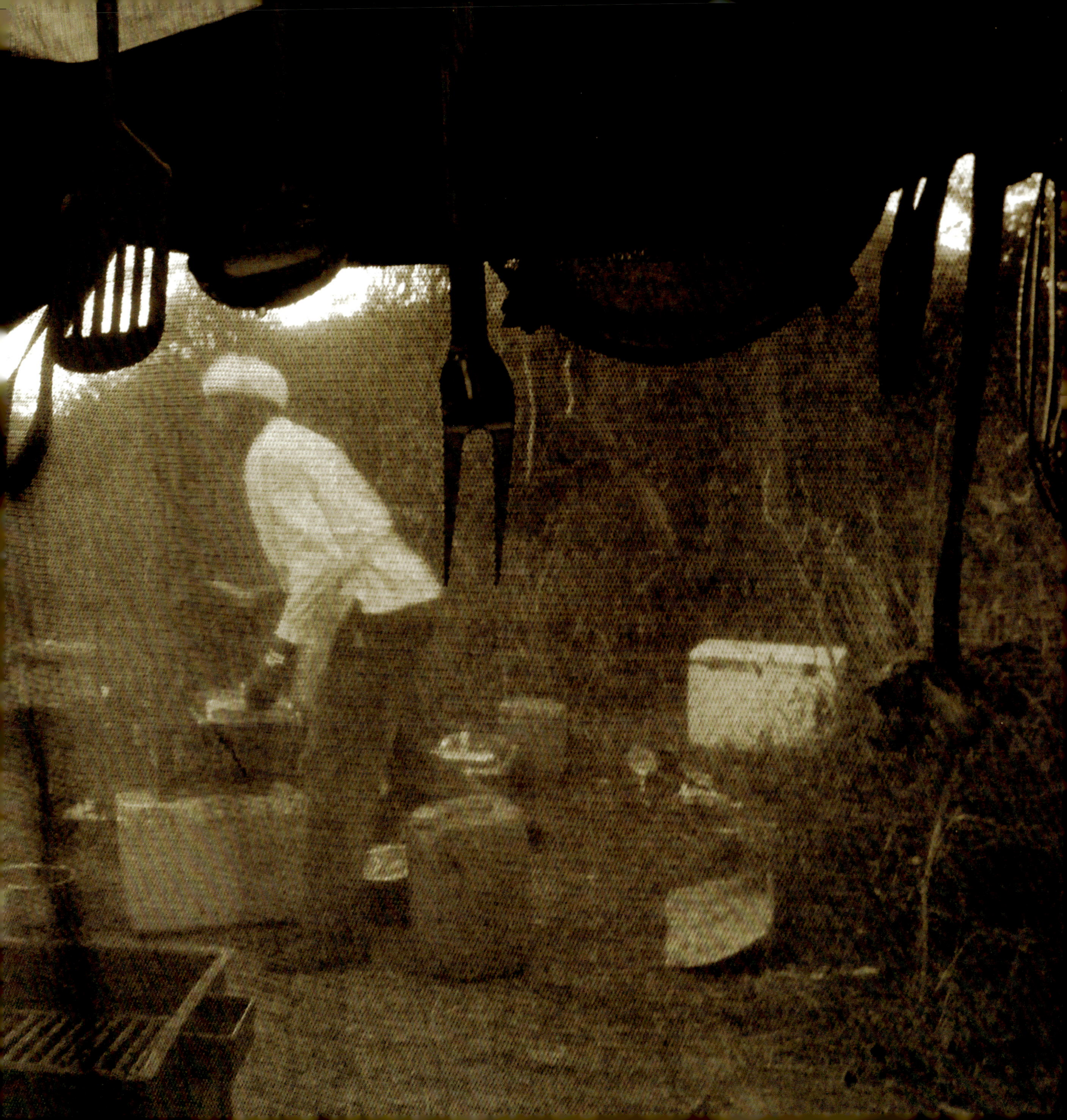

50 Safari Cuisine

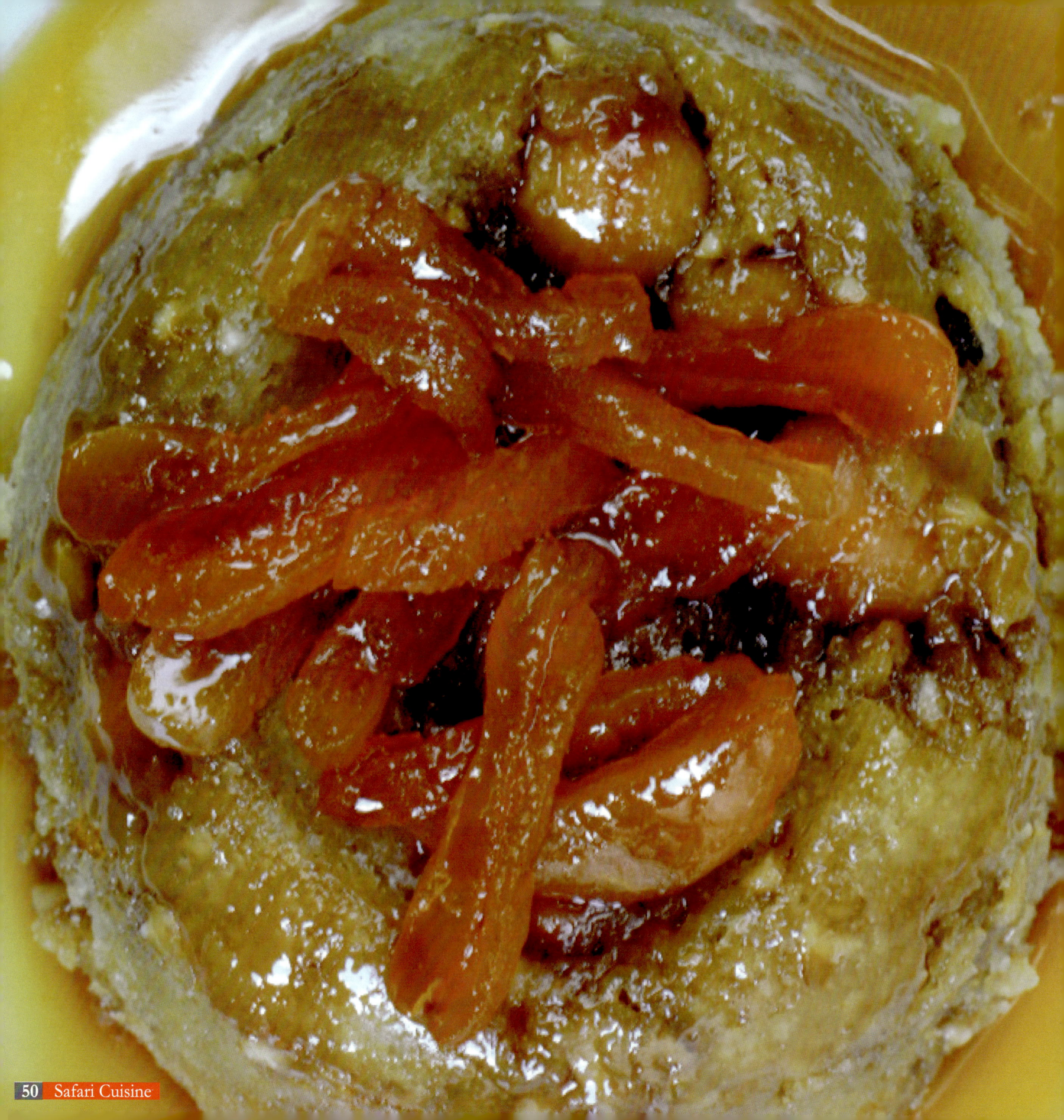

Steamed vanilla sponge with sticky macadamia and date syrup

RECIPE

Serves 8 people

Ingredients

- 1 cup self-raising flour
- ½ cup castor sugar
- ½ cup softened butter
- 4 free-range eggs
- 4 tbsp of milk
- 6 tbsp honey
- 1 tsp ground ginger

For the date syrup

- 4 tbsp muscavado sugar
- ½ cup lightly crushed macadamia nuts
- ½ cup dates
- 2 tbsp cream
- 1 tbsp rum

Method

1. To make the sponge puddings, grease and lightly flour eight ramekins.
2. Put the flour, sugar, butter, eggs and milk in a bowl, and beat into a smooth batter.
3. Mix the honey and the ground ginger, and place a spoonful in the base of each ramekin.
4. Pour in the sponge mixture.
5. Lightly place some cling film over the top of each ramekin, so it does not touch the sponge mixture.
6. Place in a saucepan with boiling water and steam the puddings for 20 minutes until they are spongy to the touch.
7. Meanwhile, place the cream and the rum in a saucepan and begin to warm.
8. Stir in the sugar until it dissolves.
9. Turn up the heat, and boil till you have a thick syrup.
10. Add the dates and the macadamia nuts, and serve with the warm pudding.

Tips/Pointers

Be sure to cover the ramekins properly, so that no water or steam can get into them. If this happens, your puddings might become soggy.

Rhino Charge 2008

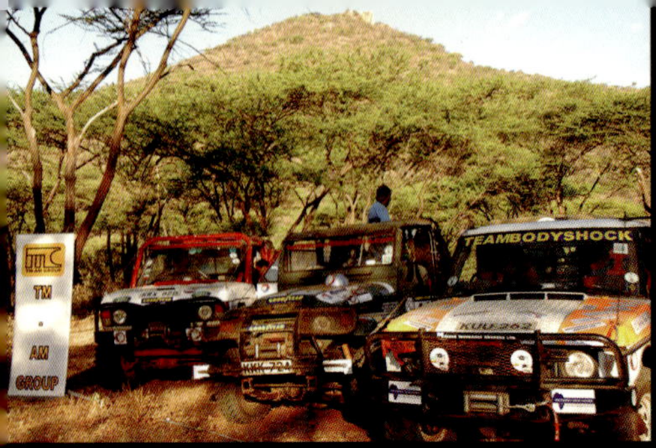
TEAMBODYSHOCK

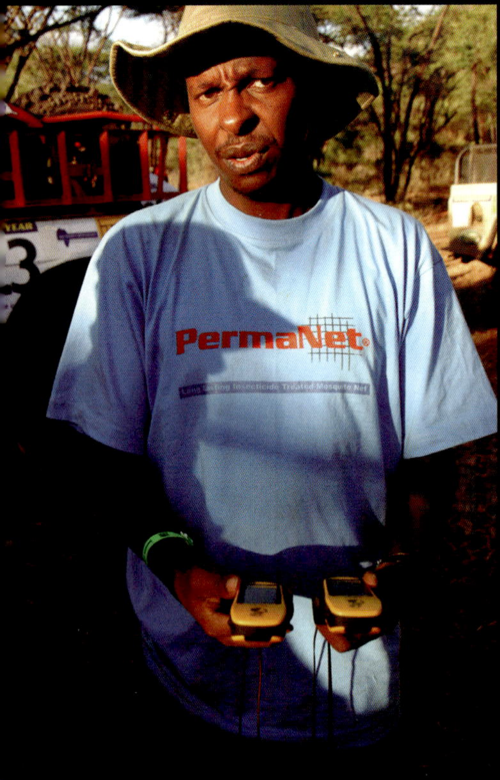
PermaNet

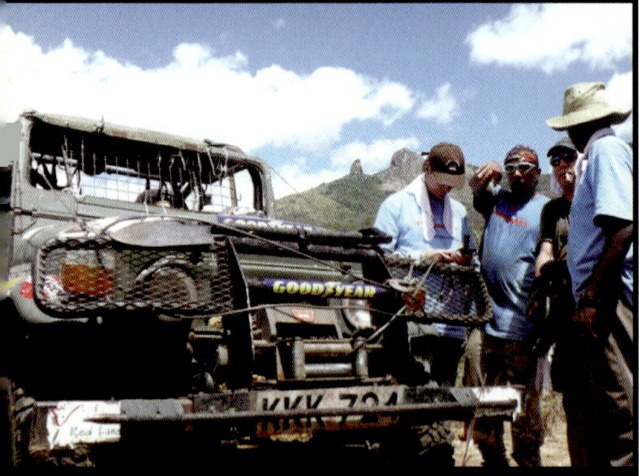
GOODYEAR

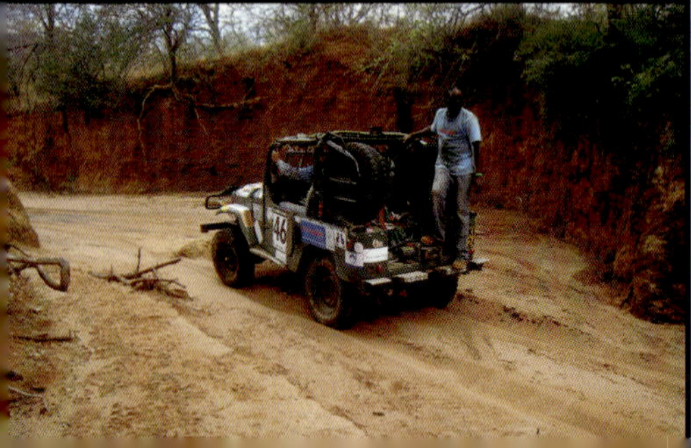

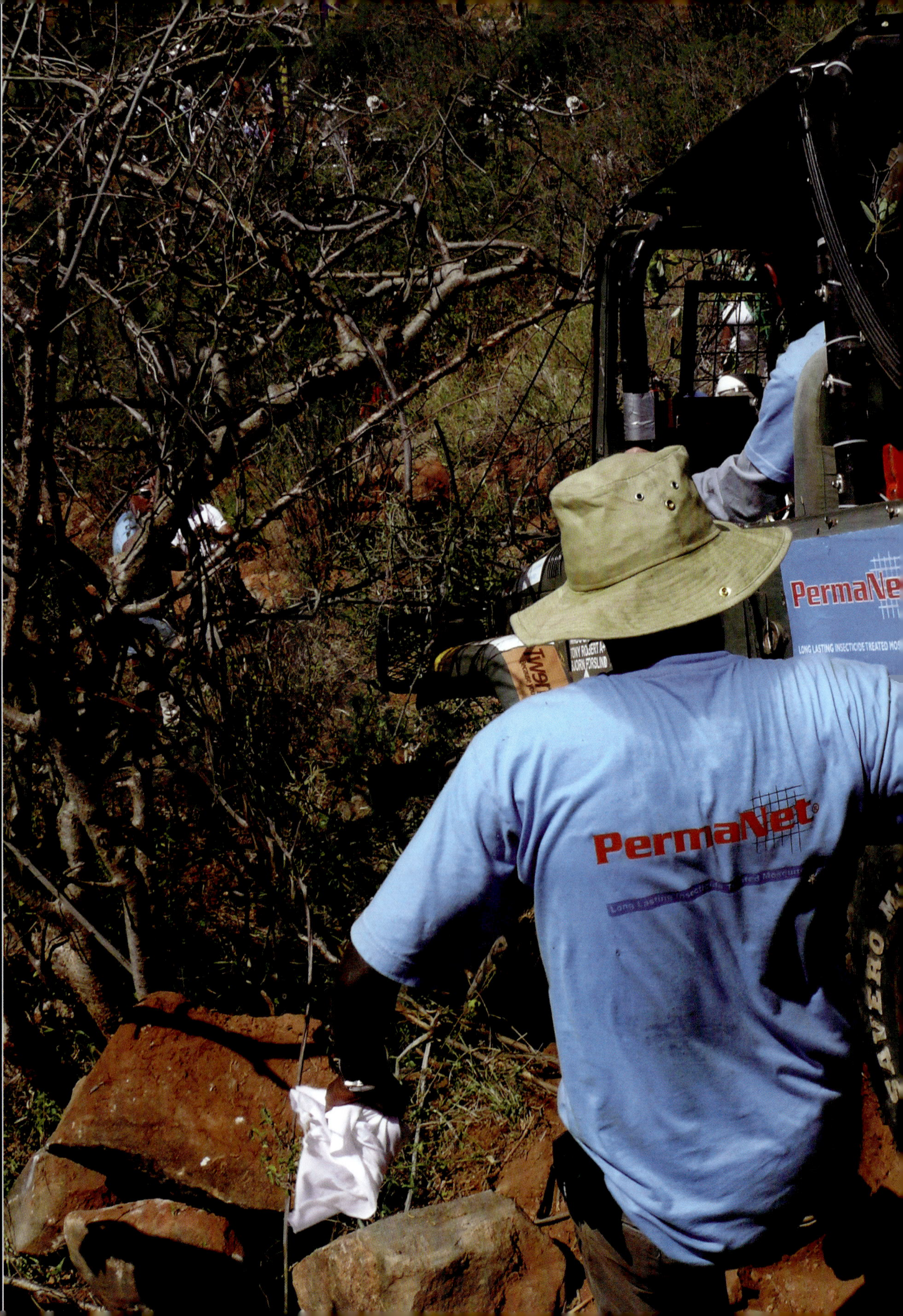
PermaNet
PermaNet

4 WHEEL DRIVE
GPRO
Red Lands Roses
Ltd.
www.braeburn.com

46

PermaVet
46
www.braeburn.com

PermaNet

SAFARICOM

MARATHON
lewa wildlife conservancy

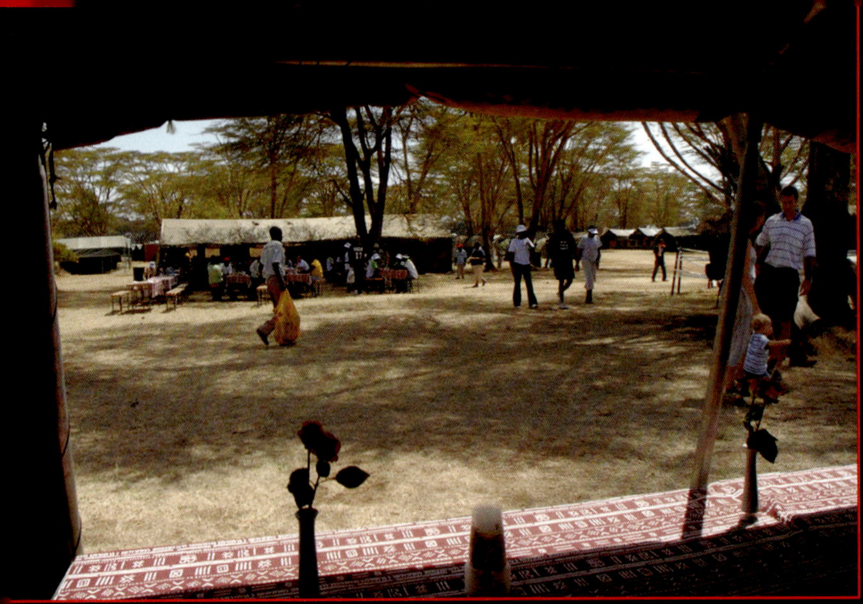

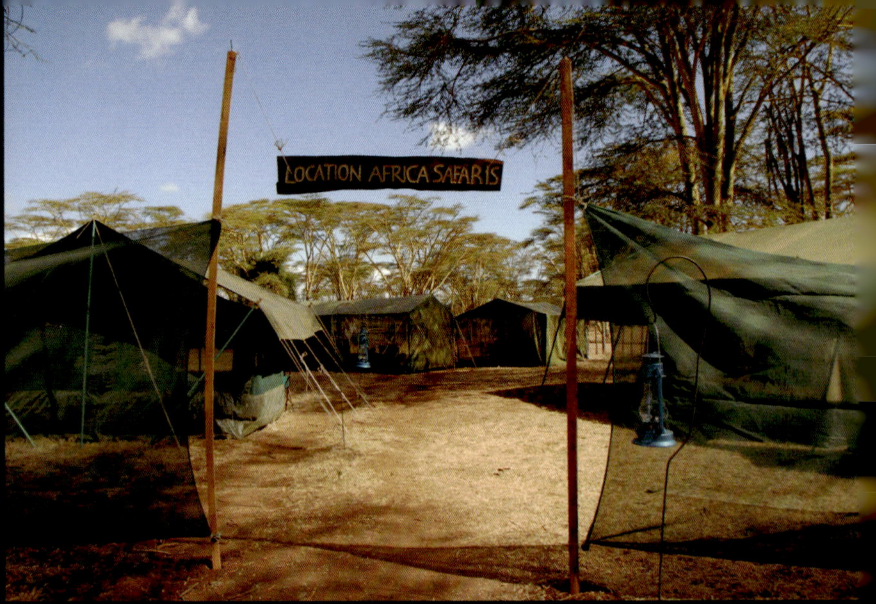
LOCATION AFRICA SAFARIS

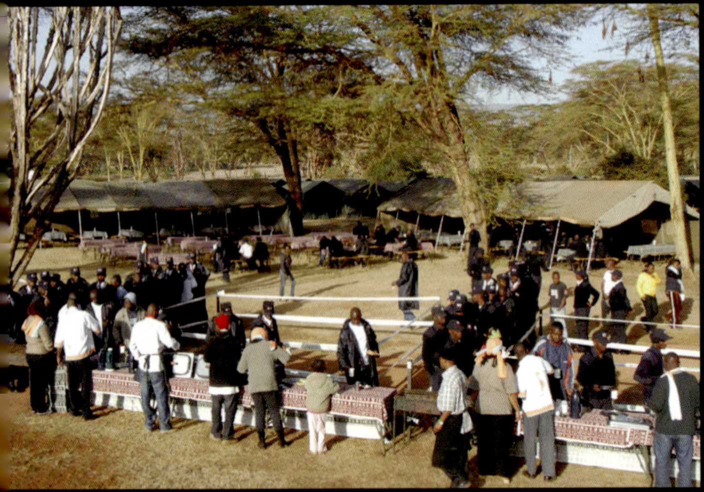

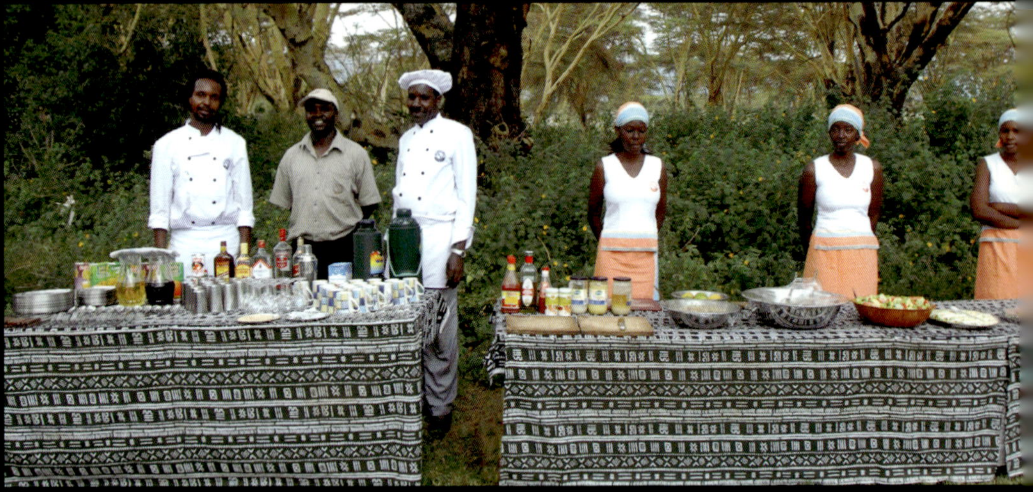

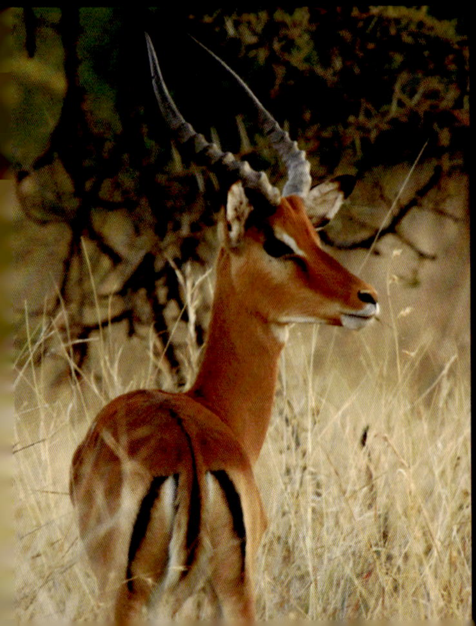

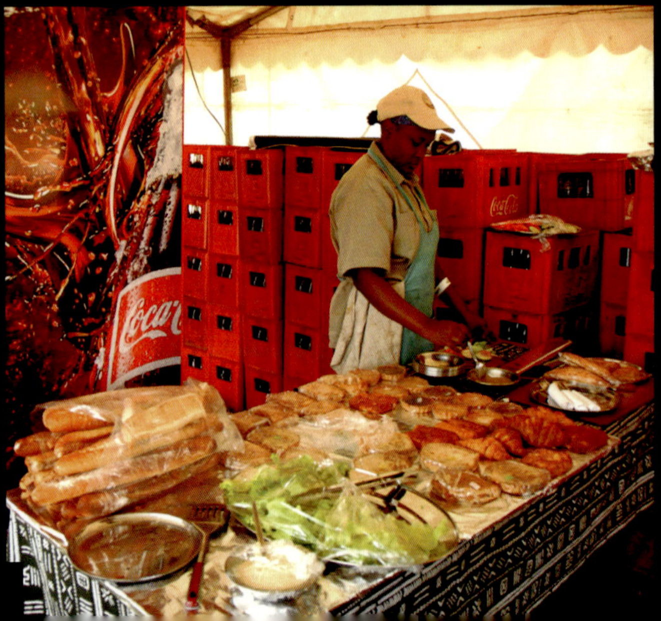

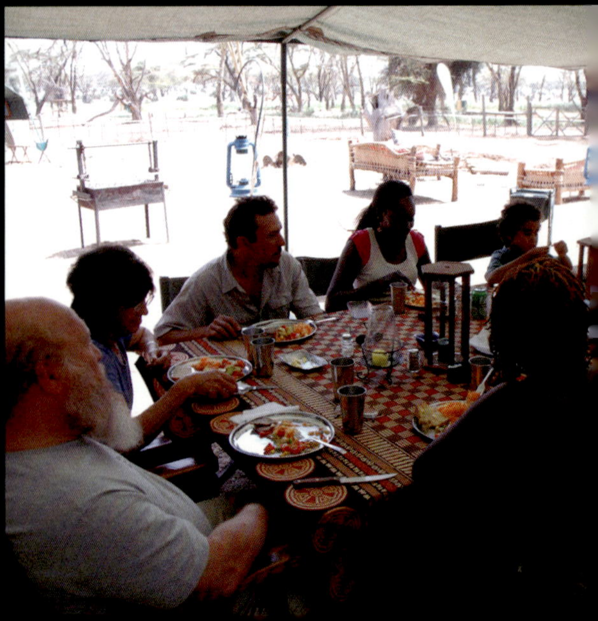

VILLAGE
Lewa Wildlife Conservancy
SAFARICOM MARATHON '09

Friday 26 June

LUNCH
Serves 150 pax TBC

Irio *(potatoes 200 g x 150 pax = 30 kg, pumpkin leaves 35 bunches & maize 40 pcs)*

Cabbage *(50 g x 150 pax = 7 kg)*

Beef Stew
(150g x 150 pax = 22.5 kg + 5 kg tomatoes + 5 kg onions)

Kachumbari
(tomatoes 6 kg, onions 4 kg, dania 10 bunches, chillies 250 g)

Fruit Salad
(100 g x 150 pax = 15 kg peeled = 30 kg raw = bananas 8 kg, watermelon 8 kg, pawpaw 8 kg, mangoes 8 kg, passion fruits 2 kg)

DINNER
420 pax + 40 pax security + 50 pax
Medics & various + 40 pax outsiders = **Serves 550 pax**

Nyama Choma: Goat Meat with Bones
(300 g x 550 pax = 165 kg: ± 12 kg per goat = 14 goats)

Sukuma *185 bunches*

Red Beans *(40 g x 550 pax = 22 kg)*

Ugali
(270 g x 550 pax = 150 kg = 75 packets)
or

Penne Bolognese
(Pasta 100 g x 150 pax = 15 kg, minced meat 80 g x 150 pax = 12 kg, onions 12 kg, tomatoes 12 kg, garlic 3 cloves, tomato paste 1 g x 150 pax = 1.5 kg)

Farfalle – Vegetables/Tomato Basil
(Pasta 100 g x 150 pax = 15 kg, TBC, tomaotes, onions, garlic, aubergines, courgettes, green beans, cauliflower, carrots, basil)

Cake & Custard
Fresh Fruits
Tea & Coffee

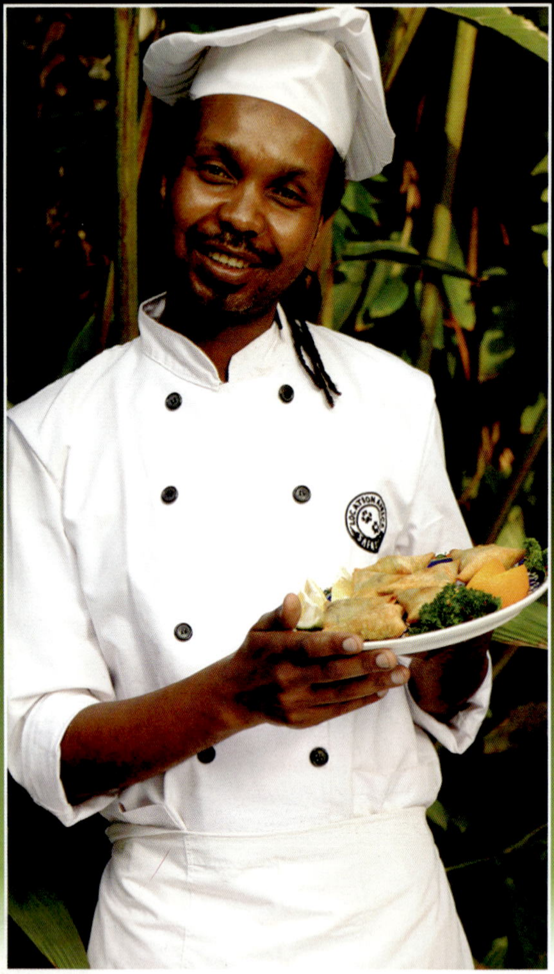

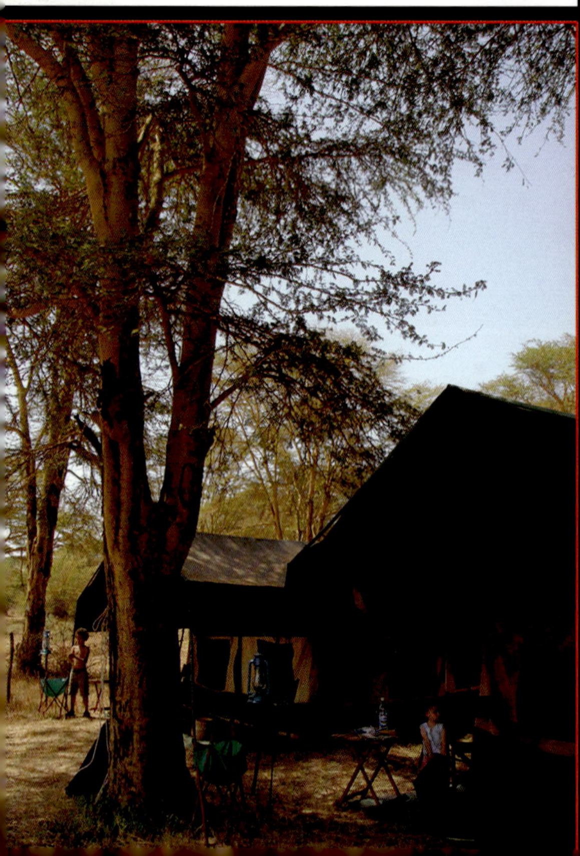

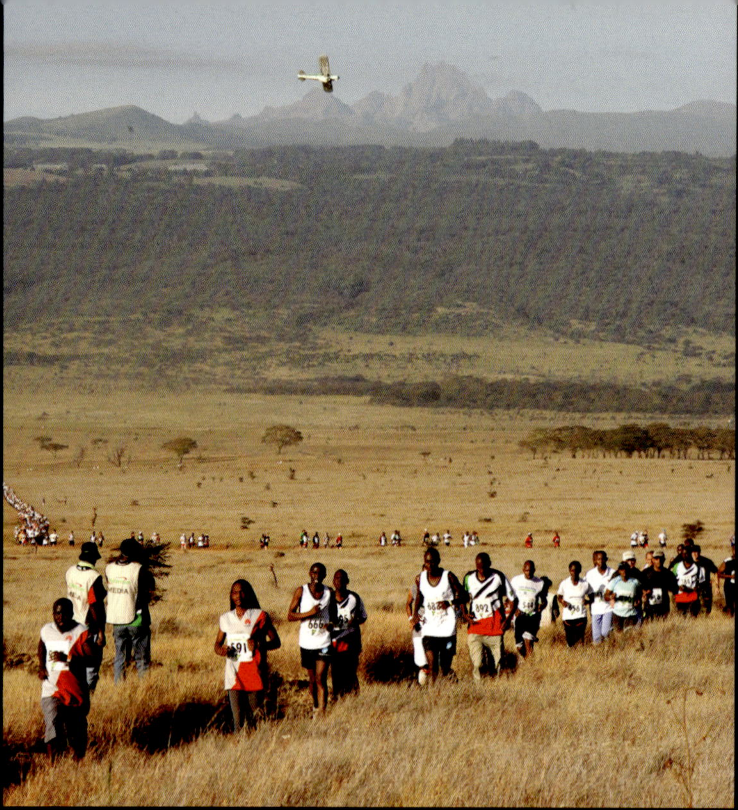

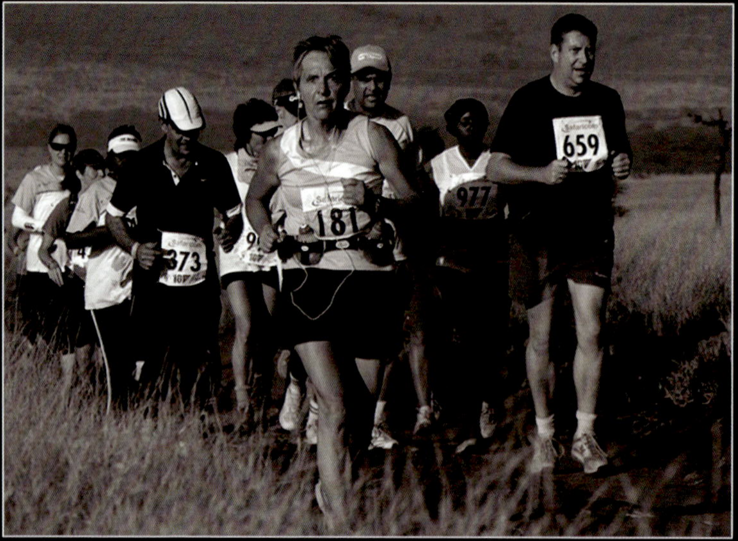
659
181
373
977

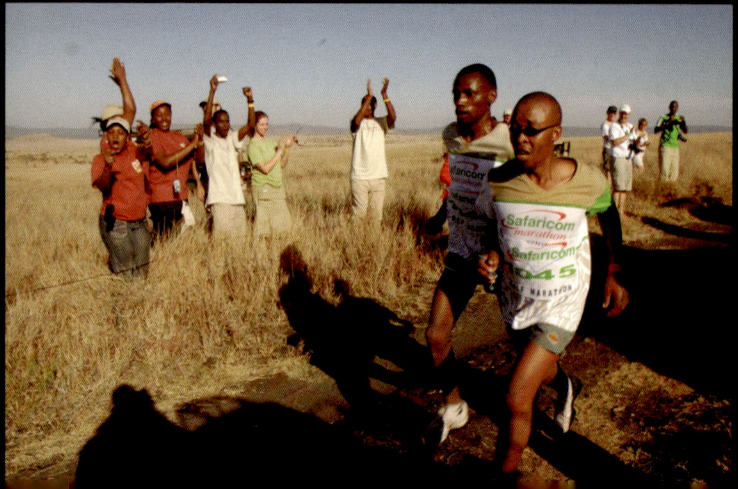
Safaricom
marathon
Safaricom

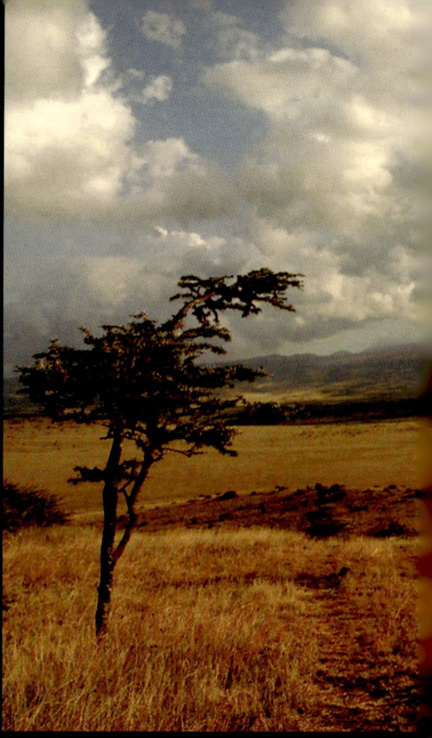

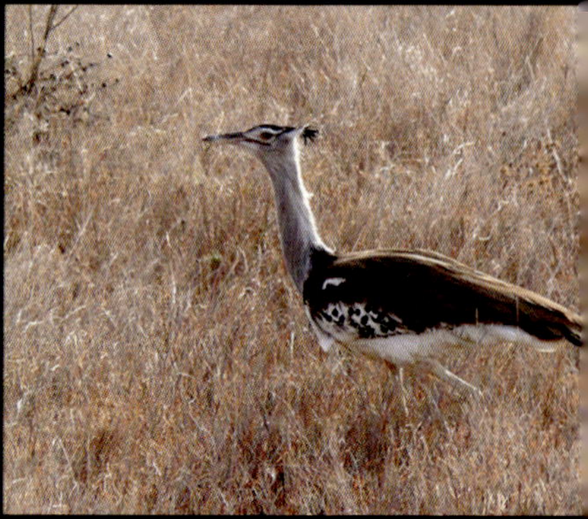

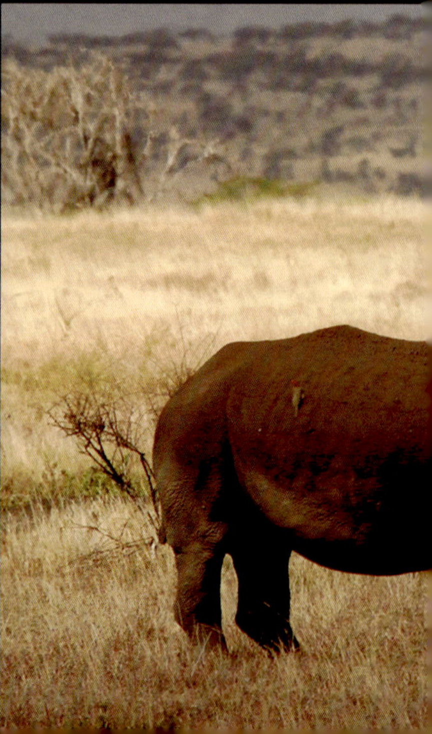

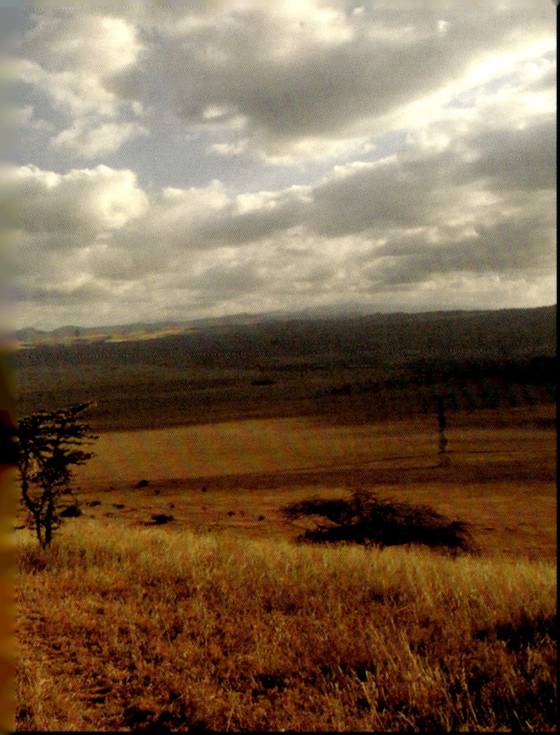
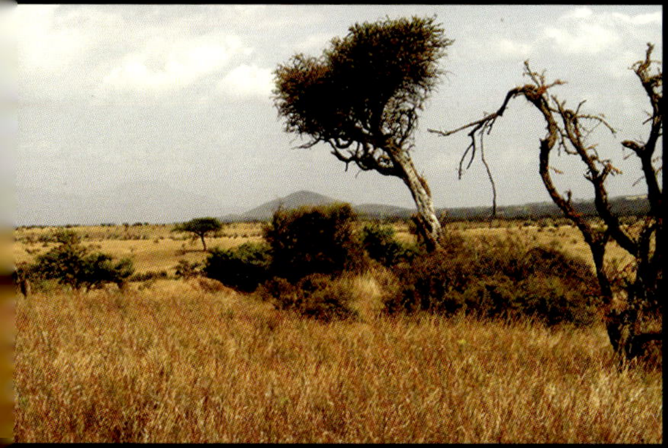
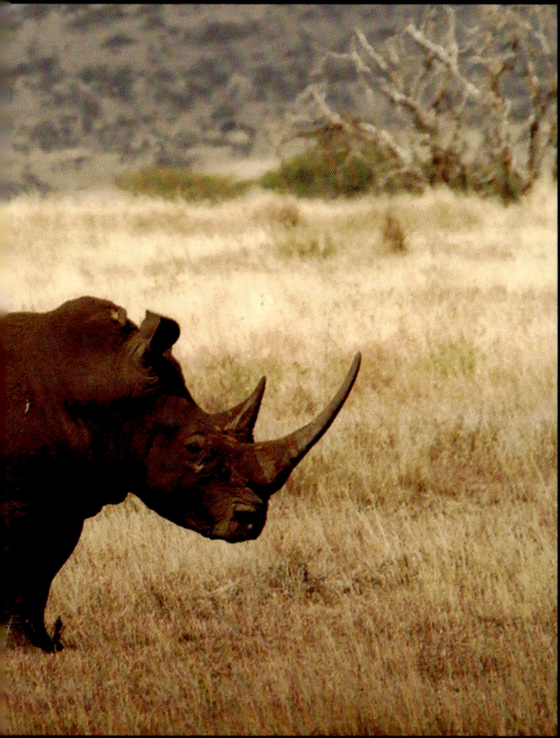
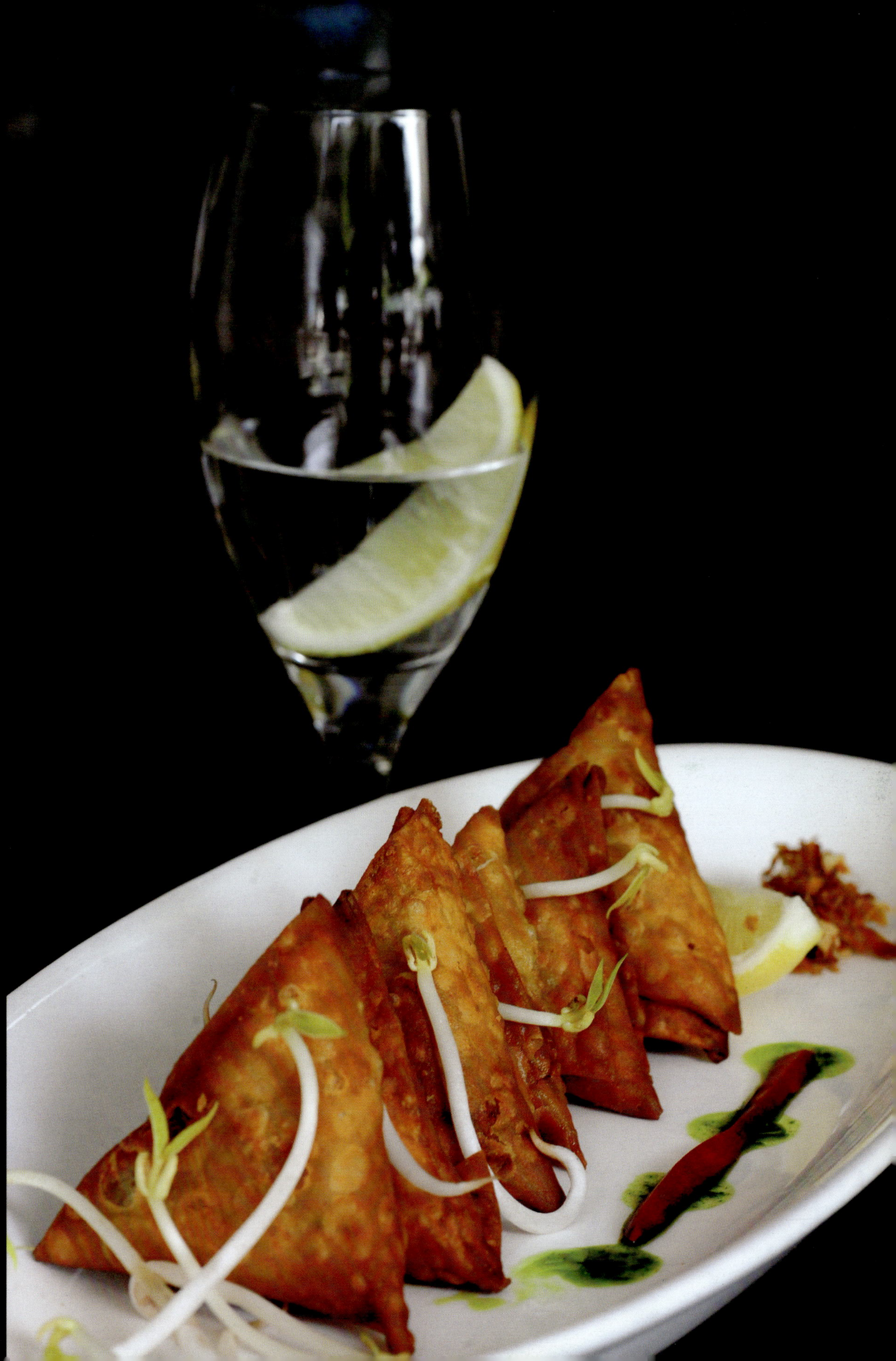

VILLAGE
Lewa Wildlife Conservancy
SAFARICOM MARATHON '09

Saturday 27 June

BREAKFAST

420 pax + 40 pax security + 50 pax
medics & various + 40 pax outsiders = **Serves 550 pax**

Selection of Cut Fresh Fruits
Pawpaw (550 pax/8 = 68.75 pcs) Mango (550 pax/4 = 137.5 pcs)
Banana (550 pax/2 = 275 pcs) Pineapple (550 pax/12 = 45 pcs)

Fruit Juice
(150 ml x 550 pax = 82.5 l)

Toast & Butter
Bread (550 pax/18 pcs per loaf x 2 slices = 61.1 loaves)
Butter (10 g x 550 pax = 5.5 kg)
Jam & Honey (Jam 550 pax x 10 g = 5.50 kg,
honey 10 g x 550 pax = 5.5 kg)

Tea & Coffee
Sugar (10 g x 550 pax = 5.5 kg)
Milk (60 ml x 550 pax = 33 l)

Cereals: Oatmeal & Cornflakes

ACTIVE STATION
Scrambled Eggs *(550 pcs = 18.33 trays)*
Bacon *(50 g x 550 pax = 27.5 kg)*
Beef Sausage *(550 pcs = 21.15 kg = 22 kg)*
Grilled Tomato *(0.5 per pax = 275 pcs)*
Arrow Roots *(20 g x 550 pax = 11 kg)*
Baked Beans *(50 g x 550 pax = 27.5 kg)*
& Fried Bread.

LUNCH
Serves 550 pax

Beef Stew, Cabbage, Potatoes, Peas & Carrots
Green Bean Balad, Tomato Salad, Fresh Fruits
Tea & Coffee

DINNER
Serves 550 pax

Chicken Curry, Vegeterian Curry, Rice
Lentils, Chapati, Kachumbari, Fruit Salad
Tea & Coffee
***

Tusk
Safaricom
START
Tusk
Safaricom
GINA DIN
CREW

Safaricom
Tusk

35
544

1150
1121

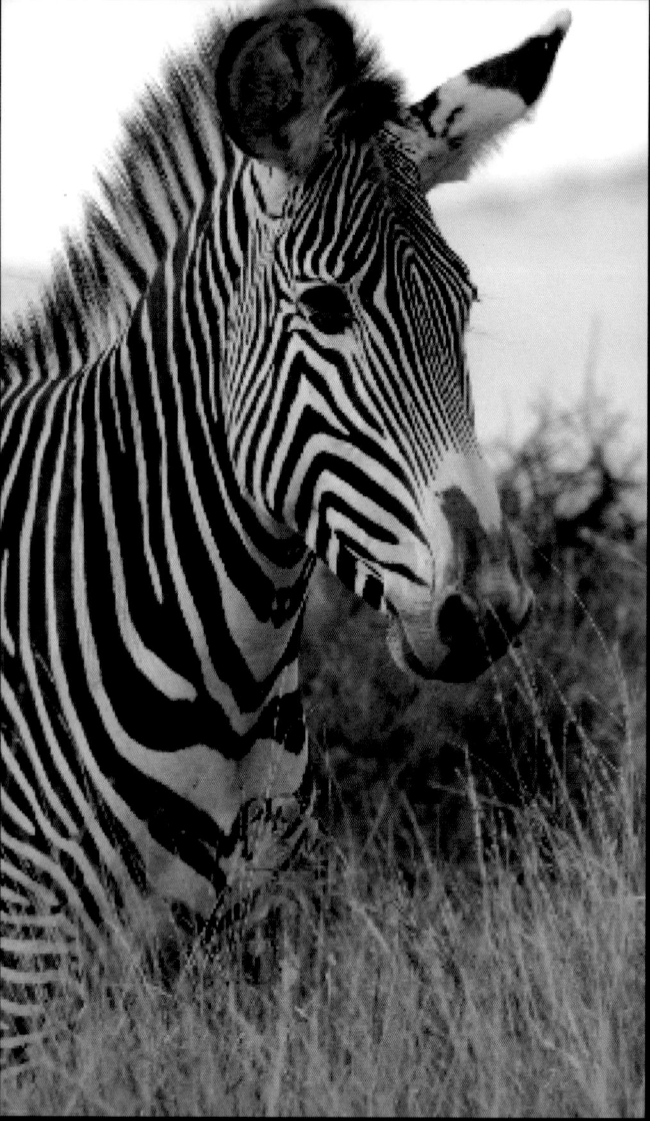

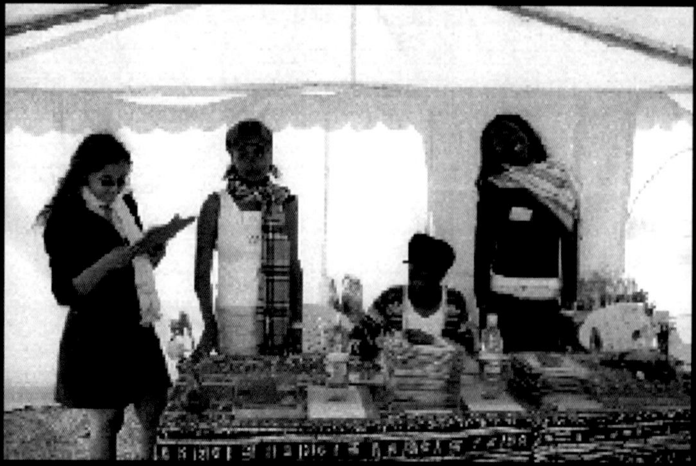

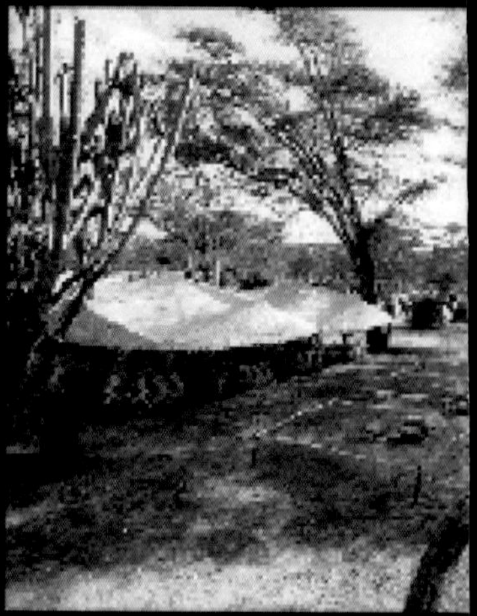

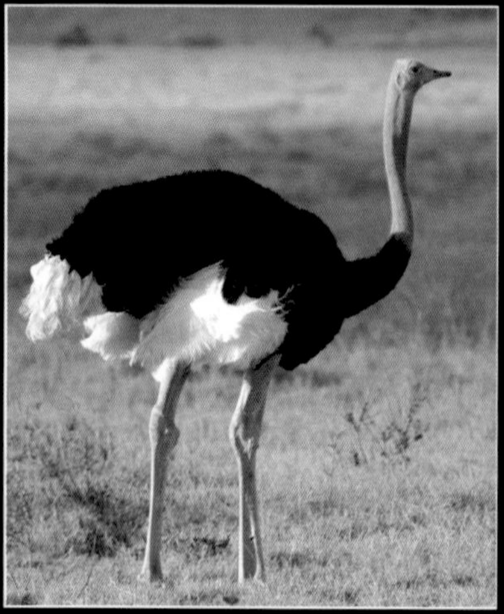

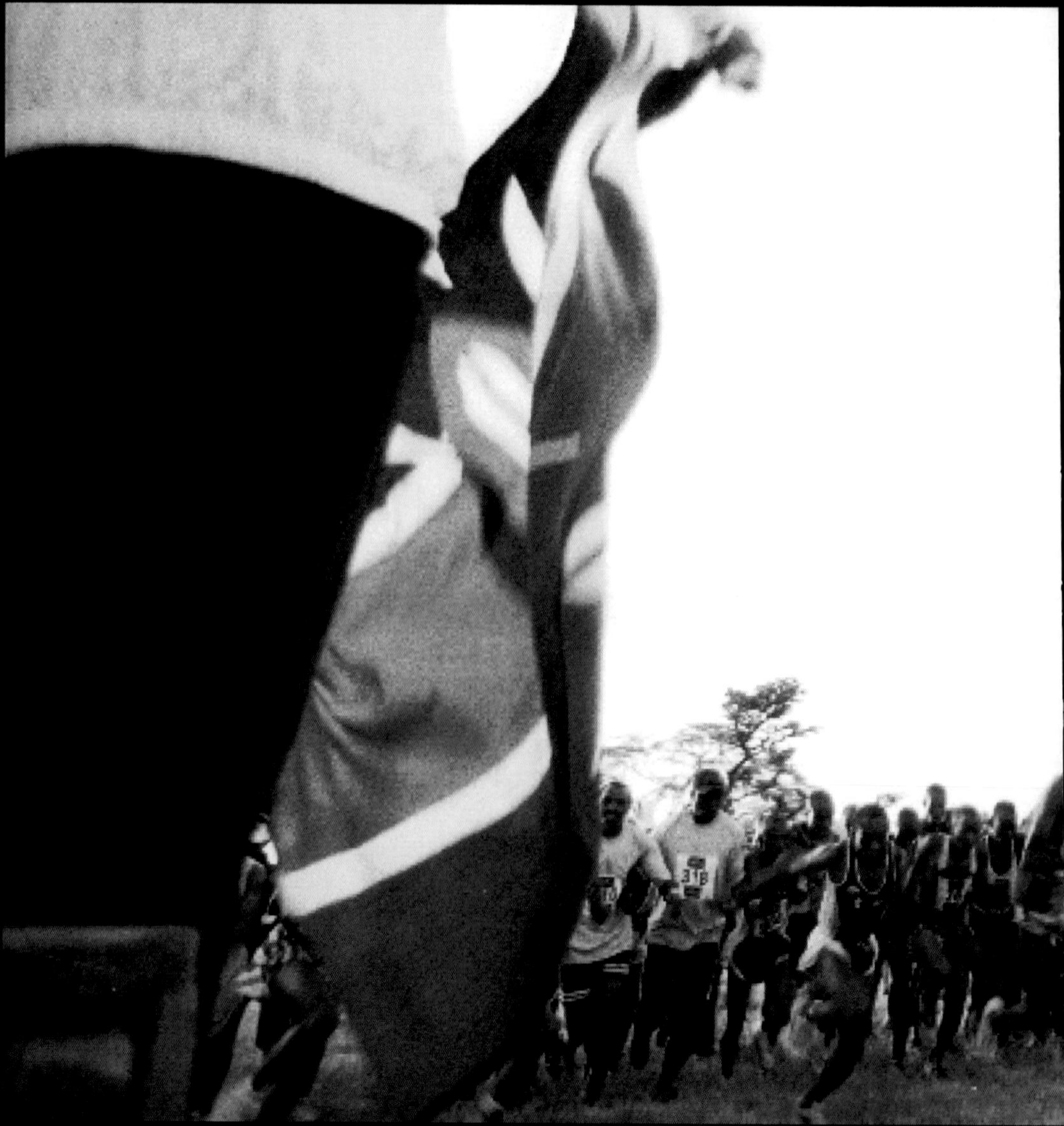

VILLAGE
lewa wildlife conservancy
SAFARICOM MARATHON

Sunday 28th June

BREAKFAST
Serves 550 pax

Selection of cut fresh fruits:
Pawpaw, mango, banana, pineapple.
Fruit Juice
Toast & Butter
Strawberry & Raspberry jam, Honey
Tea & Coffee
Cereals: Oat meal & Cornflakes
Scrambled eggs with bacon, beef sausages, grilled tomato, sweet potatoes, baked beans & fried bread.

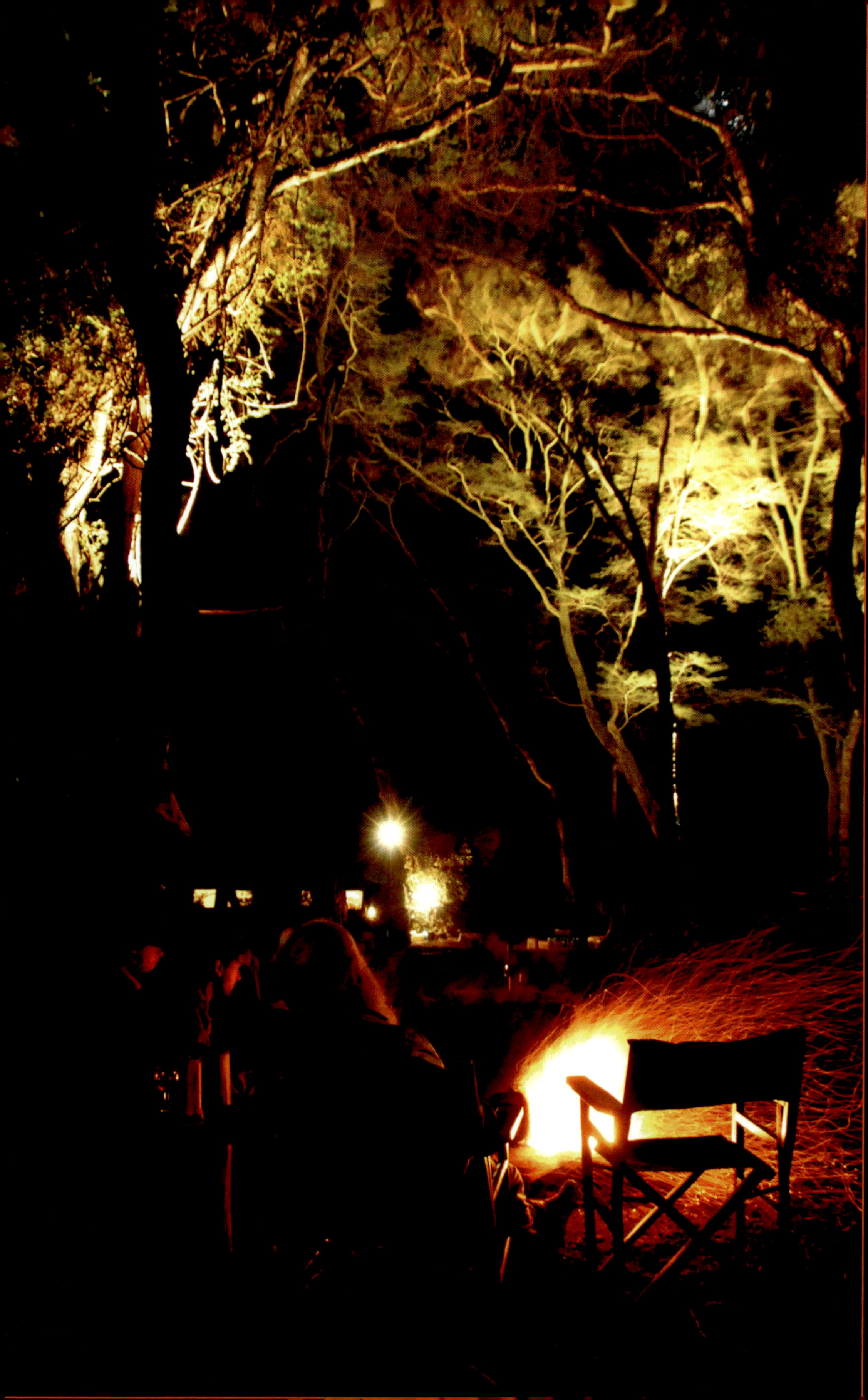

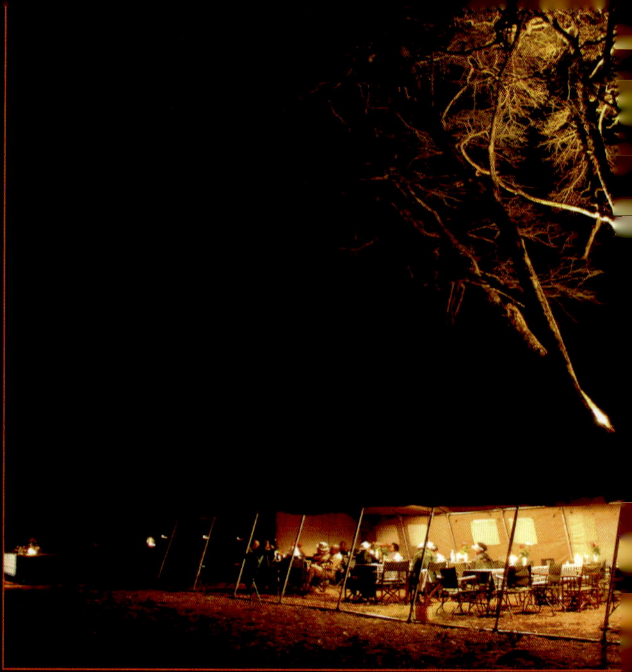

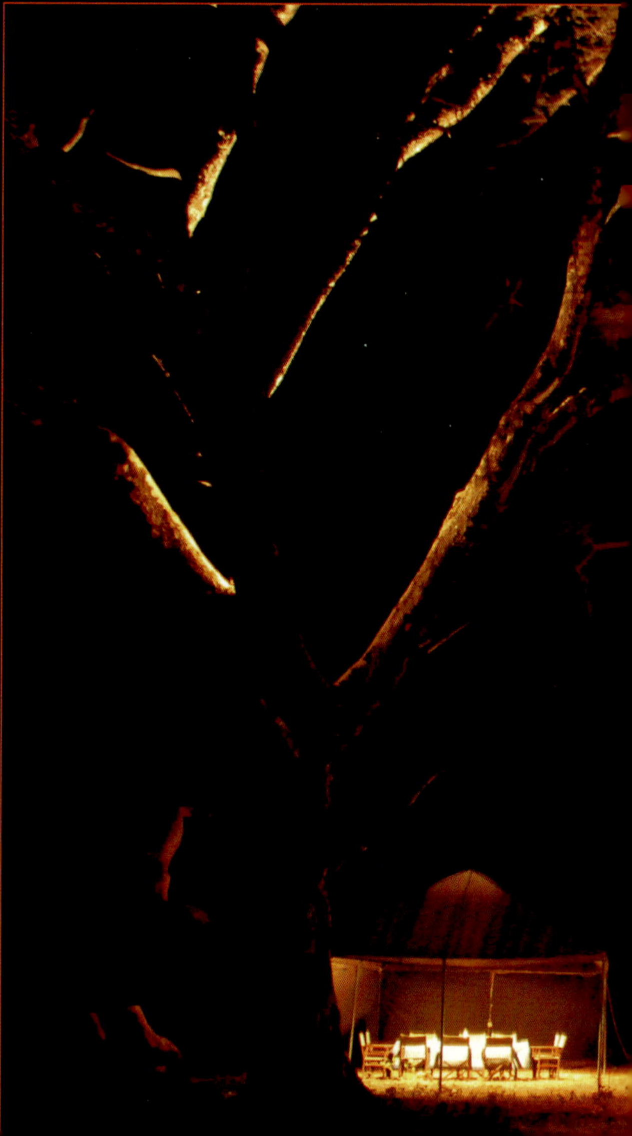

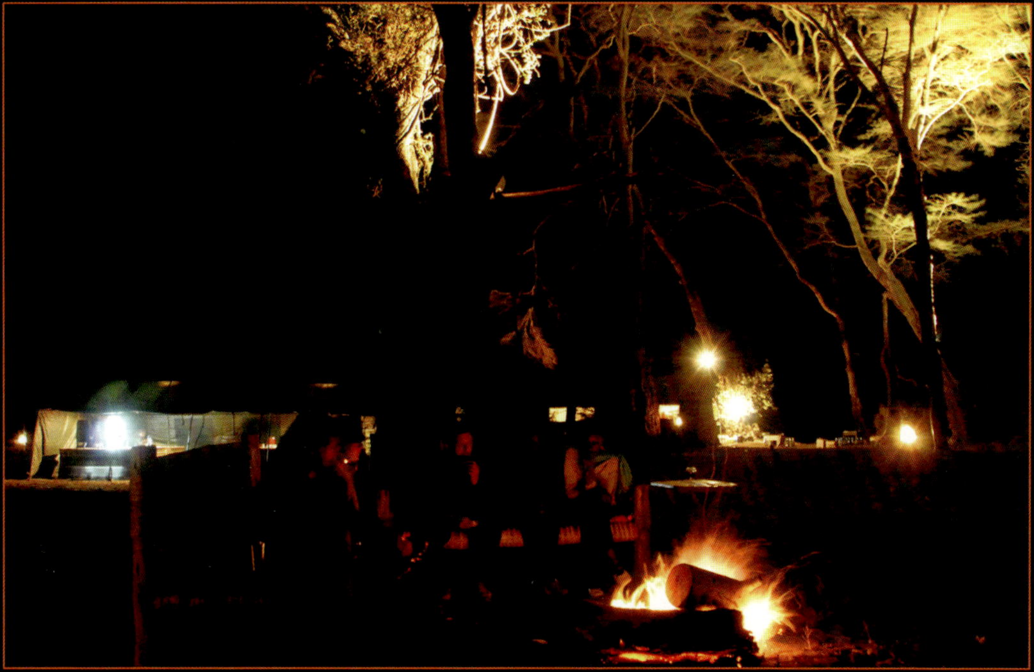
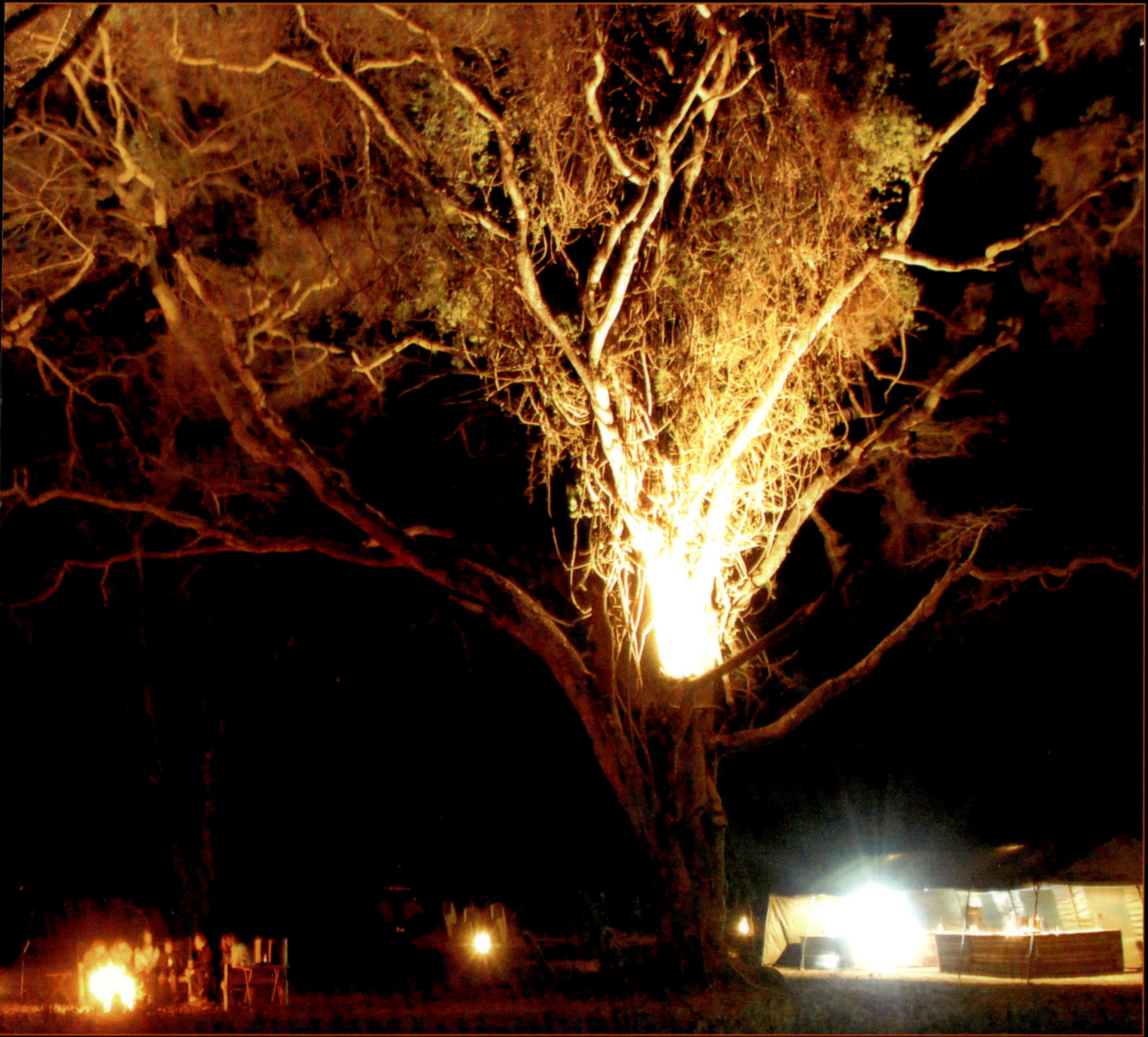
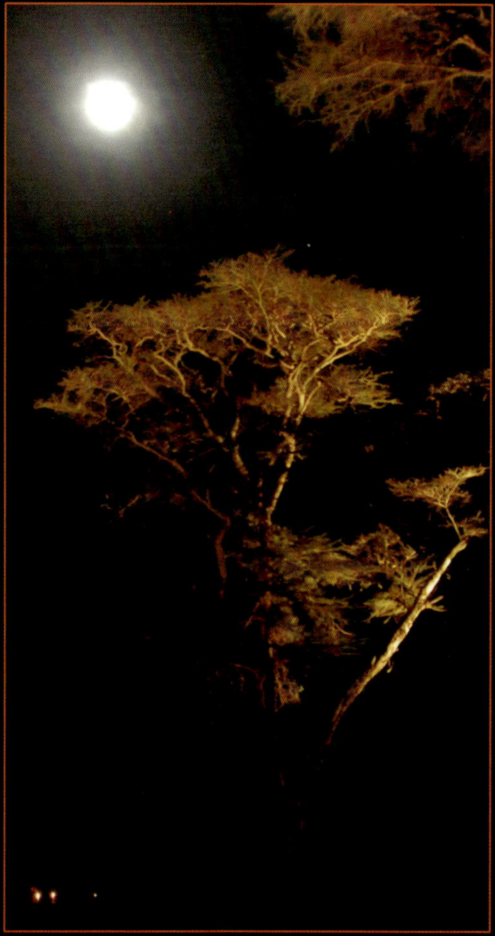

The Aberdare

National Park

68 | Safari Cuisine

Home-cured trout with onion and thyme confit and pancetta

RECIPE

Serves 10 people

Ingredients

- (1 kg) rainbow trout, filleted and de-boned
- 1.5 kg sea salt (or pink rock salt)
- Juice and zest of 9 limes
- Juice and zest of 3 lemons
- 200 g castor sugar
- 50 g crushed fennel seeds
- 9 large white onions
- 1 sprig of fresh thyme
- 1 kg butter
- 100 g thinly sliced pancetta

Method

1. Mix the sugar and the salt in a bowl. Add the juice and zest of the limes and lemons. Then add the crushed fennel.
2. Place the trout fillets, skin-side down, on a tray. sprinkle the salt mixture over them, so all are completely covered.
3. Cover and place in the fridge for 8 hours. Do not leave for longer than this, or the trout will become too salty.
4. Remove the fillets from the fridge and rinse off all the curing salt in fresh water. Soak for a further 1 hour.
5. Remove from the water, towel dry and refrigerate.
6. For the onion confit, peel and quarter the white onions.
7. Melt the butter in a saucepan and mix the onions and the thyme into it.
8. Cook on low heat, almost poaching the onions in the butter until they start to caramelise.
9. Strain off the butter from the onions, and then roughly blend the onions into a paste. Taste and season accordingly.
10. Fry the pancetta in a hot pan until it becomes crispy, and allow to rest on absorbent paper to soak up the excess fat.
11. Slice the trout thinly. Serve with the pancetta, onion confit and ideally with some oat crackers.

Tips/Pointers

If cured properly, this dish can be frozen and taken on safari as an easy and delicious starter for any meal. The key lies in the pre-preparation, and of course in making sure that you obtain fresh, good quality trout.

ANATOL'S JACOBS COFFEE
PHOTO SHOOT
ABERDARES NATIONAL PARK
MENU

Home-cured trout with onion
and thyme confit and pancetta

Poikje-braised lamb shanks with lemon
and parsley gremolata, borlotti beans,
roasted garlic and thyme

Vanilla cheesecake with dark chocolate
base and strawberry coulis

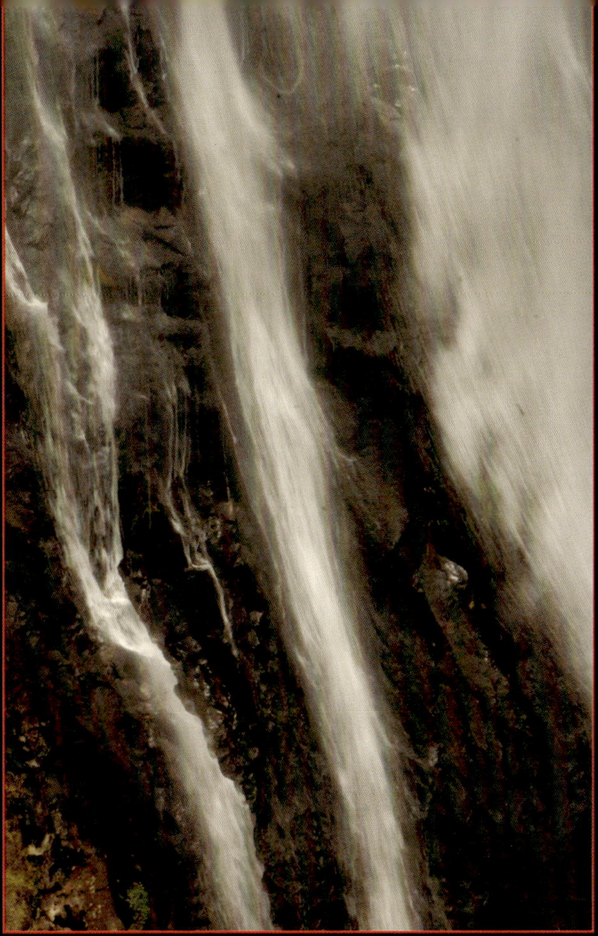
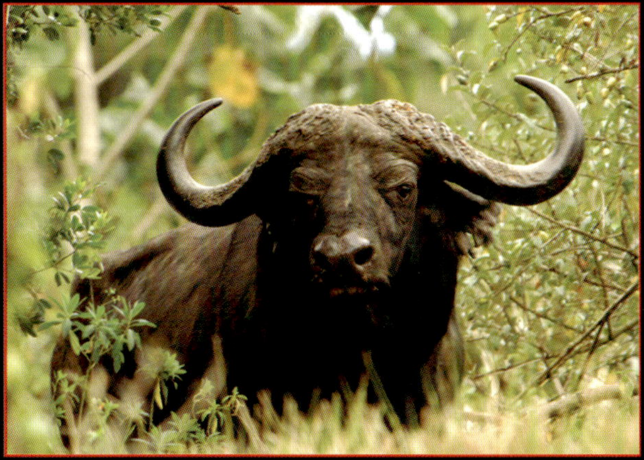
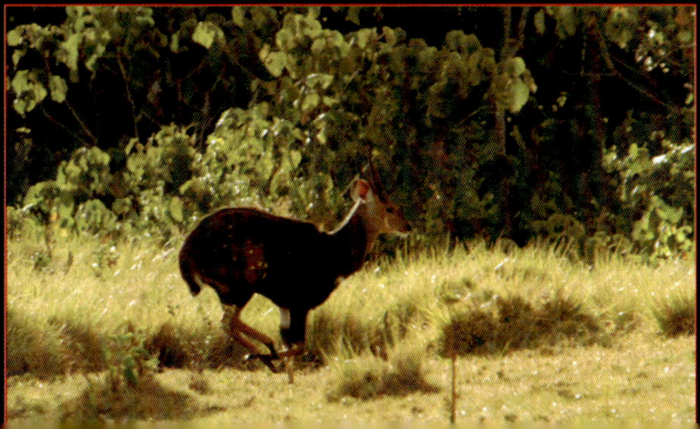
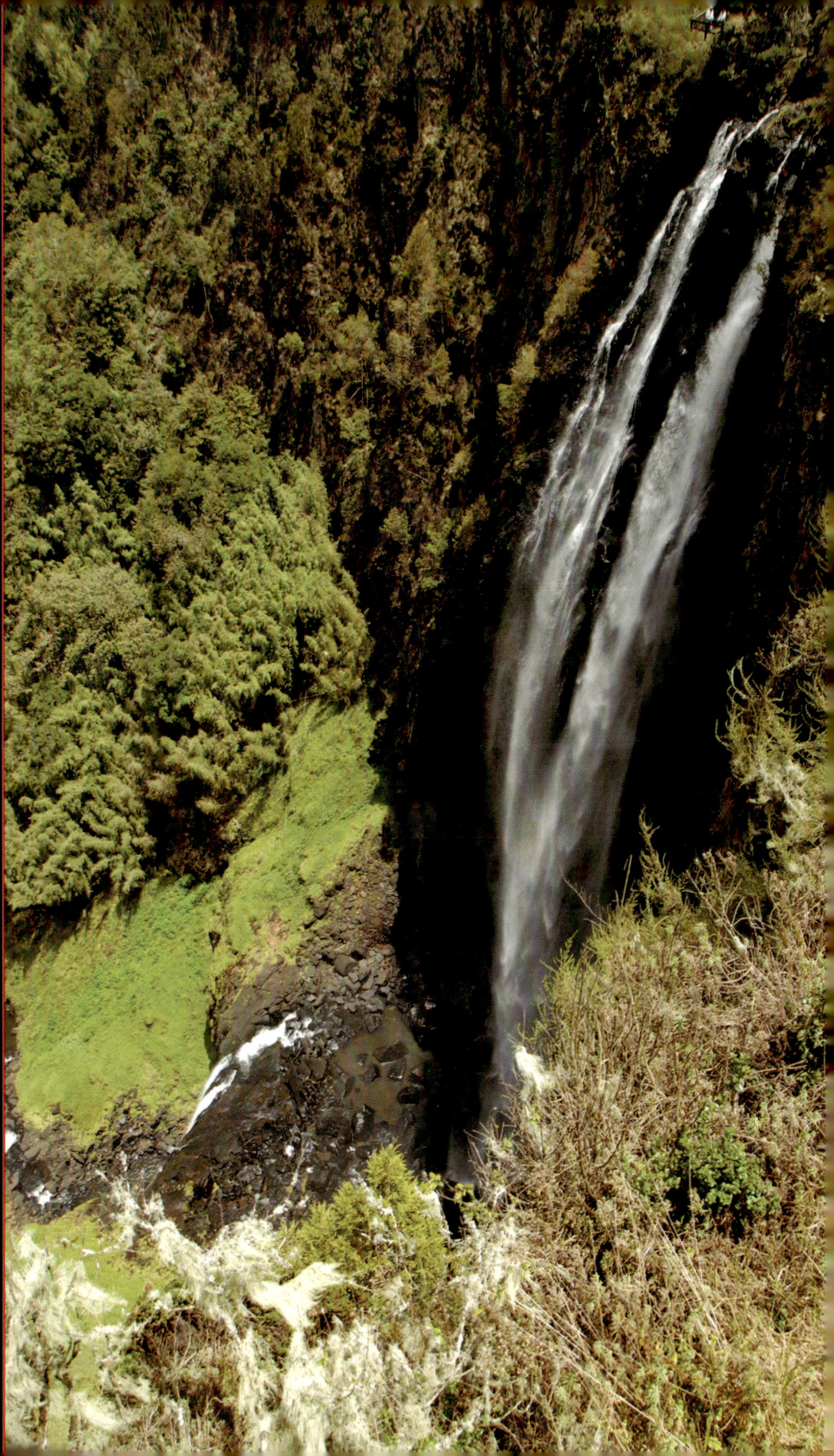

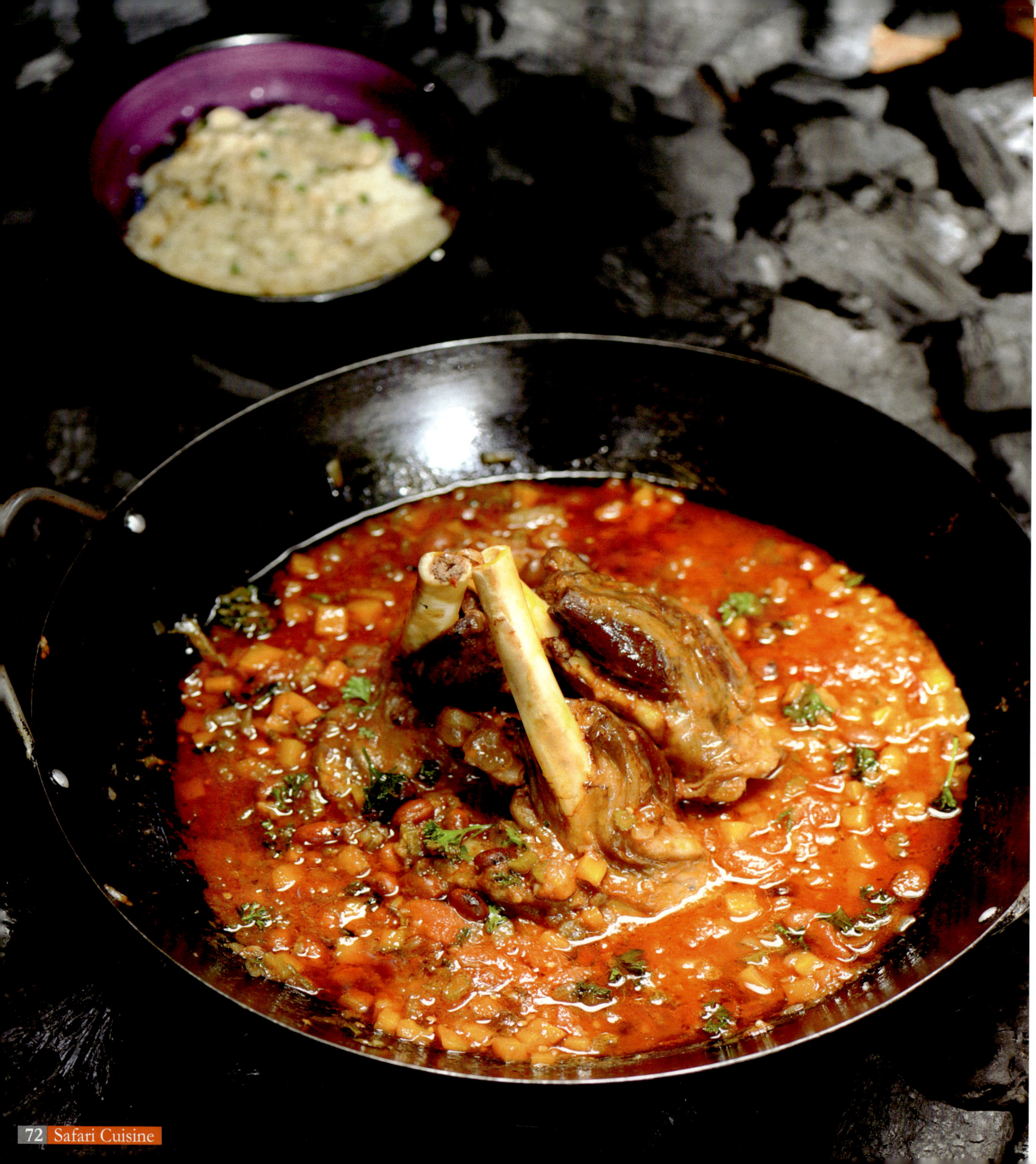

Poikje-braised lamb shanks with lemon and parsley gremolata, borlotti beans, roasted garlic and thyme

RECIPE

Serves 5 people

Bush equipment

A poikje with a stand, so it can be suspended over an open campfire.

Ingredients

- 5 lamb shanks, trimmed
- ½ tsp salt
- 1/4 tsp black pepper
- 2 cups finely chopped carrots
- 1 cup finely chopped onions
- 1 cup finely chopped celery
- 1 cup dry red wine
- ½ cup beef broth
- 1½ tsp thyme
- 2 (14.5-ounce) cans diced tomatoes
- 2 bay leaves
- 1 cup borlotti beans soaked overnight.
- 4 bacon slices
- 4 garlic cloves, sliced
- Zest of 2 lemons
- 1 bunch chopped fresh parsley
- 2 cloves crushed garlic
- 6 cloves roasted garlic
- 2 chopped anchovy fillets

Tips/Pointers

Although this recipe specifies that a poikje be used to cook the shanks, any heavy-cast iron dish that can be suspended over a campfire will suffice.

Method

1. Sprinkle the lamb shanks with salt and pepper. Heat the poikje over the campfire. Then add the lamb, and brown on all sides. Remove from the poikje.
2. Add the carrot, onion, bacon and celery to the poikje. Sauté for 3 minutes, then add the wine. Bring to the boil and cook for 5 minutes.
3. Stir into the broth: the thyme, the tomatoes, the roasted garlic and the bay leaves.
4. Return lamb to the poikje (which will be very full). Cover, and reduce the heat, then simmer for 2 hours, or until very tender, turning the lamb once.
5. Remove the lamb from the poikje and bring the liquid to a boil, reducing this until you have a thick sauce.
6. Sort and wash the beans and place them in a large saucepan in the oven. Cover with water to 2 inches above the beans; bring to the boil, and cook for 1 hour.
7. Drain the beans and add to the lamb sauce.
8. Just before serving, stir in the parsley, lemon zest and anchovy fillet.

Aberdares

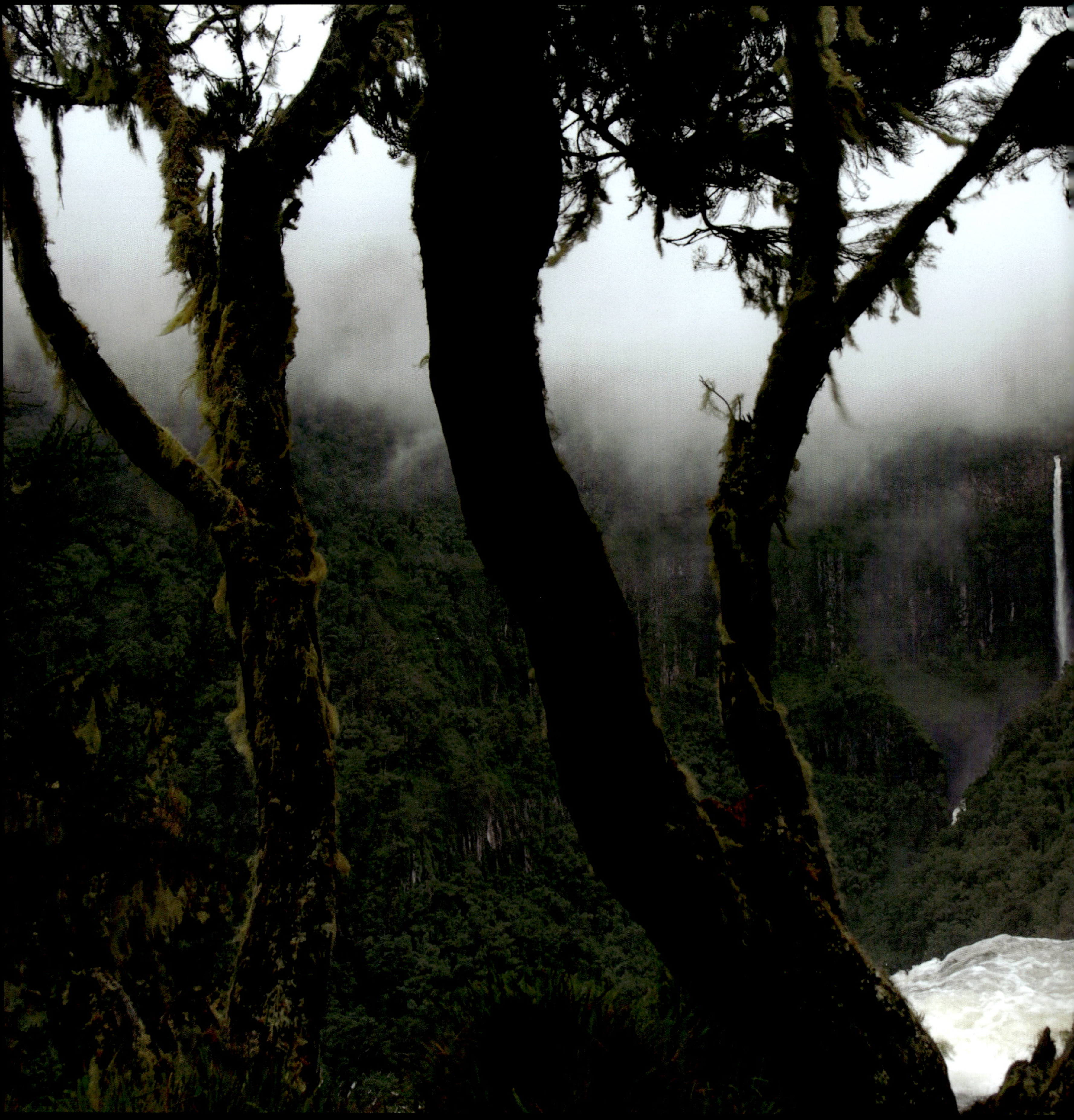

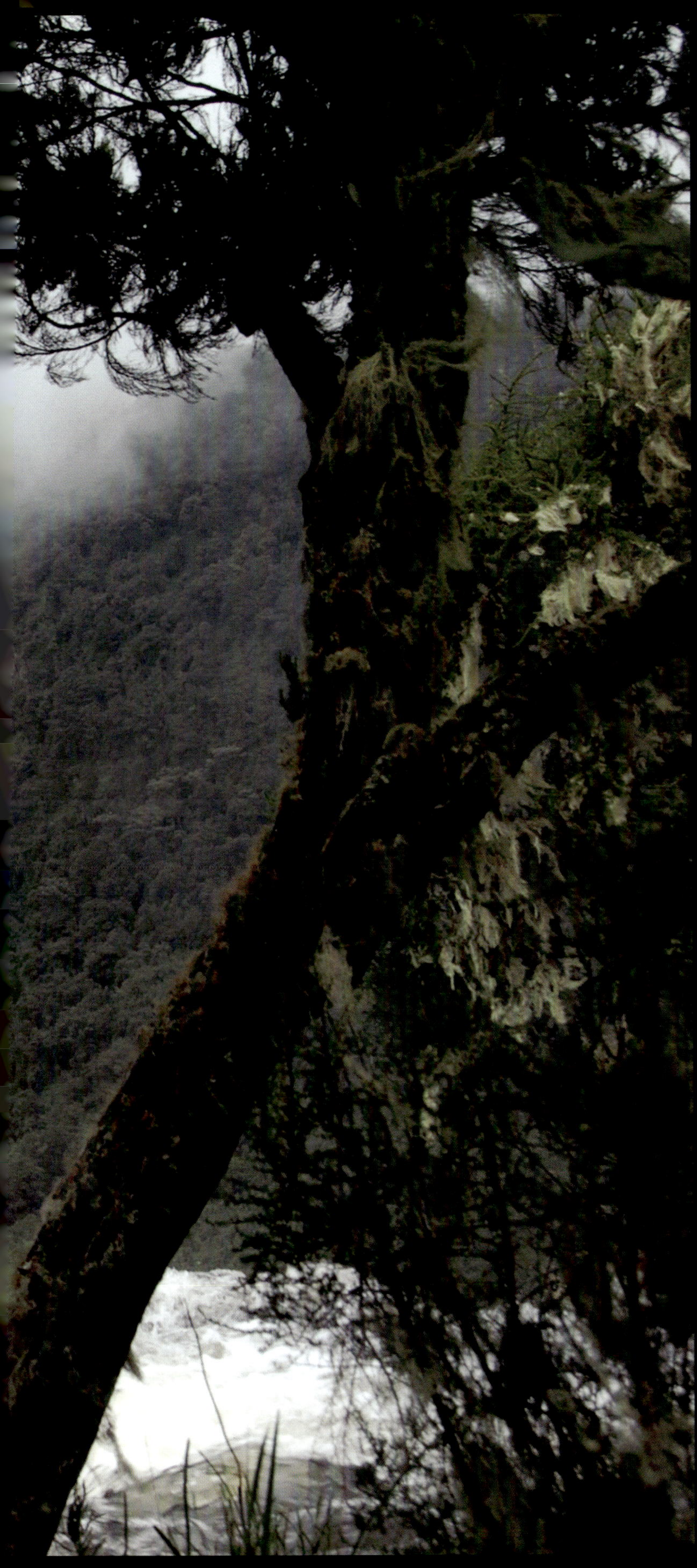
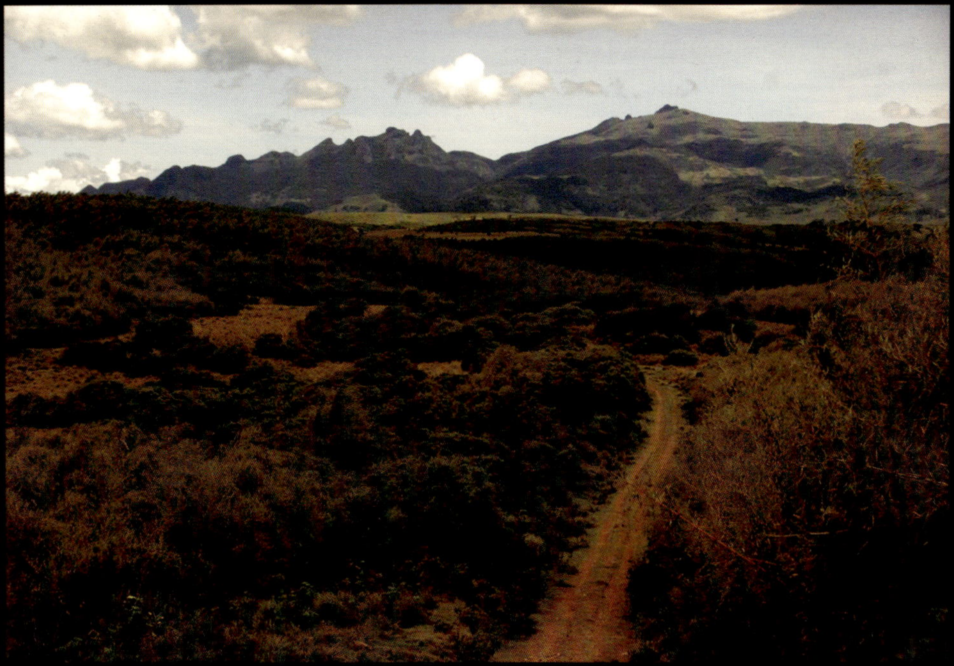
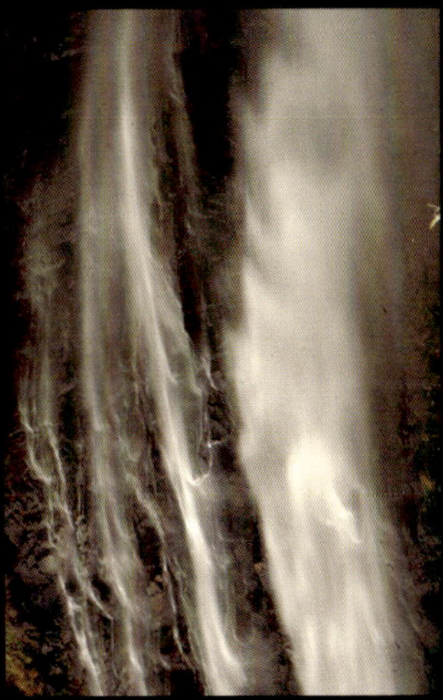
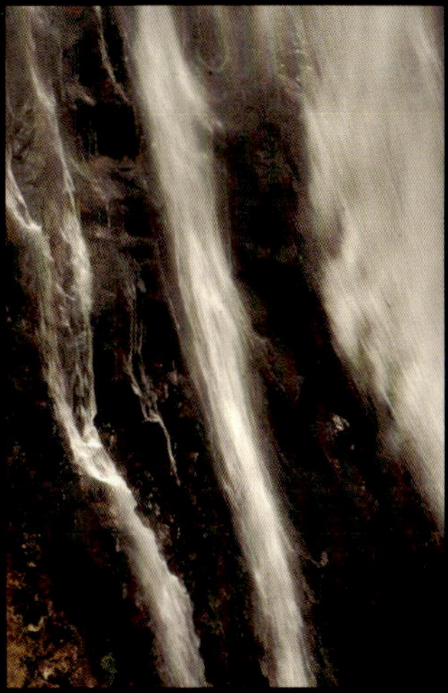
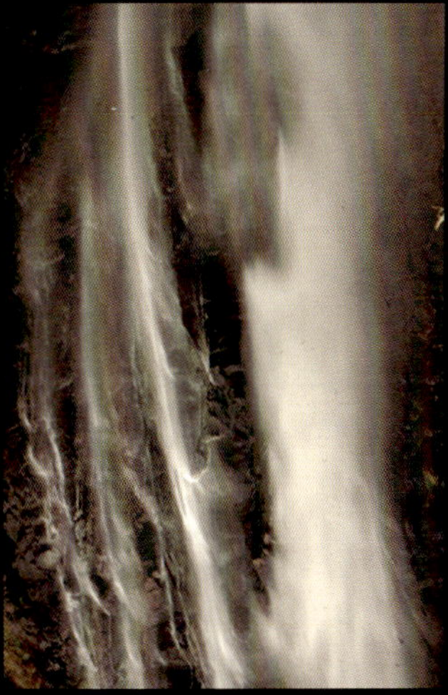
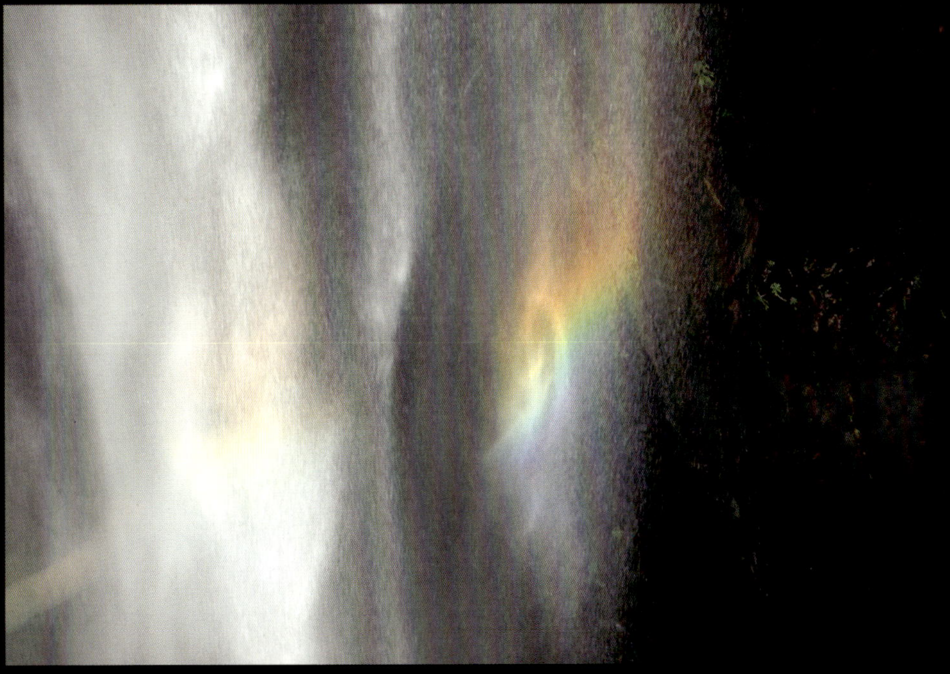

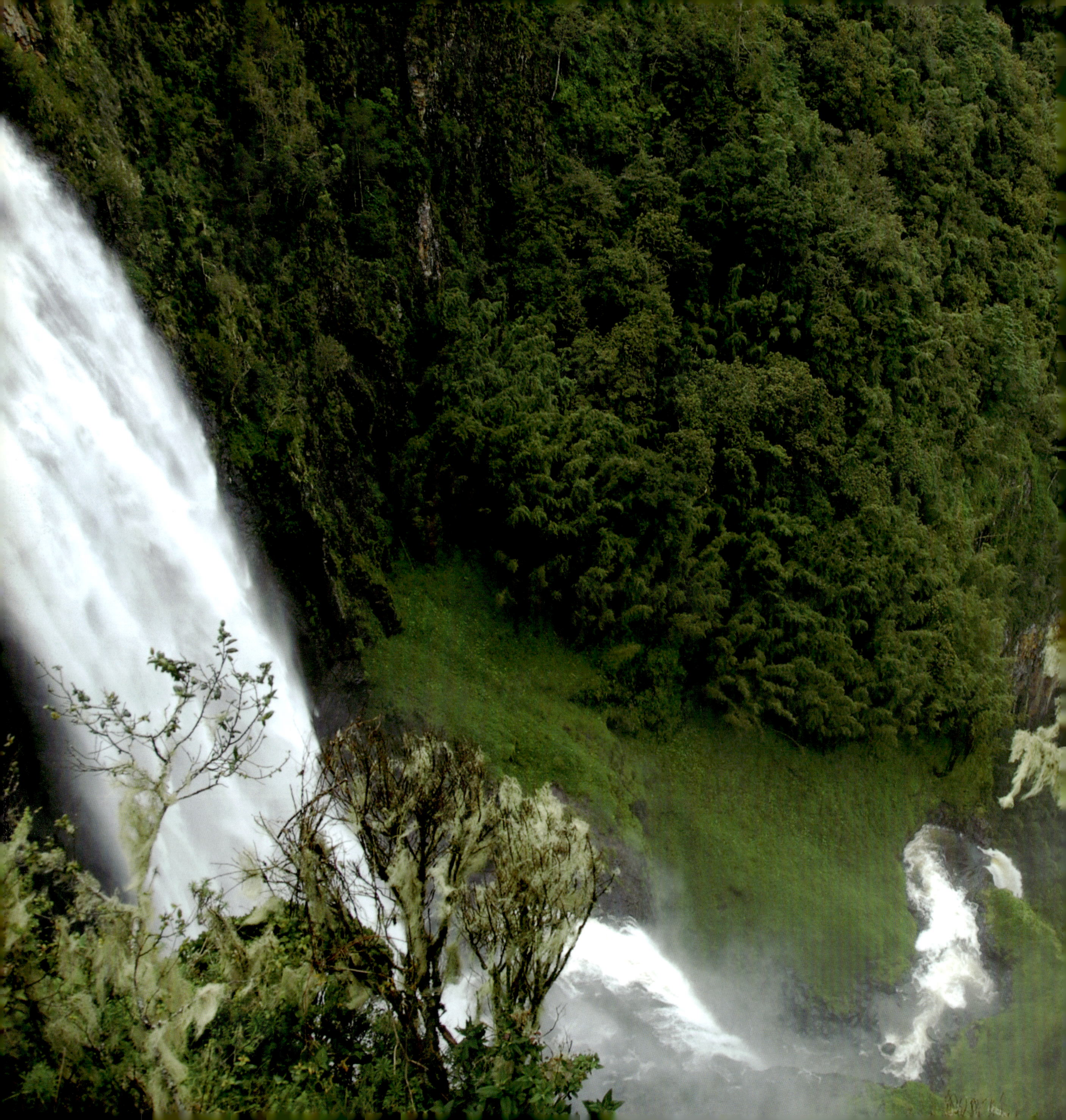

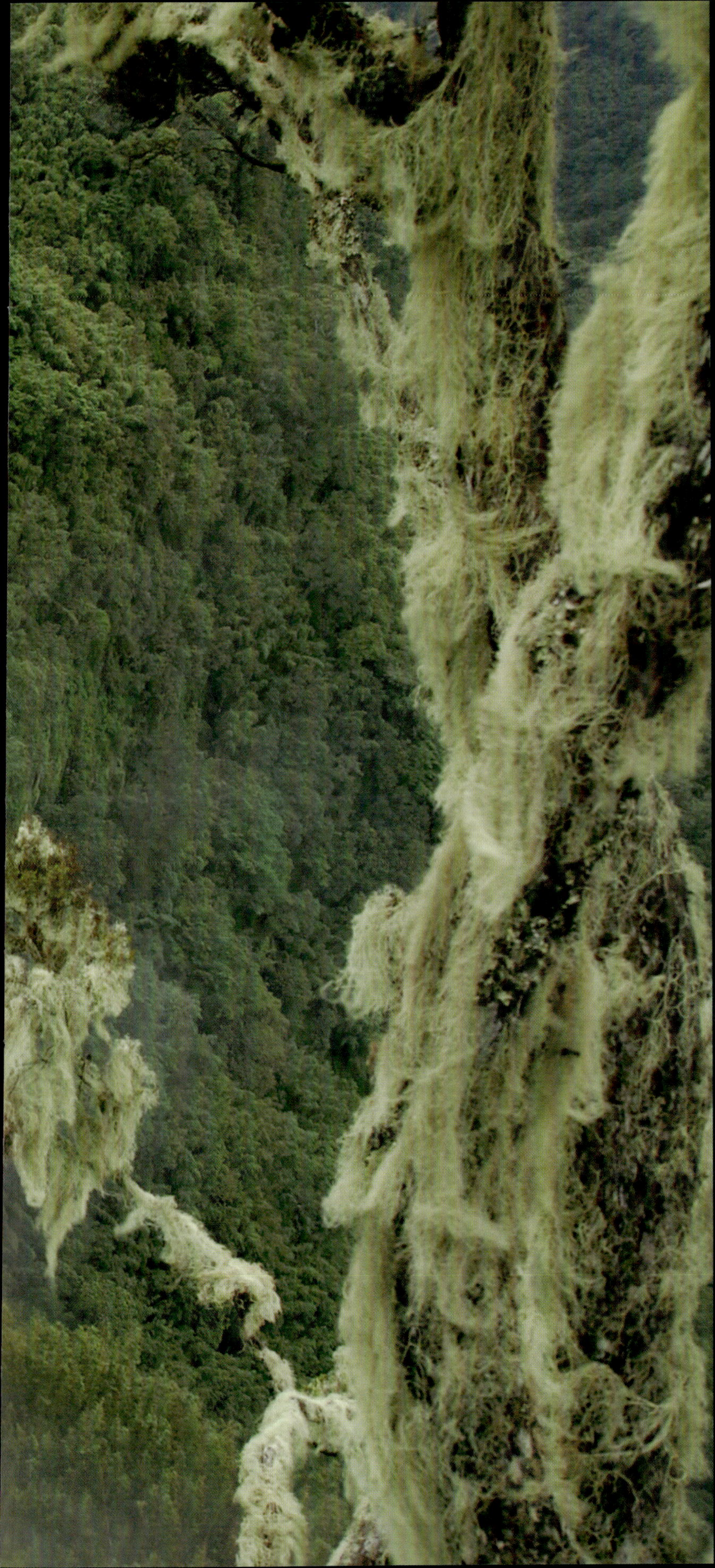
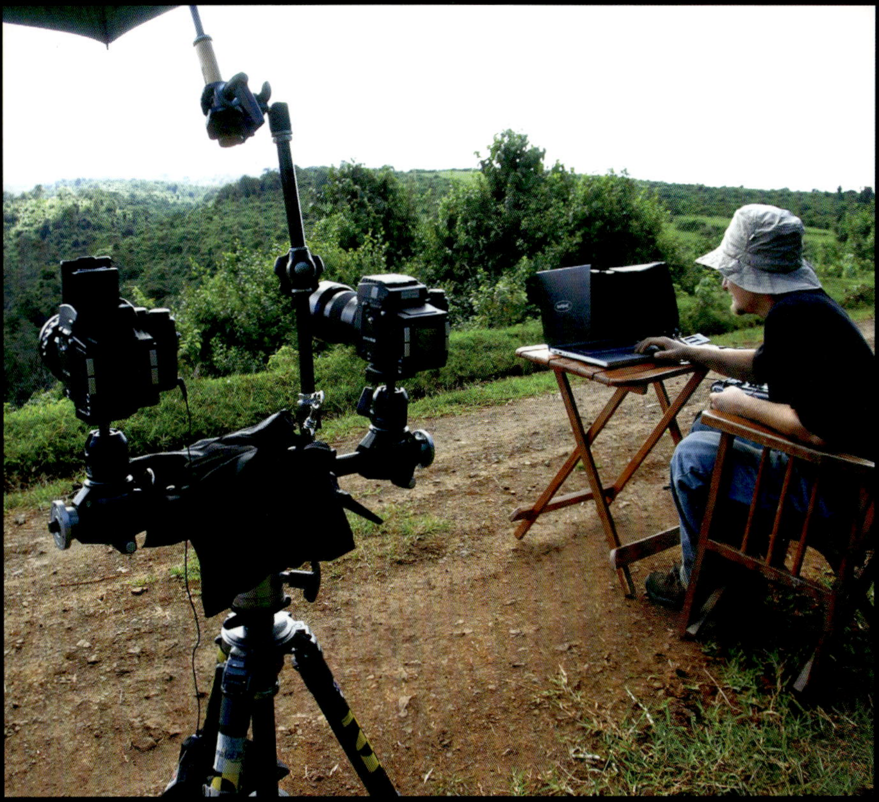
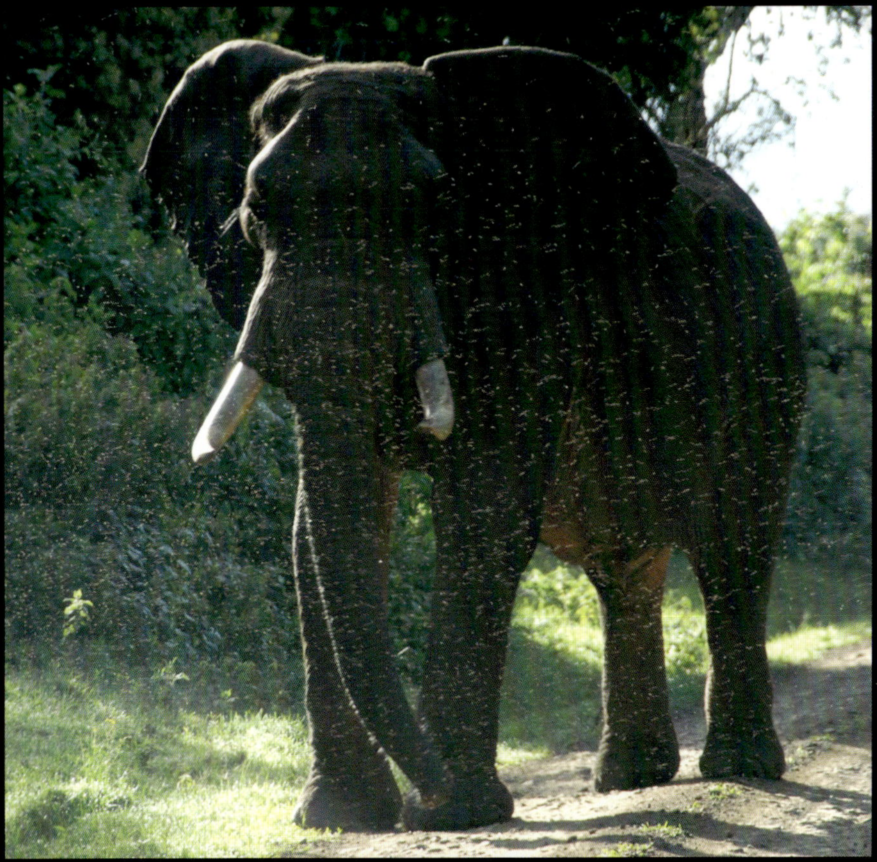

Vanilla cheesecake with dark chocolate base and strawberry coulis

RECIPE

Serves 8 people

Ingredients

- 2 cups cream cheese
- ½ cup chocolate
- ½ cup castor sugar
- 5 eggs, separated
- 1 cup double cream
- Zest of 1 lemon
- Seeds of 1 vanilla bean
- 1 cup crushed digestive biscuits
- 2 tbsp butter
- 1 punnet strawberries
- 3 tbsp unrefined sugar

Method

1. Melt the butter and the chocolate in a glass bowl over a saucepan of boiling water and mix in the crushed biscuits.
2. Line and grease an 8-inch loose-bottomed baking tin and spread out the mixture evenly. Keep in refrigerator until needed.
3. Mix the cream cheese and the cream with the grated lemon rind, the vanilla extract, and the egg yolks.
4. Whisk the egg whites with a pinch of salt and sugar until creamy and stiff.
5. Fold the egg whites gently into the cheese mixture.
6. Add the cheese mixture to the top of the biscuit base.
7. Place in an oven pre-heated to 180°C and bake for 45–55 minutes.
8. Meanwhile, add the unrefined sugar to a saucepan with 2 tbsp of water and dissolve. Boil until you have a golden brown caramel.
9. To this, add the punnet of chopped strawberries until the mixture resembles a loose jam.
10. Serve cheesecake cold with strawberry coulis.

Tips/Pointers

When baking the cheesecake, do so until the edges are firm but the centre is still slightly wobbly. This will produce a well set, but very creamy texture.

Aberdares

OUR TRADITIONAL MOBILE CAMP
location africa safaris
Feb 2010

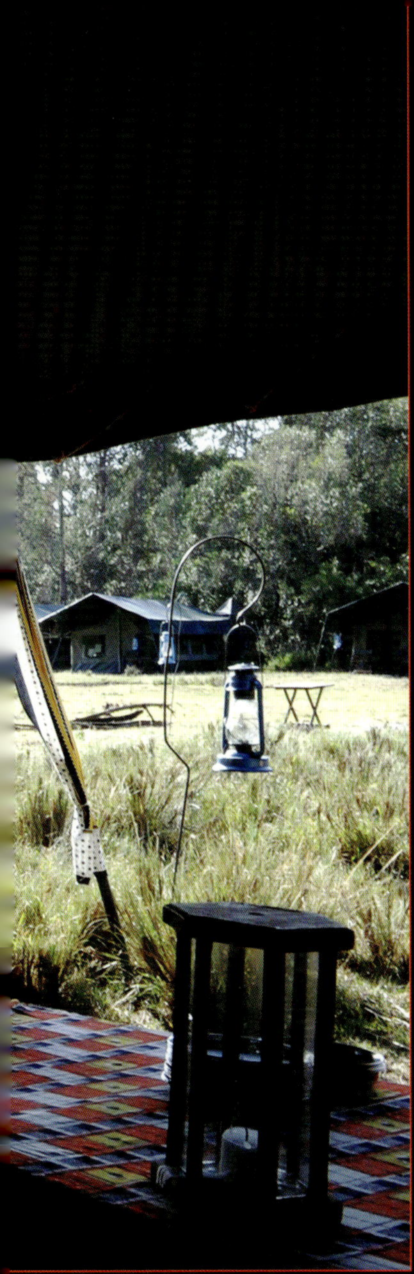
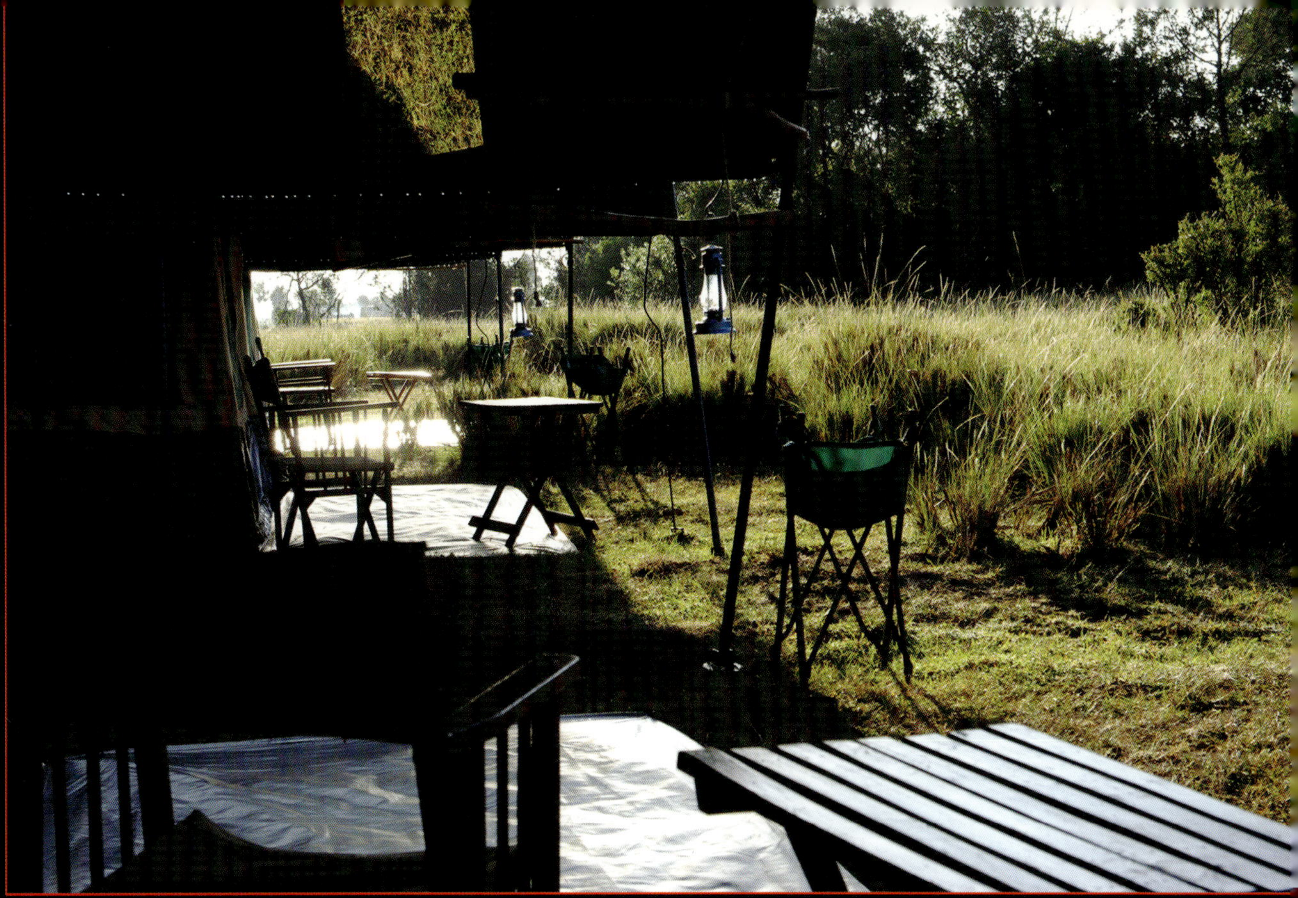
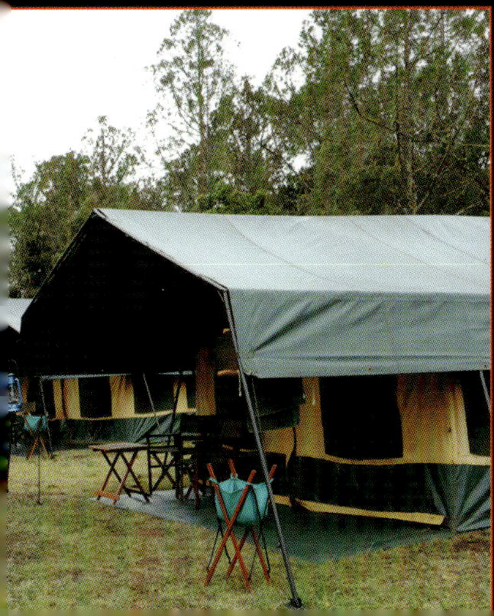
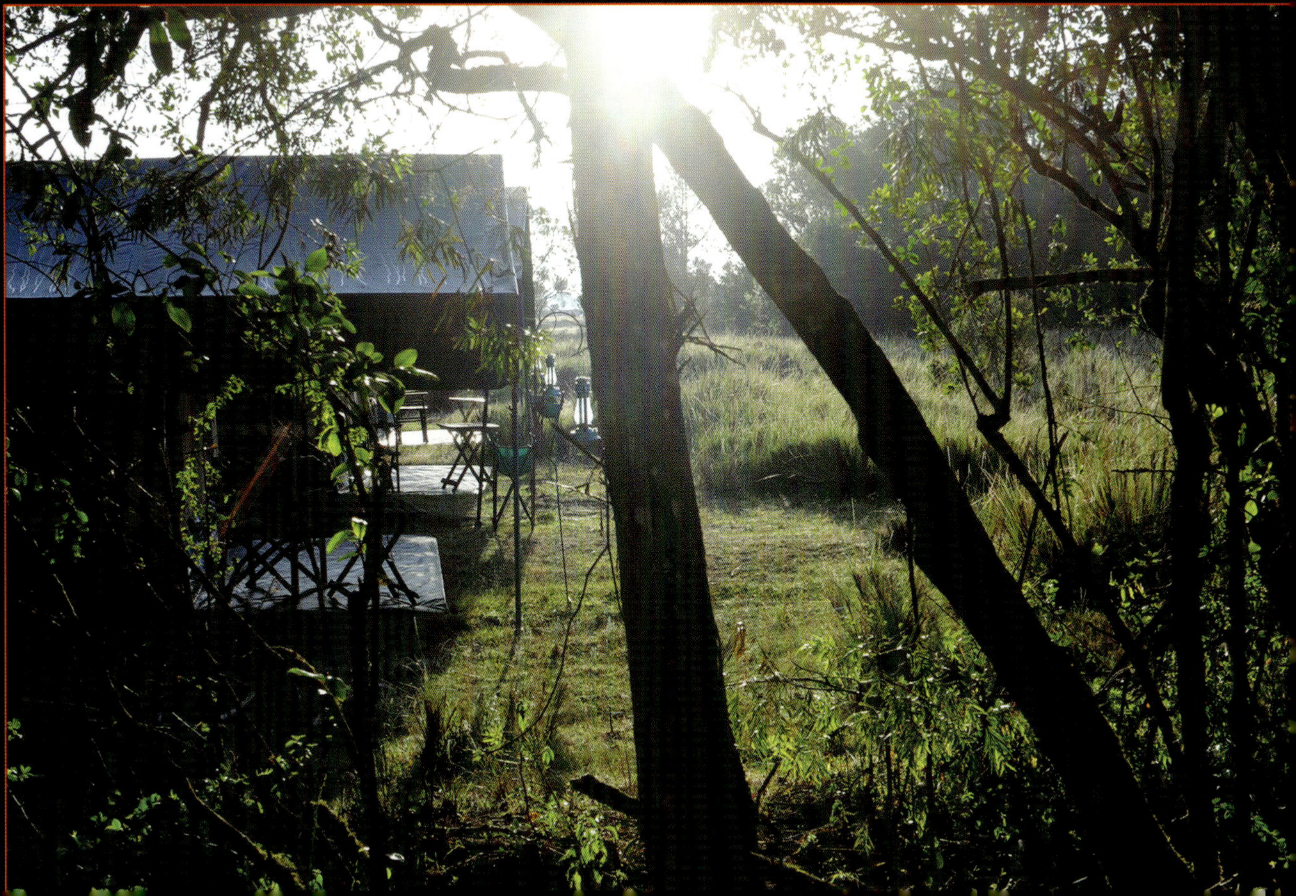

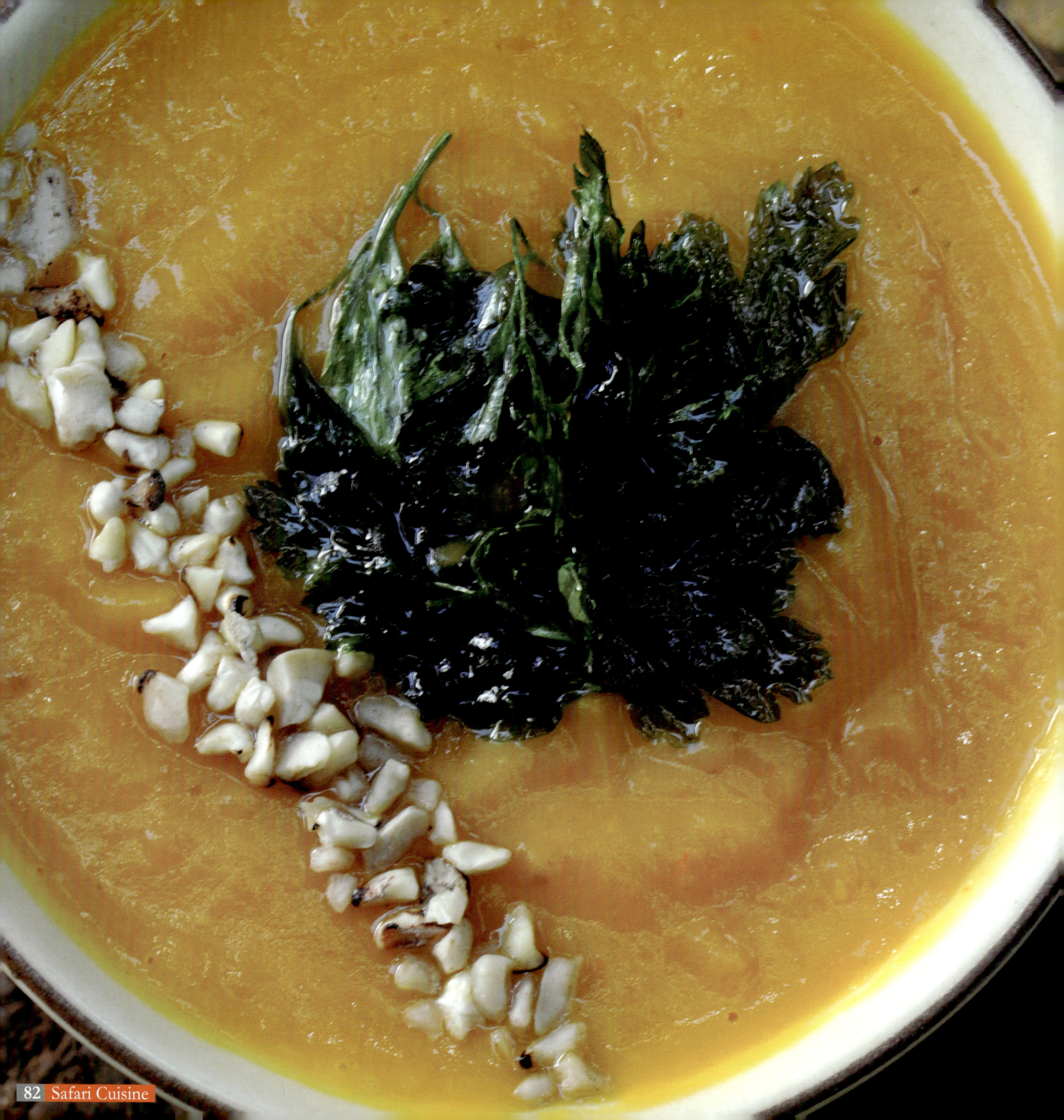

Roast butternut soup with nutmeg and hazelnut essence

RECIPE

Serves 10 people

Special equipment

A good ricer, if you do not have a blender.

Ingredients

- 3 butternuts, peeled and chopped
- 1 tbsp brown sugar
- 1 tbsp vegetable oil
- 2 tsp paprika
- 4 carrots
- 4 cloves crushed garlic
- ½ head of celery
- 3 red onions
- 200 g butter
- 2 litres vegetable stock
- 1 tsp ground nutmeg
- 1 tbsp hazelnut butter/purée

Method

1. Coat the chopped butternuts in oil and place on a baking tray. Sprinkle over the brown sugar and the paprika, and mix until the butternut is evenly coated.
2. Place the butternut in a hot oven and roast until it is golden brown and beginning to caramelise. Remove from the oven and set aside.
3. Finely dice the onions, celery and carrots, and place these in a saucepan with the butter. Cover and cook until soft and translucent.
4. Add in the garlic and fry until it starts to brown. Be careful not to burn the garlic.
5. Add the stock and butternut and bring to the boil.
6. Remove from the heat and blend, or put through a ricer, to produce a soup of thick consistency.
7. Add the nutmeg and the hazelnut purée just before serving.
8. Test for seasoning and serve.

Tips/Pointers

Roasting the butternut ensures that the rich sugars it contains will caramelise, so enriching the flavour of the soup. If you cannot find hazelnut butter, then peanut butter can be used as a substitute.

Aberdares 83

84 Safari Cuisine

Whole roast loin of pork on the bone with pan-roasted tomatoes, tomato fondue and creamed spinach

RECIPE

Serves 10 people

Ingredients

- 1 complete rack of bone in pork, with skin on
- 2 tbsp salt
- 2 tbsp pepper
- 4 onions, chopped
- 1 bulb crushed garlic
- 1 cup olive oil
- 1 kg plum tomatoes, skinned, halved and de-seeded
- Handful thyme
- 10 normal ripe tomatoes halved and skinned
- 4 large bunches of shredded spinach
- 2 cups cream
- 4 finely diced shallots
- 2 cloves crushed garlic
- Splash of dry white wine

Tips/Pointers

Starting the pork off in a very hot oven ensures that you will get excellent crispy crackling. Try, when you are baking the pork, to get the crackling to face the heat source. If (as with most charcoal ovens) the main heat comes from below cook the pork with the crackling facing downward, with a tray under the grill rack to catch the drippings.

Method

1. Score the pork skin horizontally at intervals of about half an inch. Rub the salt and pepper into the incisions, and over the joint.
2. Place in a very hot oven (hotter than 220°C) for about half an hour.
3. Reduce the heat to about 180°C and let the pork go on cooking for about 2 hours.
4. Meanwhile, for the tomato fondue, sweat the onion and the garlic with olive oil until soft.
5. Add the plum tomatoes and the thyme, and season.
6. Transfer this mixture to the oven, and roast for about 45 minutes until the tomatoes have dried out and are thick in texture. You should be left with enough to fill the normal tomatoes.
7. Cut the tops off the remaining tomatoes and scoop out the seeds. Fill with the plum tomato fondue, brush with olive oil and place in the oven for 15 minutes.
8. For the creamed spinach, sauté the shallots, add garlic and deglaze with white wine.
9. Add the spinach, and cook down until all the water has evaporated. Add the cream and reduce by half. Season to taste.
10. Remove the pork and rest for 15 minutes. Then serve with the accompaning dishes.

ABERDARES

RHINO ARK CAMP

Double chocolate tarts with frozen muscavado and nutmeg cream

RECIPE

Serves 16 people

Ingredients

For the muscavado cream
- 2 cups cream
- 3 tbsp muscavado sugar
- 1 vanilla bean

Method

1. Whip the cream into soft peaks with half the muscavado sugar and the vanilla bean.
2. Fold in the rest of the sugar and place in a bowl in the freezer.

For the short crust pastry
- 2 cups plain flour
- Pinch of salt
- 2 tbsp cubed butter
- 2–3 tbsp cold water

Method

1. Put the flour and salt in a large bowl and add the cubes of butter.
2. Use your fingertips to rub the butter into the flour until you have a mixture that resembles coarse breadcrumbs.
3. Using a knife, stir in just enough cold water to bind the dough together.
4. Wrap the dough in cling film and chill for 10–15 minutes before using.

For the dark chocolate tart
- 200 g plain chocolate, melted
- 50 g plain flour
- 500 g short-crust pastry pack, to be rolled out to the thickness of a coin and used to line four 10-cm tart tins
- 4 eggs
- Cocoa, for dusting
- 75 g butter, melted
- 100 g golden castor sugar

For the white chocolate tart
- 200 g white chocolate, melted
- 50 g plain flour
- 500 g short-crust pastry pack, to be rolled out to the thickness of a coin and used to line four 10-cm tart tins
- 4 eggs
- Icing sugar, for dusting
- 75 g butter, melted
- 100 g golden castor sugar

Method

1. Heat the oven to 180°C/fan, or to 160°C/gas 4.
2. Roll out the pastry and line two 8-inch cake tins.
3. Bake the pastry blind for 12 minutes.
4. Mix ¾ of the melted chocolate with the eggs, butter, sugar and flour.
5. Pour into the pastry cases. Bake for 20 minutes until just set.
6. Decorate with cocoa and icing sugar
7. Serve a slice of each tart with a quenelle of muscavado cream.

Tips/Pointers

Bake the tarts until the edges set, but the middles are still slightly wobbly. This will impart a range of textures, as you get closer to the centre, with the perfect gooey chocolate finish.

Aberdares 89

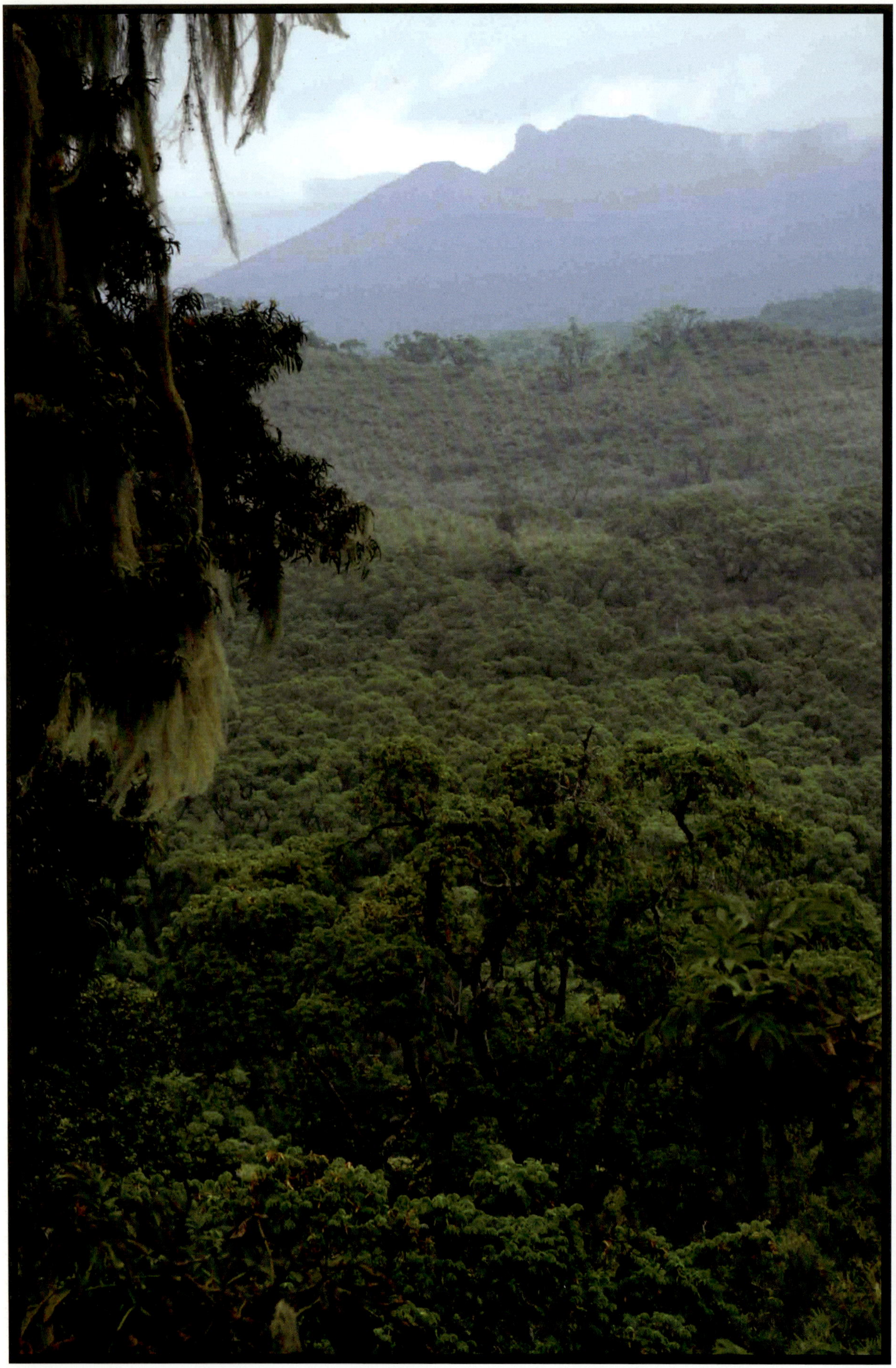
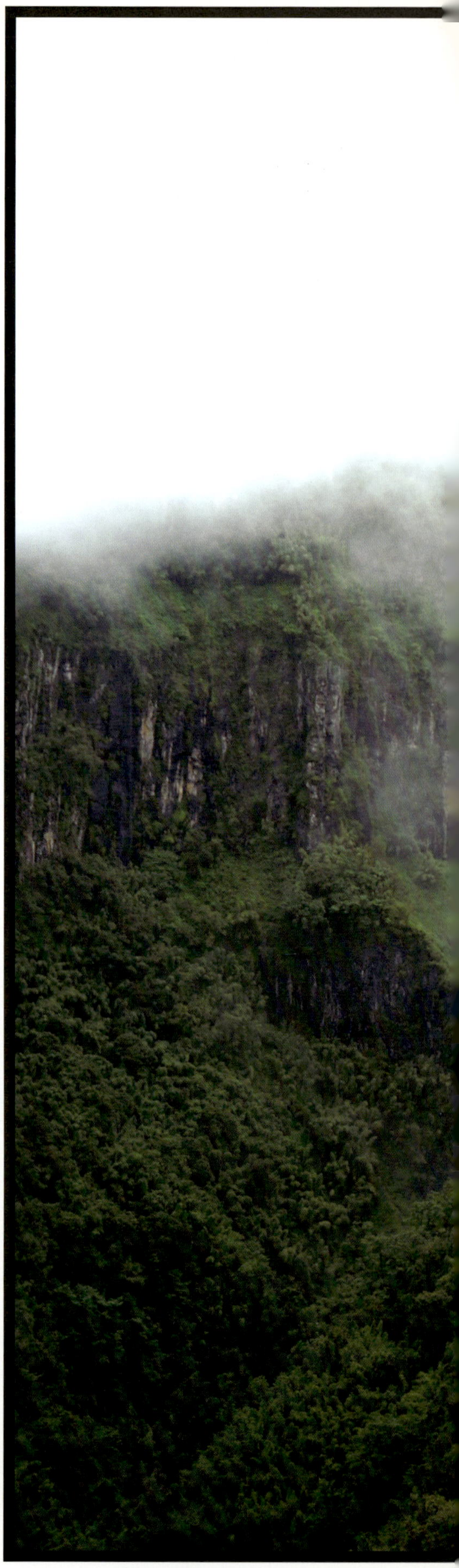

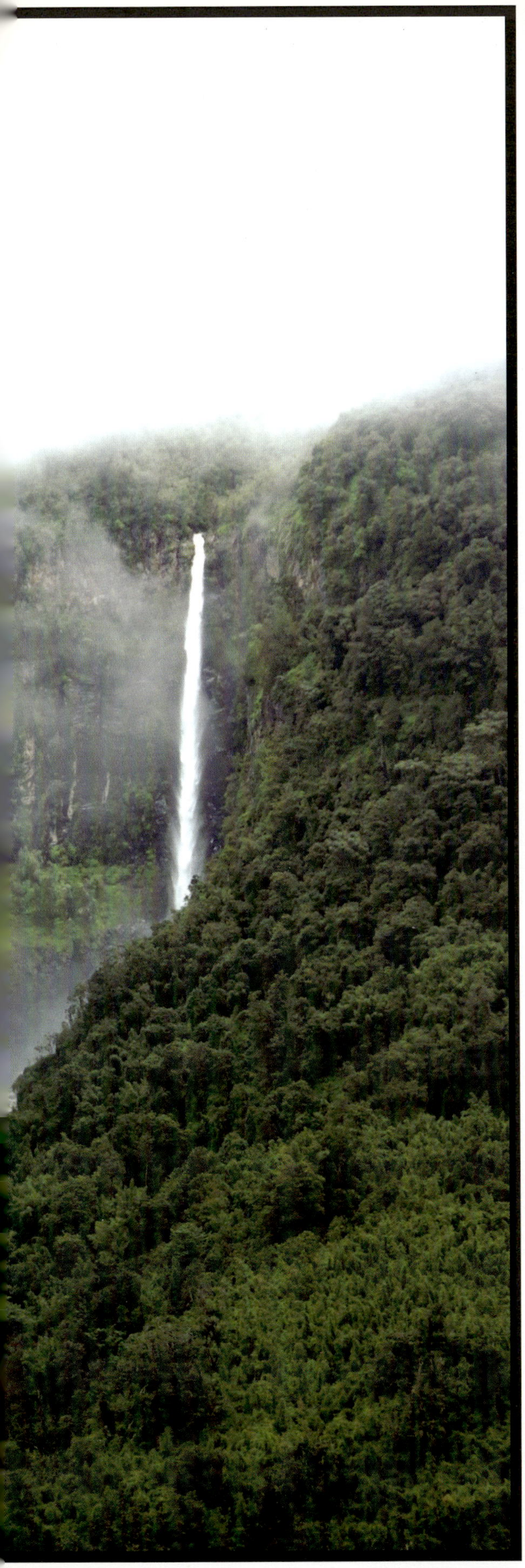
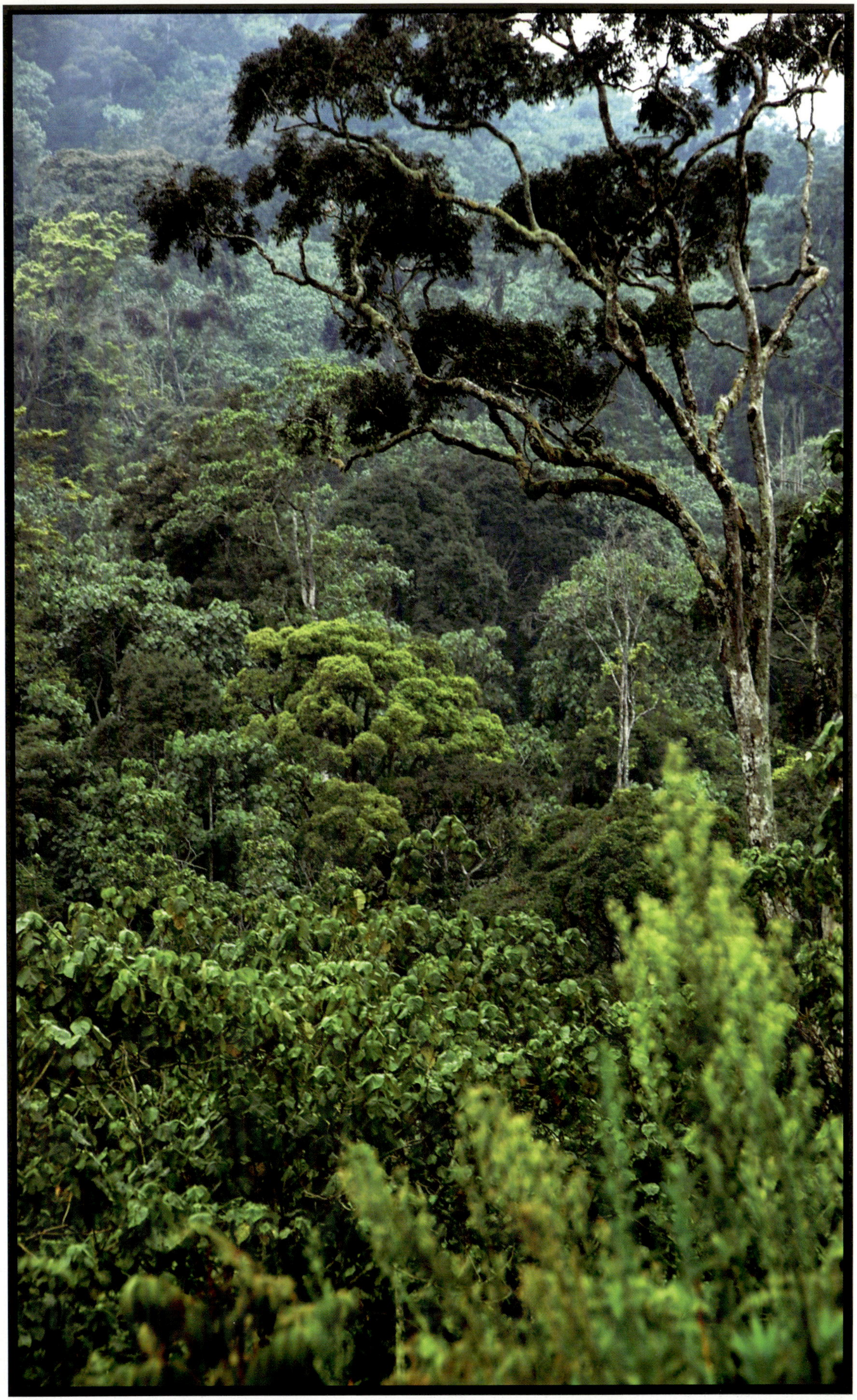

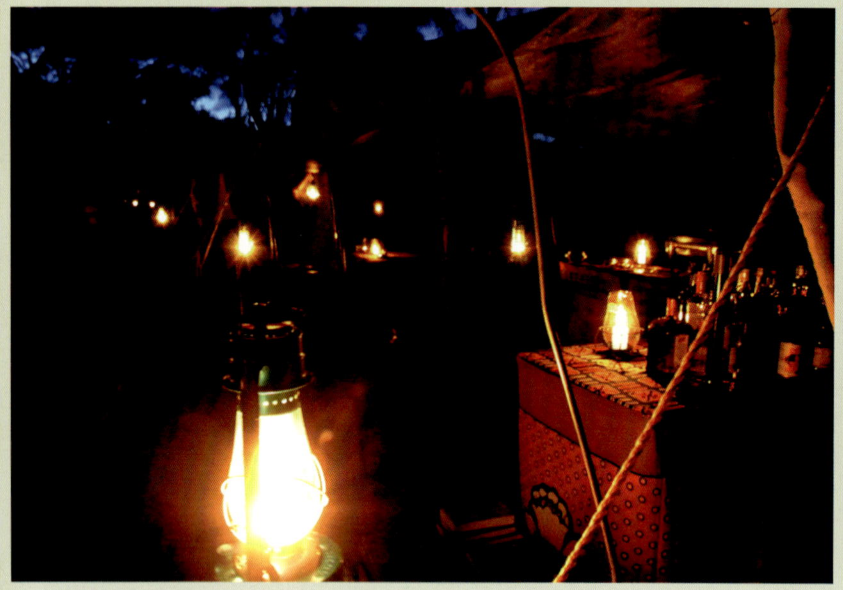

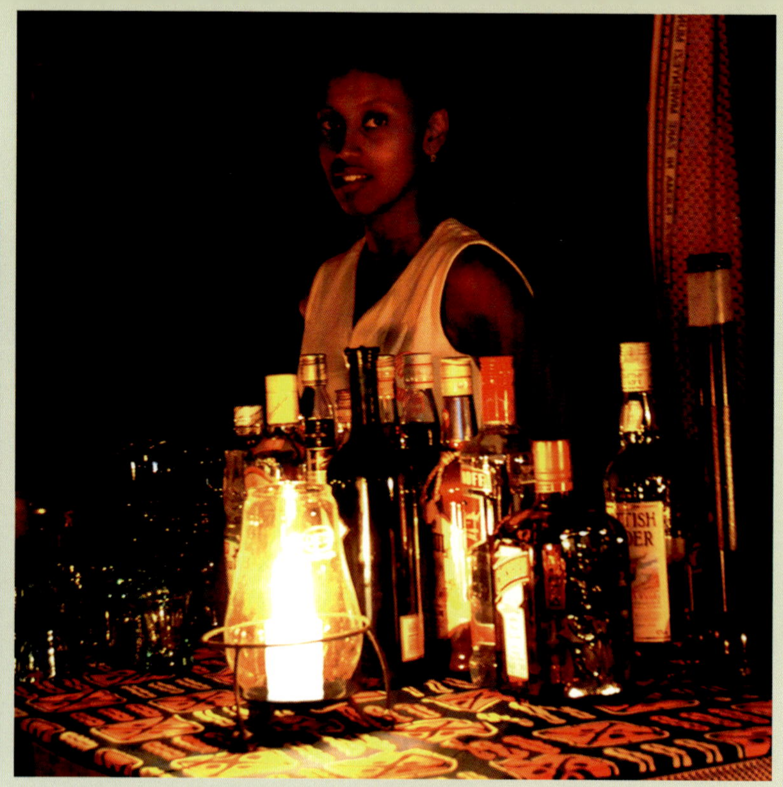

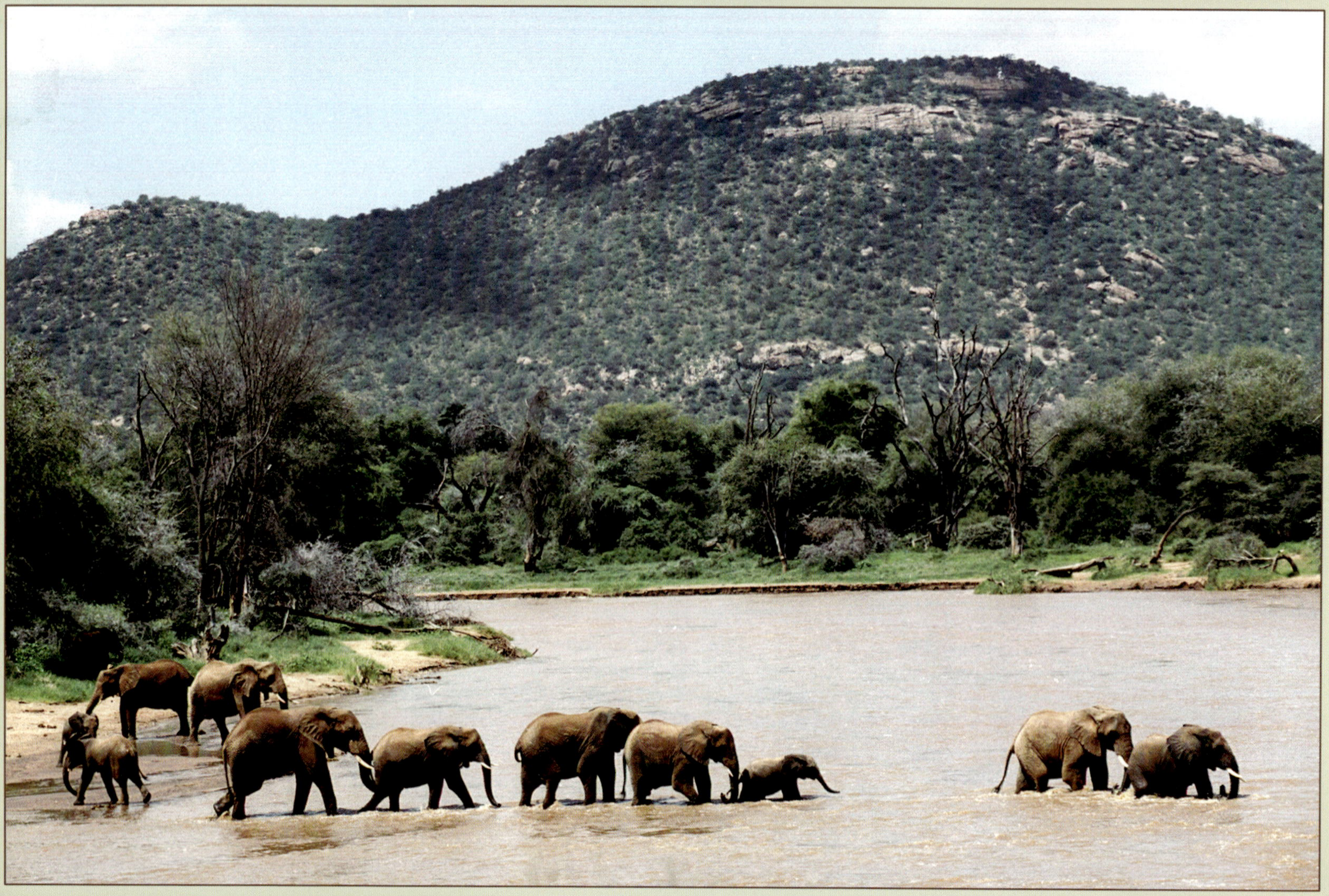

SAMBURU

THE EWASO
samburu

BASIN
country

96 Safari Cuisine

Duet of rabbit pie with fennel mash, spring onions and rich orange jus

RECIPE

Serves 10 people

Ingredients

- 1 packet of puff pastry
- 3 large rabbits, cleaned
- 1 onion, chopped
- 1 head of celery, chopped
- 3 large carrots, chopped
- 1 cup dry white wine
- 4 cloves crushed garlic
- 5 tomatoes, chopped
- 2 tsp fennel seeds
- 1 tsp juniper berries
- 1 tbsp tomato paste
- 1 punnet button mushrooms
- 1 cup cream
- 2 fennel heads
- 6 large potatoes
- 4 tbsp butter
- Juice and zest of 1 orange
- Orange gravy *(see recipe)*

Method

1. Remove the rabbit breasts from the bone and set aside.
2. In a large pan, heat some of the butter and add the carrots, onions and celery, then sauté until soft.
3. Add the garlic and brown, then deglaze with the white wine.
4. Add the rabbit legs, saddles and any bones left after cleaning the breasts.
5. To these, add the tomatoes, the tomato paste, the fennel and the juniper seeds and the mushrooms. Cook on a low heat for about 2 hours, until very tender and falling off the bones.
6. Strain the resulting liquid and return this to the heat, adding the cream. Reduce by half.
8. Allow the mixture to cool slightly. Meanwhile, season the rabbit breasts and sauté in olive oil until golden brown and partially cooked.
9. Slice the breasts and set aside.
10. Meanwhile, roll out ¾ of the pastry and line a greased 24- x 12-inch baking dish. Bake the pastry blind for 6 minutes at 180ºC
11. Remove from the oven. Spoon in the rabbit leg mixture to cover ¾ of the depth of the pie. On top of this add the half cooked rabbit breasts.
12. Roll out the remaining pastry and cover the pie. Brush with an egg wash, and place in the oven at 180˚C for 20 minutes.
13. Meanwhile, boil the potatoes and mash. Add the butter, and season.
14. Chop the fennel into a fine dice and blanch in hot water until tender.
15. Add to the mashed potatoes with the chopped spring onions and season to taste.

The orange gravy

Method

1. Place all the juices and the fat from the rabbit breasts on the heat. Begin to fry the chopped garlic. Deglaze with the juice of the orange.
2. To this, add 2 cups of water with a stock cube dissolved in it.
3. In a separate cup, dissolve 1 tsp of corn flour in about 100 ml of milk. Whisk this into the boiling gravy until the desired thickness is attained.
4. Stir in 2 tbsp of butter, test for seasoning and add the zest of half the orange.

Tips/Pointers

Any surplus liquid from the leg meat sauce should be added to the gravy, as this will make the sauce much richer and tastier.

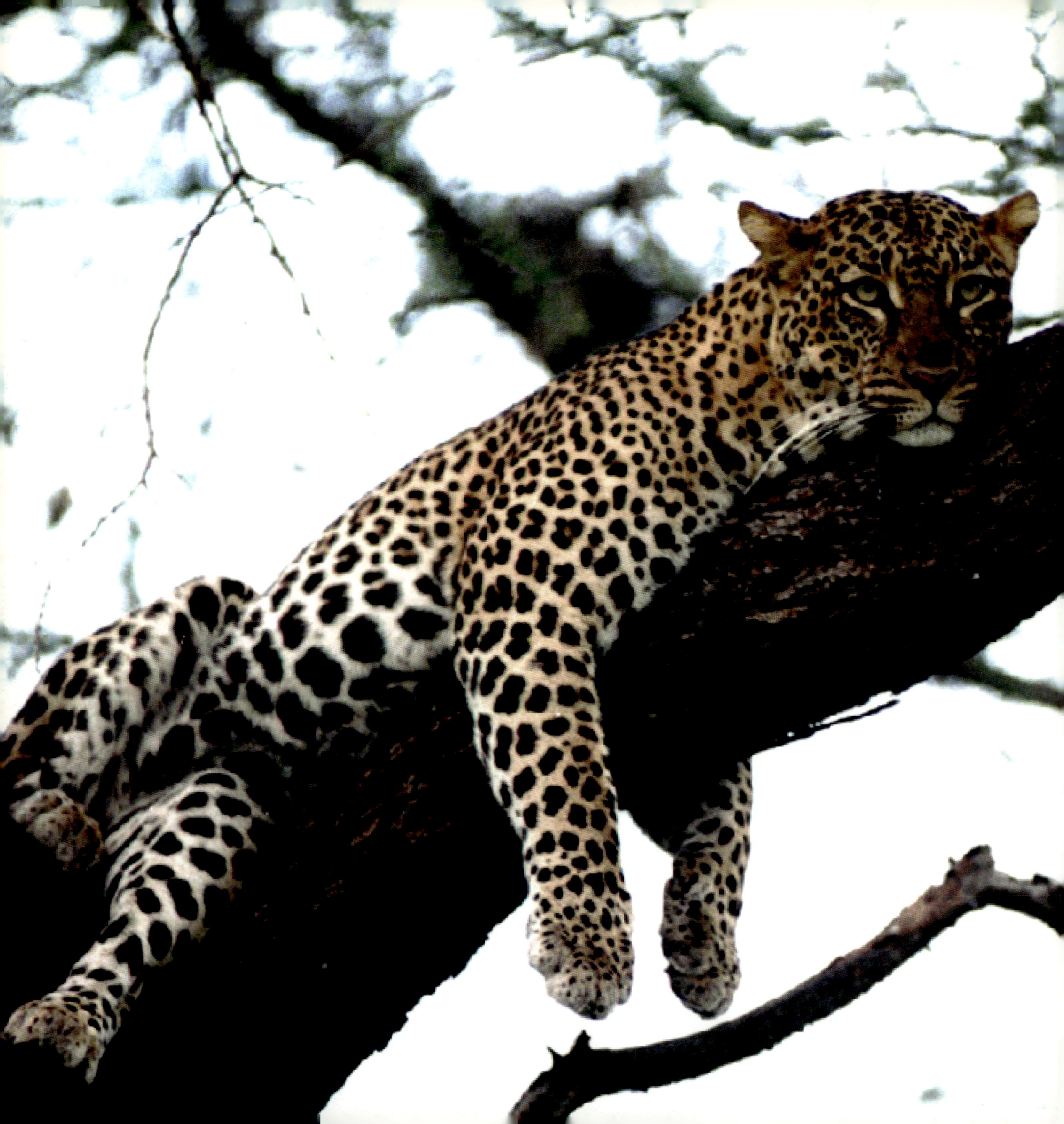

SAMBURU
GAME RESERVE
ULY'S SAFARI

MENU

Duet of rabbit pie with fennel mash,
spring onions and rich orange jus

Pot-roast chicken with sausage stuffing
and caramelised parsnips and sautéed kale

Lemon tart with caramelised goat cheese
and crème anglaise

Pot-roast chicken with sausage stuffing and caramelised parsnips and sautéed kale

RECIPE

Serves 5 people

Ingredients

- 1 large free-range chicken
- 2 tbsp softened butter
- Handful chopped oregano
- Handful chopped sage
- 200 g sausage meat
- 1 cup of bread crumbs
- 2 tbsp olive oil
- 12 parsnips, peeled
- 1 chopped onion
- 1 clove garlic
- 1 shredded kale
- ½ cup cream

Method

1. Mix the butter with half the chopped herbs and season. Push this mixture under the skin of the chicken to cover the breast.
2. Mix the other half of the herbs with the sausage meat and breadcrumbs. Stuff these into the body cavity of the chicken.
3. Heat the oil in a pan and drop in the parsnips. Fry for a couple of minutes. Then place the chicken on top of the parsnips and push it down so it sits properly in the pan.
4. Pour 200 ml of water over this, and close with a tight-fitting lid. Place in the oven for 40 minutes.
5. Meanwhile, cook the kale in boiling water until tender.
6. Sauté the chopped onion and garlic and toss the kale into this. Add the cream and reduce by half. Season to taste with salt and pepper.
7. Remove the chicken from the oven and reduce the heat slightly. Take off the lid and return to the oven for 1 hour until the chicken is golden brown.
8. Remove from the oven and serve with the parsnips and kale.

Tips/Pointers

Pot-roasting is a great method of outdoor cooking. It allows for the variations in cooking temperature that often occur with outdoor ovens, while helping to make sure that you do not burn the chicken. The end result is a tender, moist roast, complete with a wonderful stock from which to make your gravy.

Samburu

FRIDAY 27 FEB 2009

LUNCH

Beef Fajitas, Tortillas, Guacamole Salsa
Kachumbari, Grated Cheese, Sour Cream
Fruit Salad
Tea & Coffee

SUNDOWNERS

Carrot Crudités
Crisps with Cottage Cheese Dip
Fish Fingers & Tartar Sauce
Dates wrapped in Bacon
Green Olives

DINNER

Dahl Soup
Chicken Curry,
Steamed Basmati Rice
Chapattis & Papadums

Condiments (chopped tomatoes, bananas, onions, green peppers, mango chutney, fresh chilies, grated coconut)
Crêpes à l'Aranca
Fruit Salad
Tea & Coffee

S A M B U R U

Cottage Cheese Dip

2 tsp moutarde de Dijon, handful of Spanish capers, a little mayonnaise, a few drops of Tabasco and of Worcestershire Sauce, chopped fresh coriander, salt and pepper

SATURDAY 28 FEB 2009

BREAKFAST
Selection of cut fresh fruits: pawpaw, mango, banana, pineapple
Fruit Juice
Toast & Butter, Strawberry Jam, Raspberry Jam, Honey
Tea & Coffee

ACTIVE STATION:
Eggs (Fried, Scrambled, Boiled, Omelettes)
Garnishes for omelettes (green pepper, grated cheese, tomatoes, chilies, onions)

Bacon, Beef Sausage, Grilled Tomato
Baked Beans, Fried Bread,
Pancakes à la Zedan

GAME RESERVE

Lemon tart with caramelised goat cheese and crème anglaise

RECIPE

Serves 8 people

Ingredients

- Juice and zest of 5 lemons
- 5 eggs, gently beaten
- 500 ml cream
- 200 g castor sugar
- 200 g goat cheese
- 2 tbsp icing sugar
- Short-crust pastry *(see recipe)*

Method

1. Grease a 12-inch tart tin.
2. Roll out the pastry and line the tin. Bake blind for 6 minutes at 180°C.
3. Meanwhile, gently beat the eggs and sugar. Be sure not to add too much air while doing this.
4. When the sugar has dissolved, stir in the cream and then add the juice and zest of the lemons. You should have a smooth, silky mixture.
5. Remove the pastry from the oven. Immediately pour 2 tbsp of the mixture into the pastry case, making sure it covers the bottom.
6. Set aside to cool. Then pour all the remaining mixture into the pastry and bake for 35 minutes at 180°C
7. Remove from the oven. Allow to cool slightly.
8. Cover the tart with the goat cheese, and sprinkle the icing sugar all over it.
9. Return to the oven, allowing the goat cheese to melt and caramelise.
10. Place in the fridge and chill before serving.

Short crust pastry

Ingredients

- 2 cups plain flour
- Pinch of salt
- 2 tbsp cubed butter

Method

1. Put the flour and salt in a large bowl and add the cubes of butter.
2. Use your fingertips to rub the butter into the flour until you have a mixture that resembles coarse breadcrumbs.
3. Using a knife, stir in just enough of the cold water to bind the dough together.
4. Wrap the dough in cling film and chill for 10–15 minutes before using.

Tips/Pointers

When you remove the pastry from the oven after baking it blind it is important to pour in some of the lemon mixture while the pastry is still hot. This allows the egg to soak into the pastry and to set, thereby preventing the remaining mixture from soaking through during the baking process.

Samburu 105

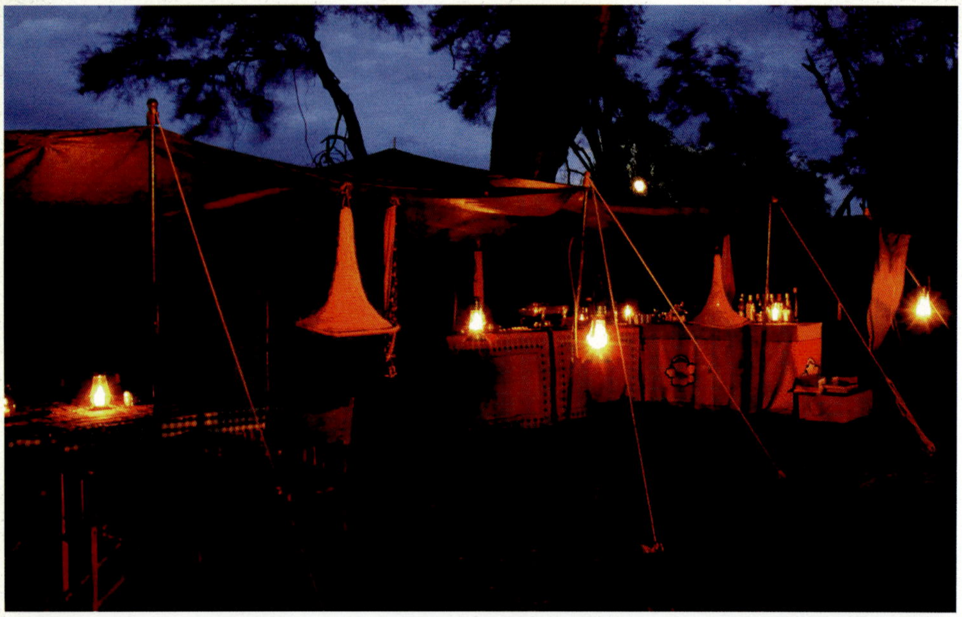

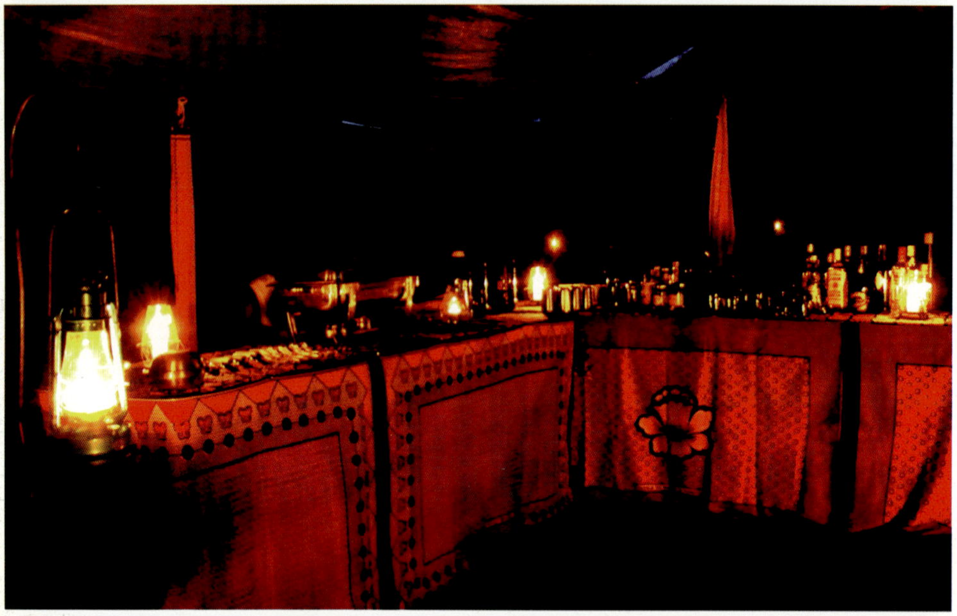

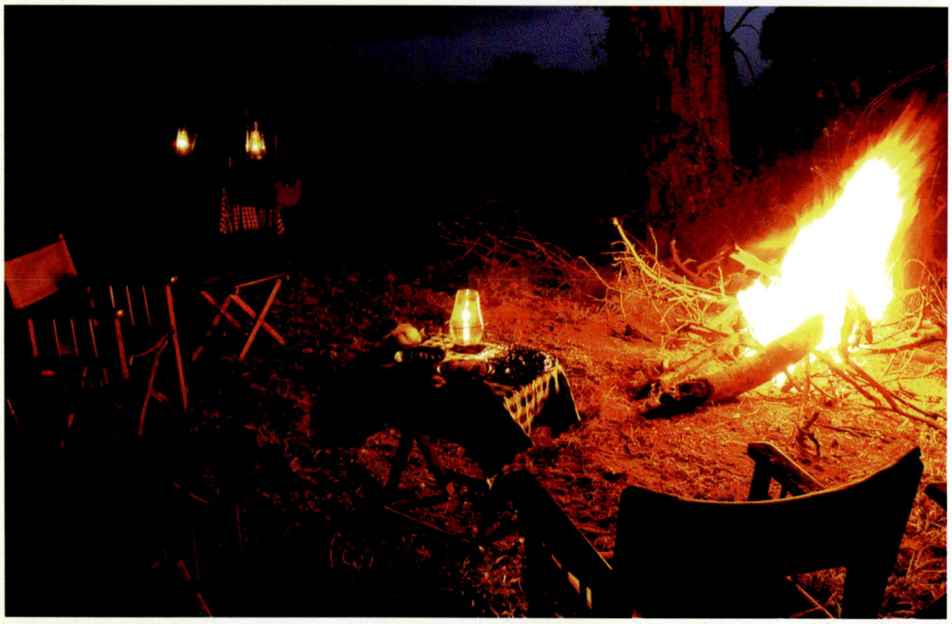

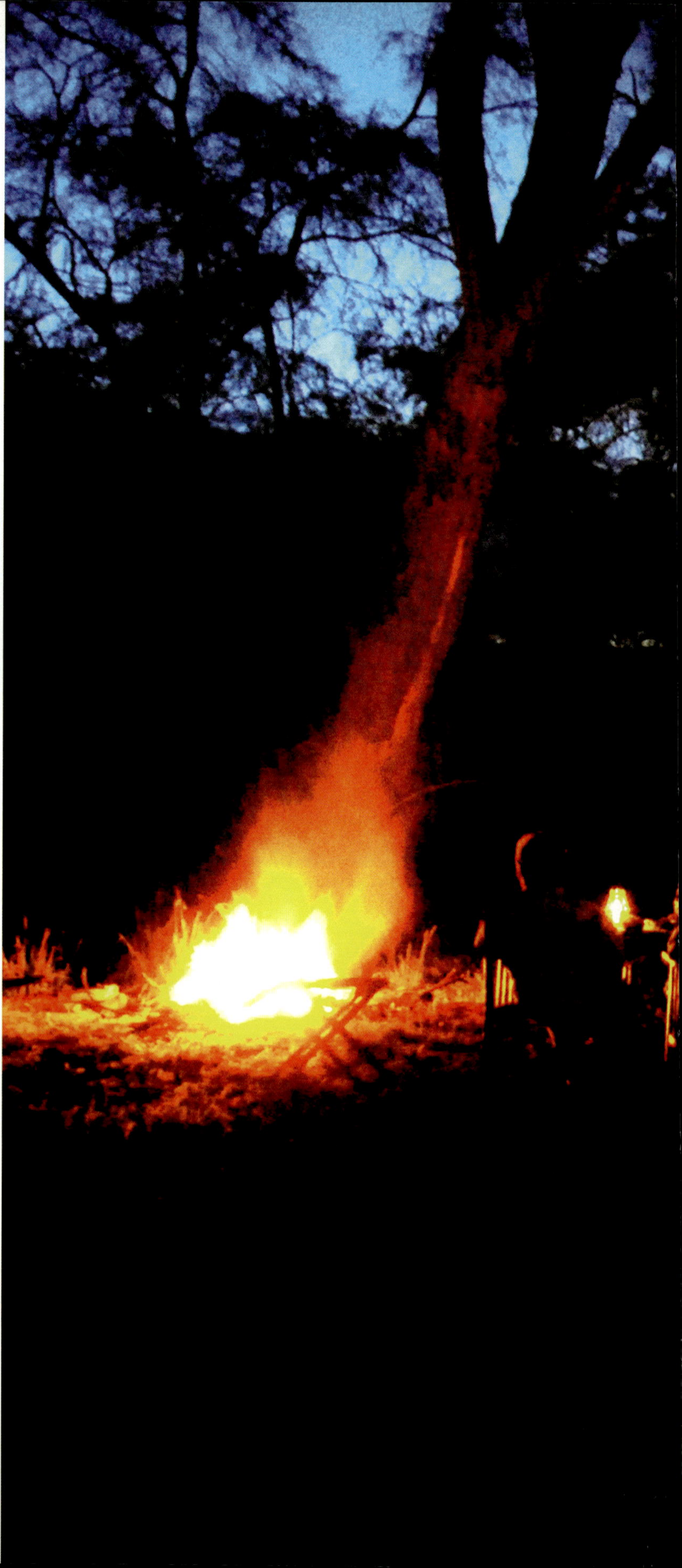

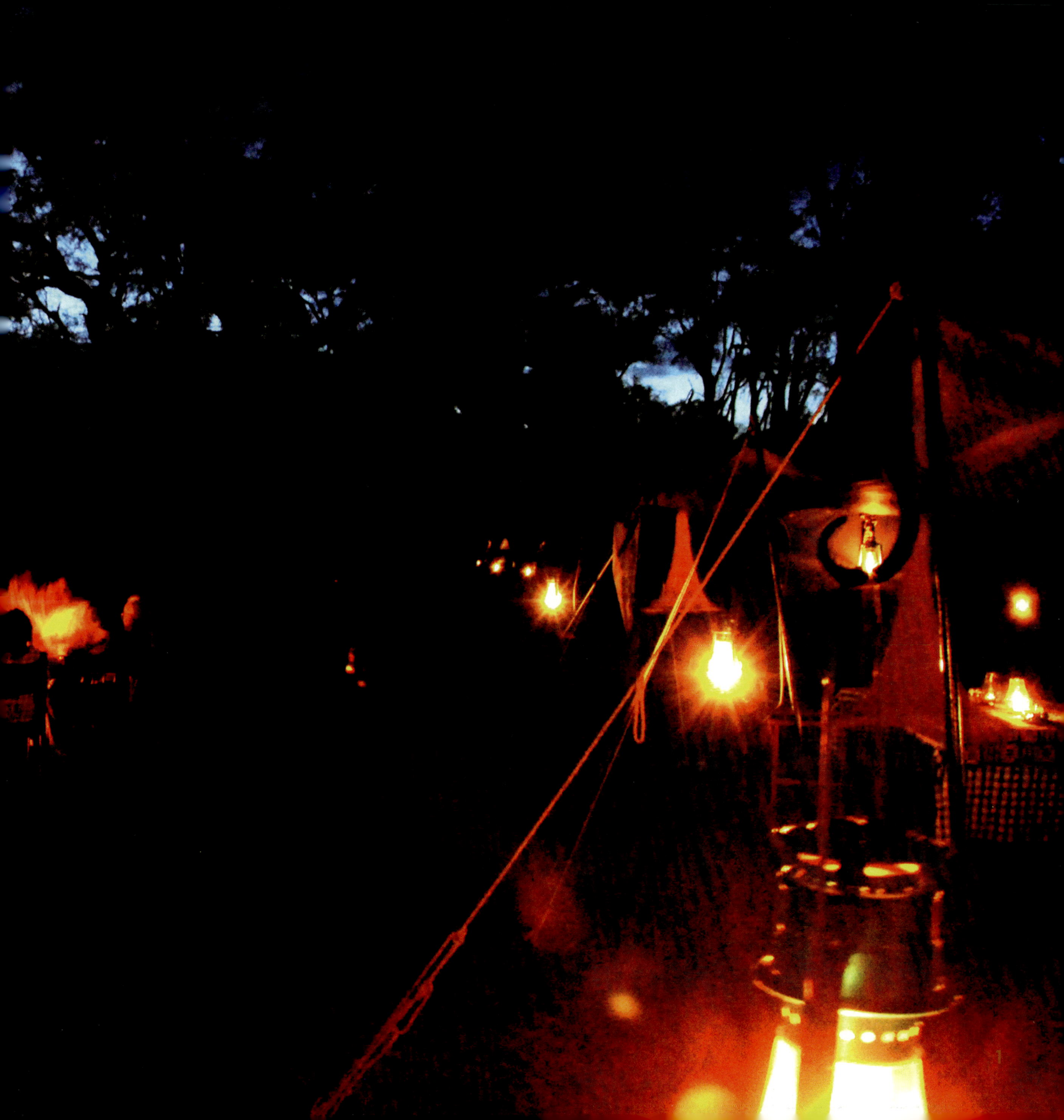

SHOMPOLE
sampu camp

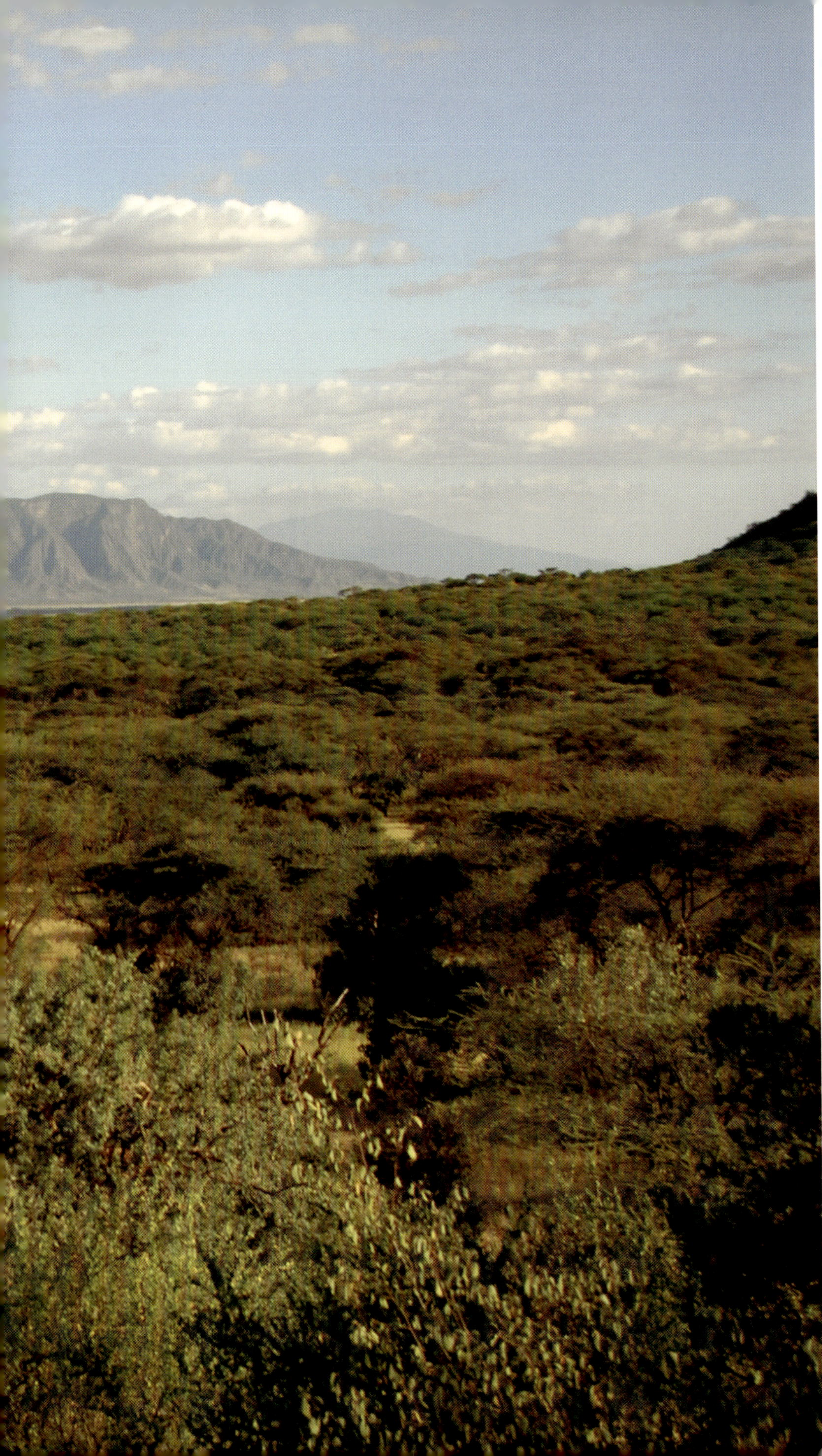

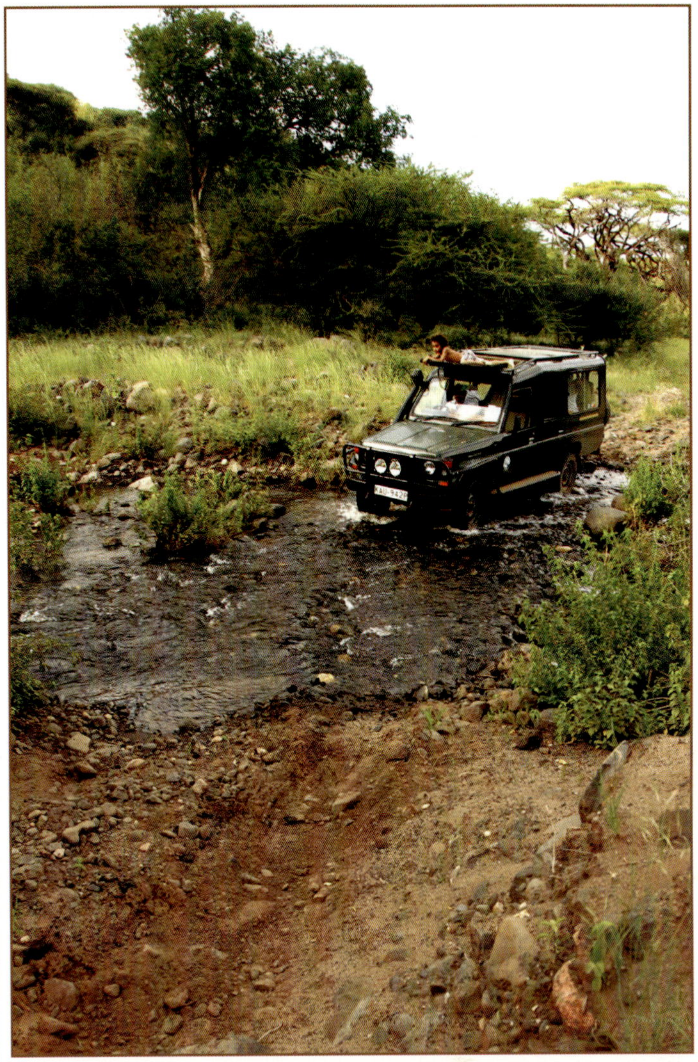

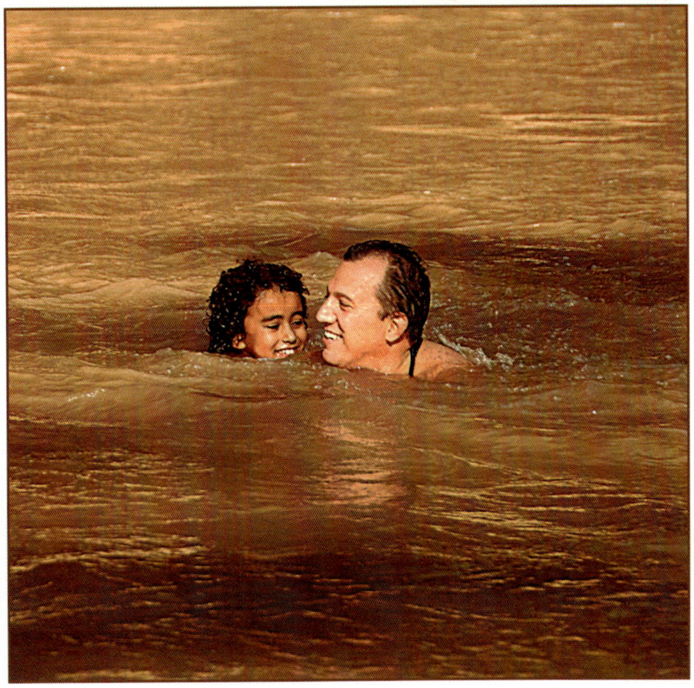

Poached salt beef with potato croutons, rocket and mustard butter

RECIPE

Serves 5 people

Ingredients

- 500 g salt beef
- 4 red-skin potatoes
- 2 shallots
- Pinch of fresh thyme
- Seasoning
- 4 handfuls of rocket
- 5 tbsp softened butter
- 1 tbsp wholegrain mustard
- 1 tbsp chopped capers
- 3–4 medium chopped gherkins
- Drizzle of olive oil

Method

1. Soak the salt beef in water overnight to remove excess salt.
2. Poach the beef in the water for 3 hours, or until cooked and tender.
3. Remove from the water and allow to cool.
4. Meanwhile, skin and cut the potatoes into cubes about the size of an average crouton.
5. Place the potato cubes in cold water and bring to the boil. Then strain the liquid from the potatoes. Set these aside and allow to steam themselves dry.
6. Once dry, drop the potato cubes into hot oil, and fry until brown and crispy.
7. Place the softened butter into a bowl and mix in the mustard and the capers and gherkins. Place in the fridge to set.
8. Cut the salt beef into cubes of the same size as the potato cubes.
9. Sauté the chopped shallots and the thyme in olive oil. Throw in the beef and potato cubes. Toss lightly and season.
10. Plate and serve with rocket and mustard butter.

Tips/Pointers

Red-skin potatoes, being less floury than other potatoes, will give you superior croutons. This dish, complete with a perfectly poached egg and a dash of Tabasco, makes for an excellent brunch.

Shompole 111

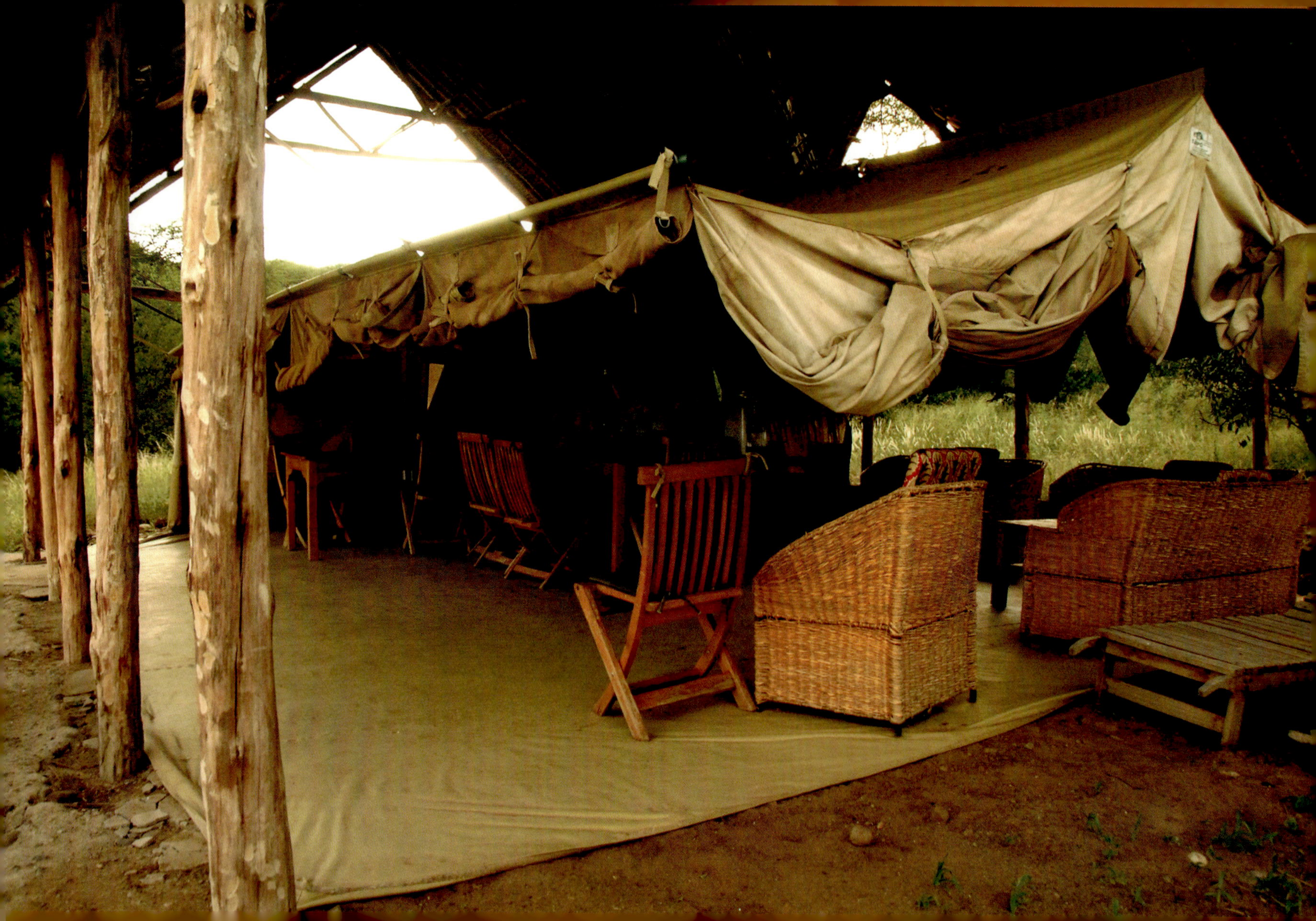

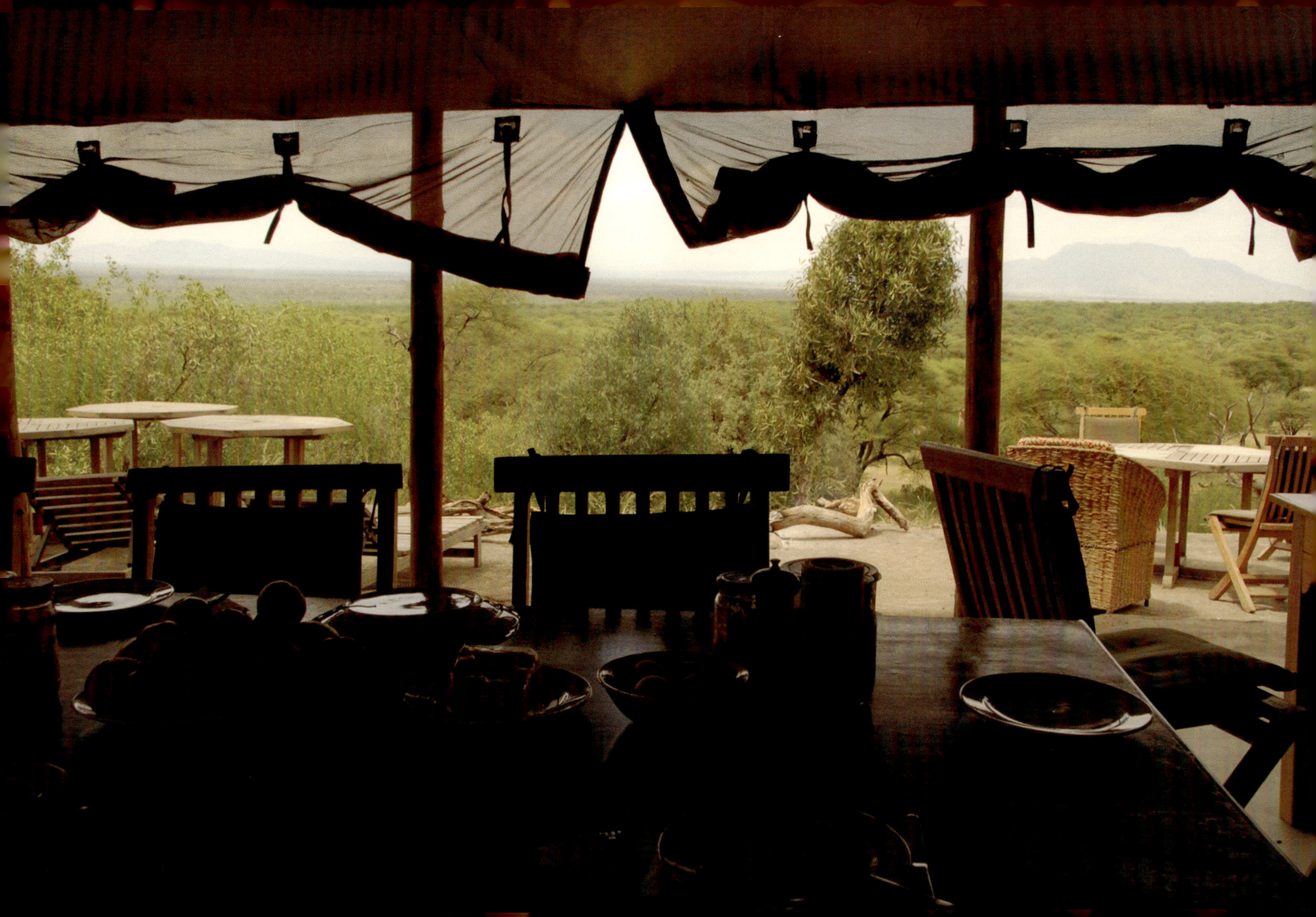

Safari Cuisine

Tandoori-baked quail with onion strings and cucumber and yoghurt salsa with roasted cumin

RECIPE

Serves 5 people

Special equipment

Out in the bush, baking or roasting can be very tricky. With crude charcoal ovens, temperatures are hard to control. Here, an improvised tandoori oven may be called for. For this, you will need a medium-sized alluminium saucepan with a tight-fitting lid and no handles. Dig a hole in the ground of roughly double the size of the saucepan. Fill the bottom 5–6 cm of the hole with burning embers from a fire. Line the saucepan with some scrunched-up tin foil, and insert a grill. The foil will act as a buffer between your food and the direct heat. With your quail on the grill, and the lid closed, lower the saucepan into position over the burning embers. Then fill in the sides of the hole around the saucepan with soil, to seal in the heat. (if you are using a normal oven, then simply bake at 200ºC.)

Ingredients

- 5 whole quails
- 2 pots natural yoghurt
- 1 tbsp crushed ginger
- 1 tbsp crushed garlic
- 1 tbsp crushed green chilies
- ½ tsp turmeric powder
- 1 tsp dana-gira (roasted pounded cumin and coriander)
- ½ tsp ground chili
- ½ tsp garam masala
- 1 bunch chopped fresh coriander
- Juice and zest of 1 lemon
- Seasoning
- 3 tsp roasted whole cumin seeds
- 1 grated cucumber
- 5 white onions sliced thinly into rings
- 1 cup of seasoned flour

Method

1. Take the grated cucumber, salt heavily and set aside.
2. Take 1 pot of the yoghurt and place in a bowl.
3. To this, add the garlic, the ginger, the chilies, all the spices (except the whole cumin seeds), the lemon juice and half of the fresh coriander.
4. Coat the quails in this basting, and set aside to marinade for 3–4 hours.
5. Meanwhile, thoroughly wash the salt from the cucumber, squeezing out the excess liquid in a cloth.
6. Add this to the pot of yoghurt, along with the roasted cumin seeds
7. Place the quails in the oven and bake for about 20 minutes until cooked.
8. Remove and allow to rest for 5 minutes.
9. Dust the thinly sliced onions in the flour, and deep fry for about 1 minute in hot oil until crispy.
10. Serve the quail over the onions with the cucumber salsa.

Tips/Pointers

With the cucumber salsa, the salting of the cucumber has a strong bearing on the quality of the sauce. Proper salting, for about 1 hour, will remove excess liquid, giving the cucumber an almost pickled texture. Just as important is a thorough washing to remove the salt, before the cucumber is mixed into the yoghurt.

Shompole

Triple chocolate mousse

116 Safari Cuisine

RECIPE

Serves 8 people

Ingredients

For the dark chocolate

- 1 ¾ cups whipping cream
- 1 cup quality semi-sweet dark chocolate chips
- 3 ounces espresso or strong coffee
- 1 tbsp dark rum
- 4 tbsp butter
- 1 tsp flavourless, granulated gelatin

For the milk chocolate

- 1 ¾ cups whipping cream
- 1 cup quality milk chocolate chips
- 3 tbsp Grand Marnier
- 4 tbsp butter
- 1 tsp flavourless, granulated gelatin

For the white chocolate

- 1 ¾ cups whipping cream
- 12 ounces quality white chocolate chips
- 4 tbsp butter
- 1 tsp flavourless, granulated gelatin

Method

Applies to all layers

1. Chill 1½ cups of whipping cream in the fridge. Chill metal mixing bowl and mixer beaters in the freezer.
2. Over boiling water boiler, combine chocolate chips, (coffee), alcohol and butter. Melt over gently simmering water, stirring constantly.
3. Remove from the heat while a couple of chunks are still visible. Cool, stirring occasionally, to just above body temperature.
4. Pour the remaining ¼ cup of whipping cream into a metal measuring cup and sprinkle in the gelatin. Allow 10 minutes for the gelatin to dissolve.
5. Then heat gently by swirling the measuring cup over a low gas flame or a candle. Do not boil, or the gelatin will be damaged. Stir mixture into the cooled chocolate, and set aside.
6. In the chilled mixing bowl, beat cream to medium peaks. Stir ¼ of the whipped cream into the chocolate mixture to lighten it.
7. Fold in remaining whipped cream in two doses. There may be streaks of whipped cream in the chocolate, but that is fine. Do not overwork the mousse.
8. Spoon a layer of the dark chocolate into the bottom of the serving glasses. Set in the fridge for 20 minutes. Remove and spoon a layer of milk chocolate over this. Repeat the process for the white chocolate layer.
9. Allow the whole mousse to set for 2 hours.

Tips/Pointers

Make each mousse one after the other. While one layer is cooling in the glasses you can be making the other layer.

Shompole 117

T H E

TROUT TREE

Trout Pâté
Brown bread, butter & salad garnish

Grilled Trout
… as fresh as it gets, with garlic butter
& a glass of Nederberg Sauvignon Blanc

Carrot Cake
with fresh cream from the farm

… and freshly ground Kenya Coffee

THE TROUT

Whole Smoked Trout
with brown bread,
horseradish sauce, &
a trimming of fresh
organic salad

(Served Cold)

Trout Curry
Spicy hot trout chunks in curry sauce,
served with rice, chapattis, condiments
& a glass of Nederberg Pinotage

Rolled Banana Pancake
in nuts and cream, & with a
chocolate sauce topping

Freshly ground Kenya Coffee

T R E E

LOISIIJO
ECO BANDAS
COMMUNITY PROJECT
EWASO NJIRO
SHAMPOLE CONSERVANCY

LOISIIJO

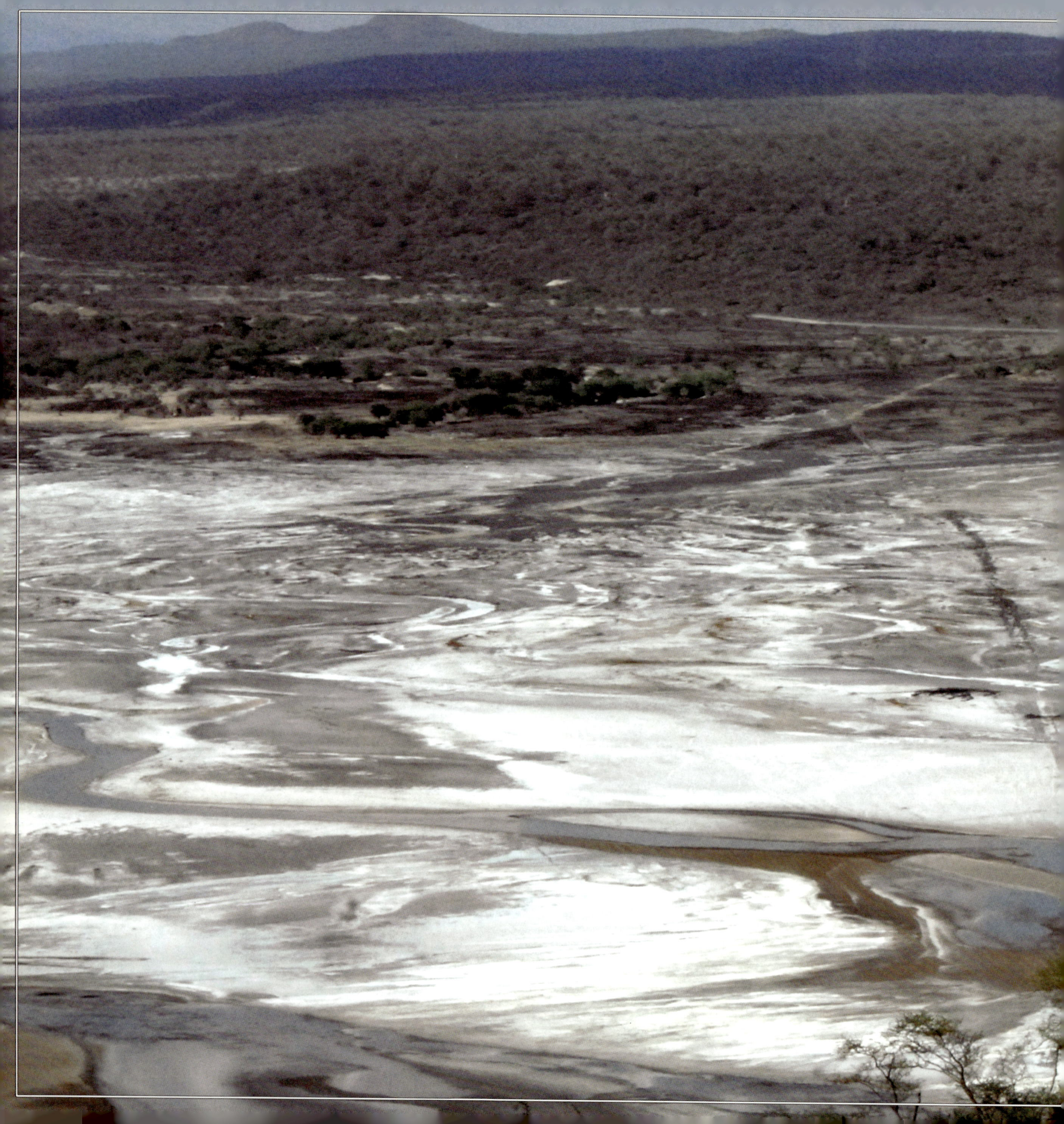

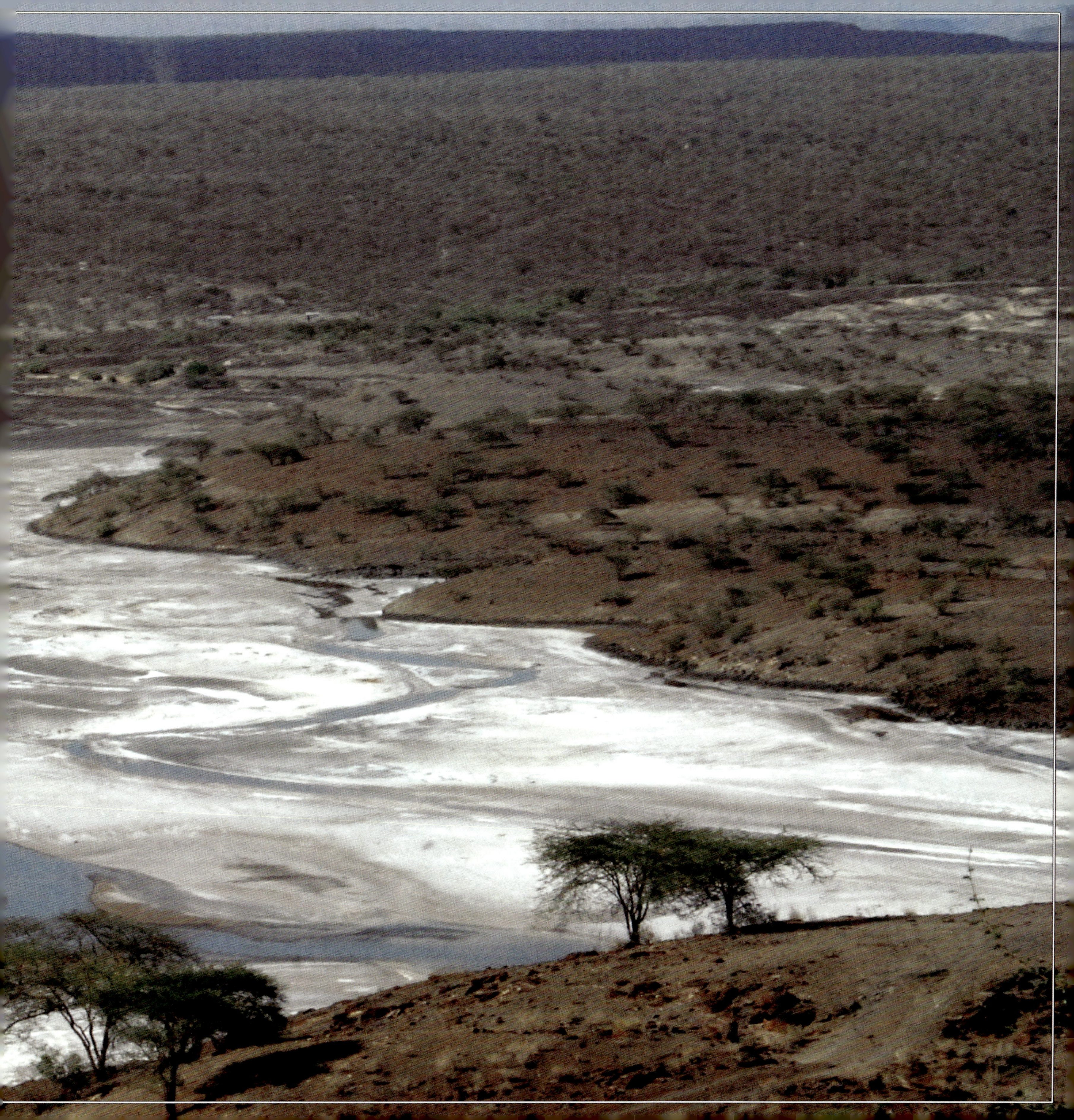

126 Safari Cuisine

Seared chicken liver with horseradish, port cream and crisp belly of pork

RECIPE

Serves 4 people

Ingredients
- ½ kilo chicken liver
- Handful chopped shallots
- 2 tsp crushed garlic cloves
- 1 good slug port
- Equally good slug of double cream
- ½ bunch roughly chopped flat leaf parsley
- 4 slices of pork belly (or, alternatively, streaky bacon)
- 1 freshly minced horseradish (or, alternatively, horseradish cream)
- 1 tbsp butter

Method
1. In a hot pan, fry the pork belly until it is crispy and the fat has rendered (melted).
2. Melt the butter in the same frying pan, together with the pork fat. Allow the butter to brown, while being careful not to let it burn.
3. Throw in the shallots and the garlic, and fry until they start to get some colour.
4. Toss in the chicken livers, and sear until their liquids are squeezed out.
5. Deglaze with the port and cream, and reduce by half.
6. Finally stir in horseradish and parsley and serve.
7. Garnish with crispy pork belly.

Tips/Pointers
This is not a dish for people experiencing cholesterol problems. Keeping the rendered pork belly fat in with the butter will give you a much richer, tastier and altogether more decadent sauce.

Loiisijo 127

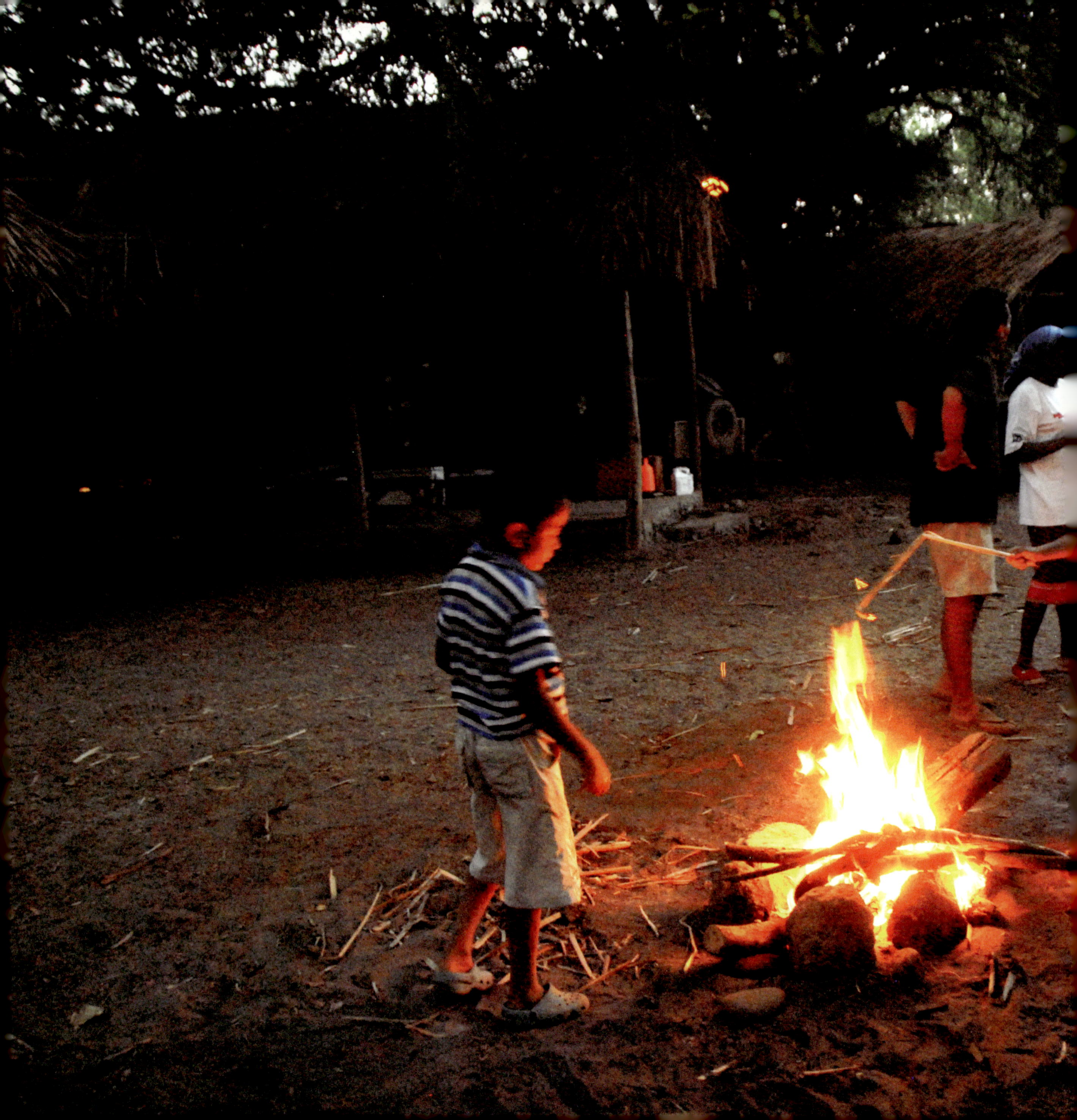

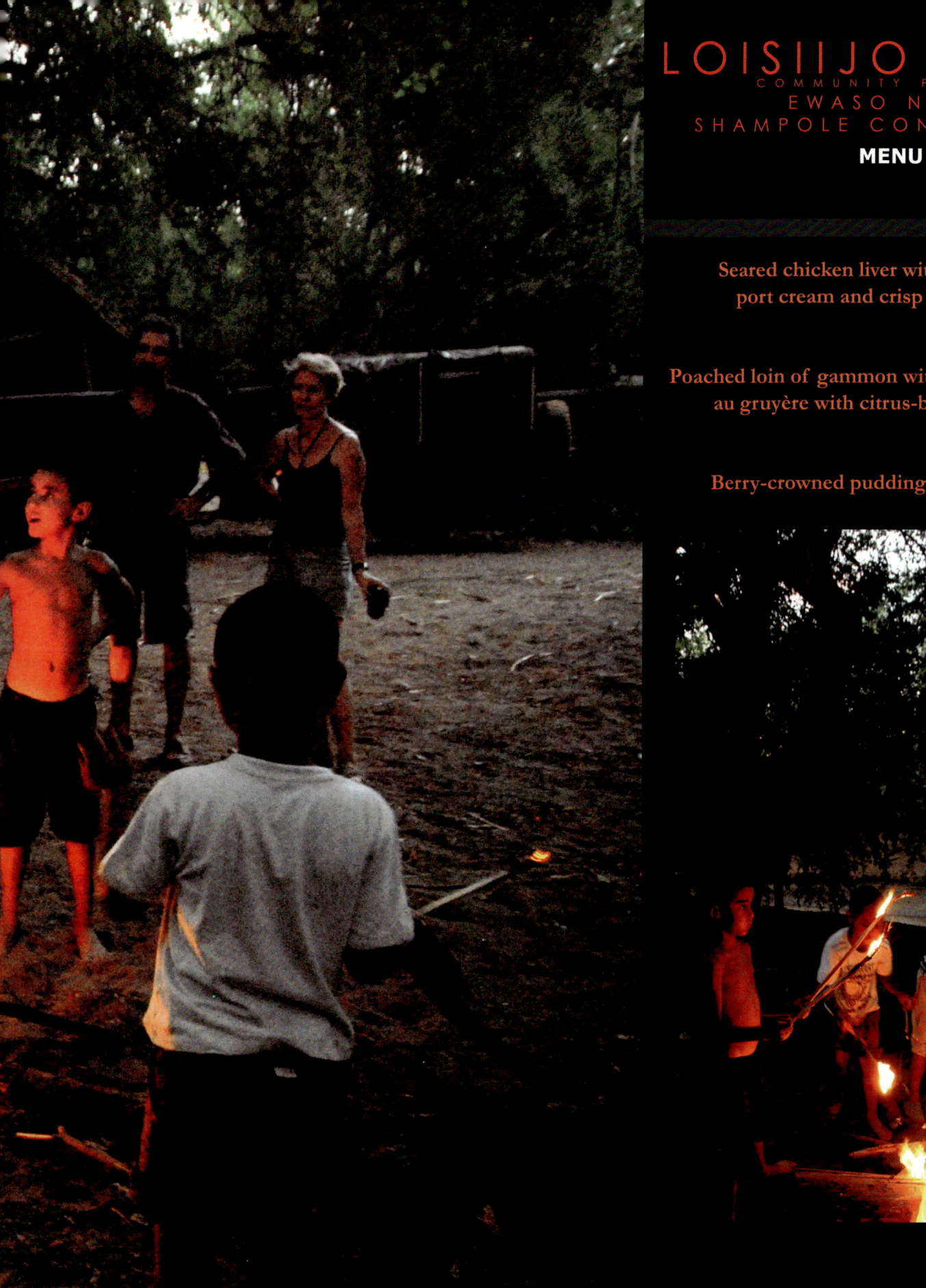

LOISIIJO ECO BANDAS
COMMUNITY PROJECT
EWASO NJIRO
SHAMPOLE CONSERVANCY

MENU

Seared chicken liver with horseradish,
port cream and crisp belly of pork

Poached loin of gammon with cauliflower gratin
au gruyère with citrus-braised pok choi

Berry-crowned pudding with port syrup

Safari Cuisine

Poached loin of gammon with cauliflower gratin au gruyère with citrus-braised pok choi

RECIPE

Serves 5 people

Ingredients

- 1 kg gammon loin (boiling bacon)
- 2 litres water
- 1 tsp cloves
- 1 cinnamon stick
- 1 large cauliflower
- 1 tbsp plain flour
- 2 tbsp butter
- 200 ml whole milk
- 1 white onion
- 2 bay leaves
- 1 tsp black pepper corns
- ½ tsp ground nutmeg
- 100 g grated gruyère cheese
- Juice and ½ zest of 1 lemon
- Juice and ½ zest of 1 orange
- Juice and ½ zest of 1 lime
- 1 pok choi ('Chinese cabbage'), shredded
- Seasoning

Method

1. Place the gammon loin in the water with the cinnamon and cloves and bring to the boil.
2. Simmer for 1 hour, then turn off the heat and allow to sit in the hot water for a further half-hour.
3. Place in a pan, the juice and zest of the lemon, orange and lime.
4. Reduce the citrus liquor by ¾, by which time it should have an intense flavour.
5. Remove from heat and immediately add the pok choi to this.
6. To prepare the milk for the béchamel, place it in a saucepan with the roughly chopped onion, bay leaves and the black pepper. Simmer for 5 minutes.
7. Melt the butter in a saucepan and add the flour, to prepare the béchamel sauce for the cauliflower au gratin.
8. Cook the flour out for 5 minutes on a medium heat, being sure not to burn it.
9. Slowly add the warm milk, whisking the mixture until the desired thickness is achieved.
10. Cook this mixture out for a further 5 minutes.
11. Add the gruyère cheese and the nutmeg.
12. Cut up the cauliflower. Place this in an oven dish. Then cover generously with the cheese béchamel.
13. Bake the cauliflower in the oven for 30–40 minutes until the top has browned and the whole cauliflower is tender.
14. Serve the dish, making sure the gammon is still hot, re-heating this in the water if necessary.

Tips/Pointers

Gammon loin is also known as boiling bacon. It is a relatively cheap cut of meat and one that is grossly undervalued. Delicious and easy to cook, it can be pre-prepared and eaten cold, although it is better served hot. If pok choi is not available, then shredded red cabbage can be used instead.

Loiisijo

LOISIIJO
ECO BANDAS
COMMUNITY PROJECT
EWASO NJIRO
SHAMPOLE CONSERVANCY

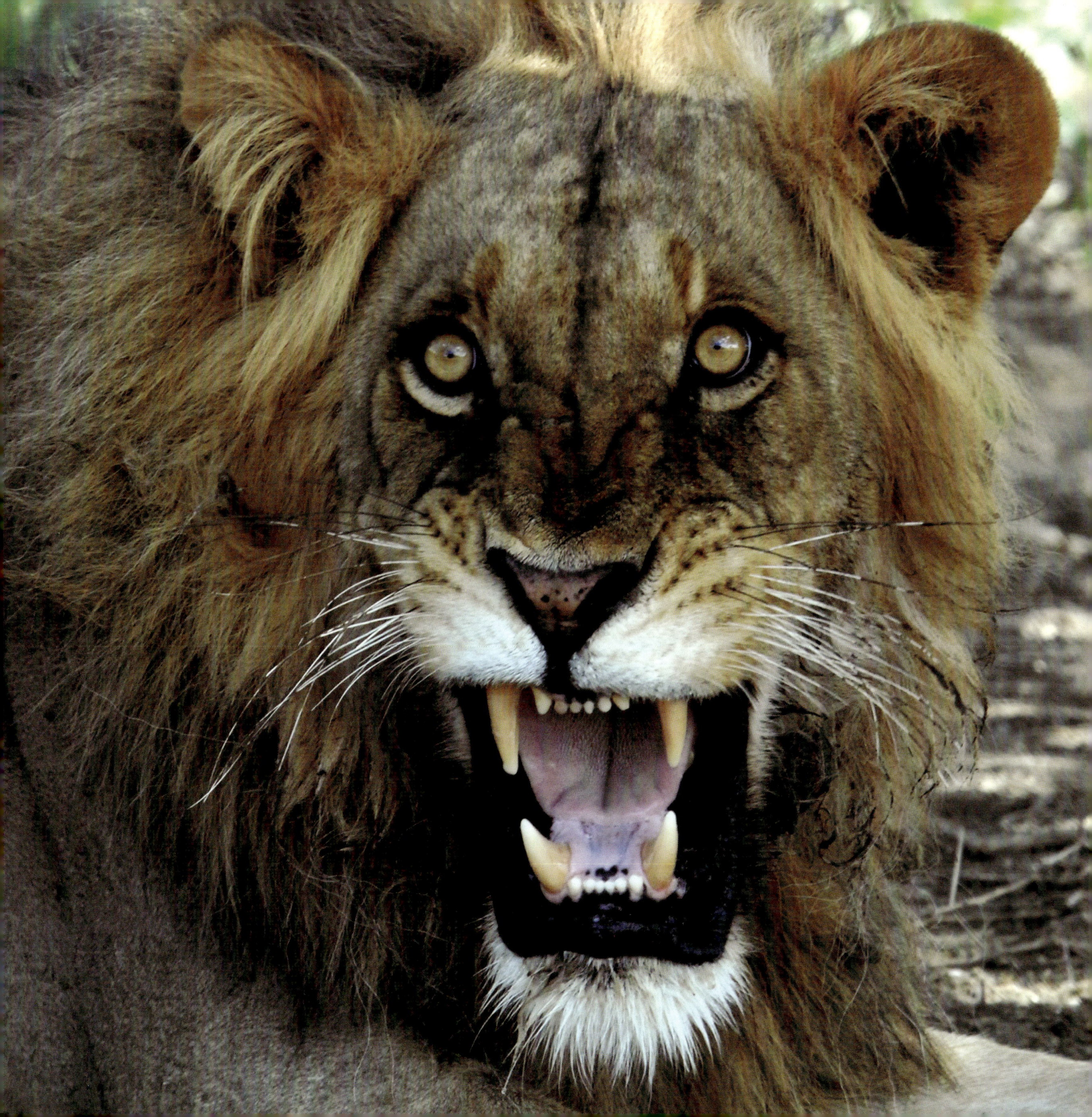

Berry-crowned pudding with port syrup

RECIPE

Serves 4 people

Ingredients

- 5 tbsp softened butter
- 1 cup castor sugar
- 2 eggs, beaten
- 1 cup self-raising flour
- 5 tbsp milk
- 300 g mixed berries
- 4 tbsp unrefined sugar
- ½ cup port
- Whipped cream to serve

Method

1. Heat the oven to 200°C, and butter 4 individual 175-ml oven-proof pudding moulds.
2. Beat the castor sugar and butter until light and creamy. Gradually beat in the eggs until the mixture is smooth. Carefully fold in the flour.
3. Take half the berries and distribute evenly into the four moulds. Spoon the cake mixture over these, until each mould is ¾ full.
4. Stand the puddings in a deep oven tray, and surround with boiling water so this reaches half way up the sides of the moulds.
5. Cook for 35–40 minutes until springy to the touch.
6. Meanwhile, dissolve the sugar in the port over a medium heat, and bring to the boil.
7. Add the rest of the berries until these are just warmed and stir gently, being careful not to break up the berries.
8. Serve each pudding with port and berry syrup and some thick cream or custard.

Tips/Pointers

If you do not have an oven, this pudding can be steamed. In that case, cover each pudding mould with some pleated foil (to allow for expansion) and tie each with string to secure it and make it water-tight. Then place in a large saucepan with a tight-fitting lid, and steam for about 1 hour.

Loiisijo 135

RHINO CHARGE
mogoswok BARINGO

2 0 0 9
D I S T R I C T

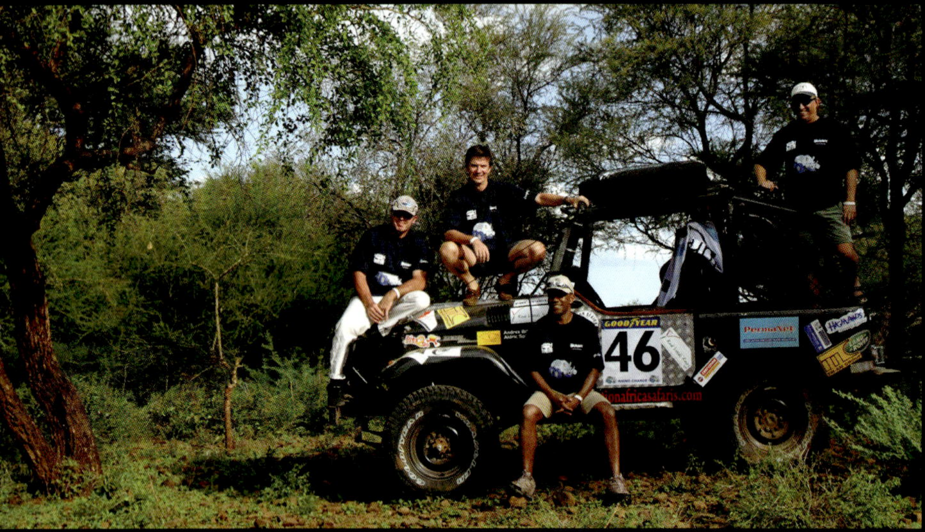
GOODYEAR
46

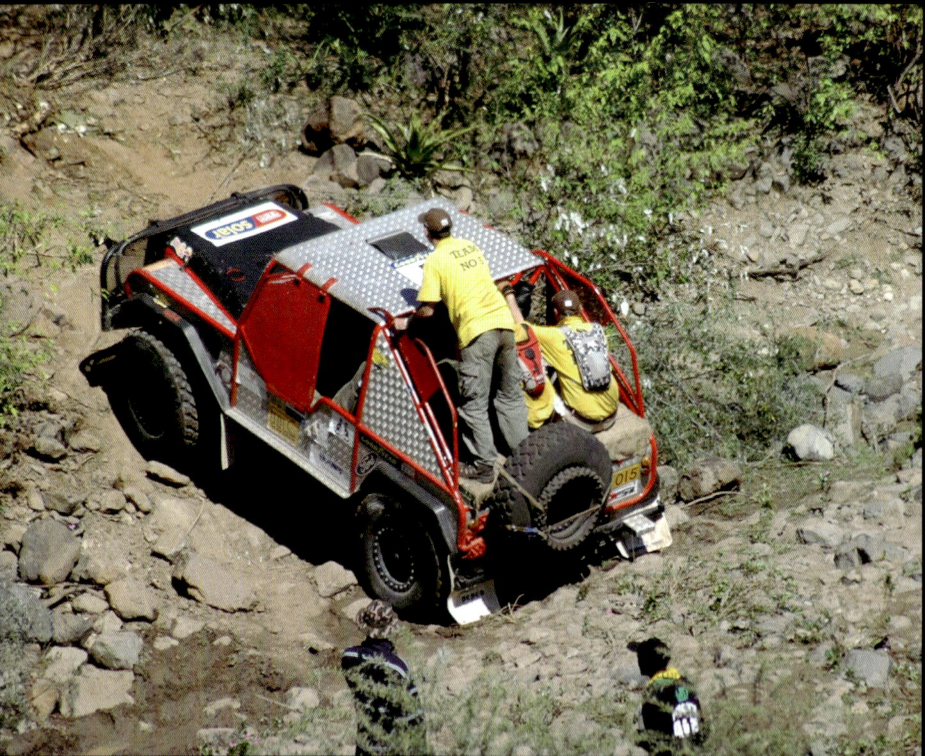

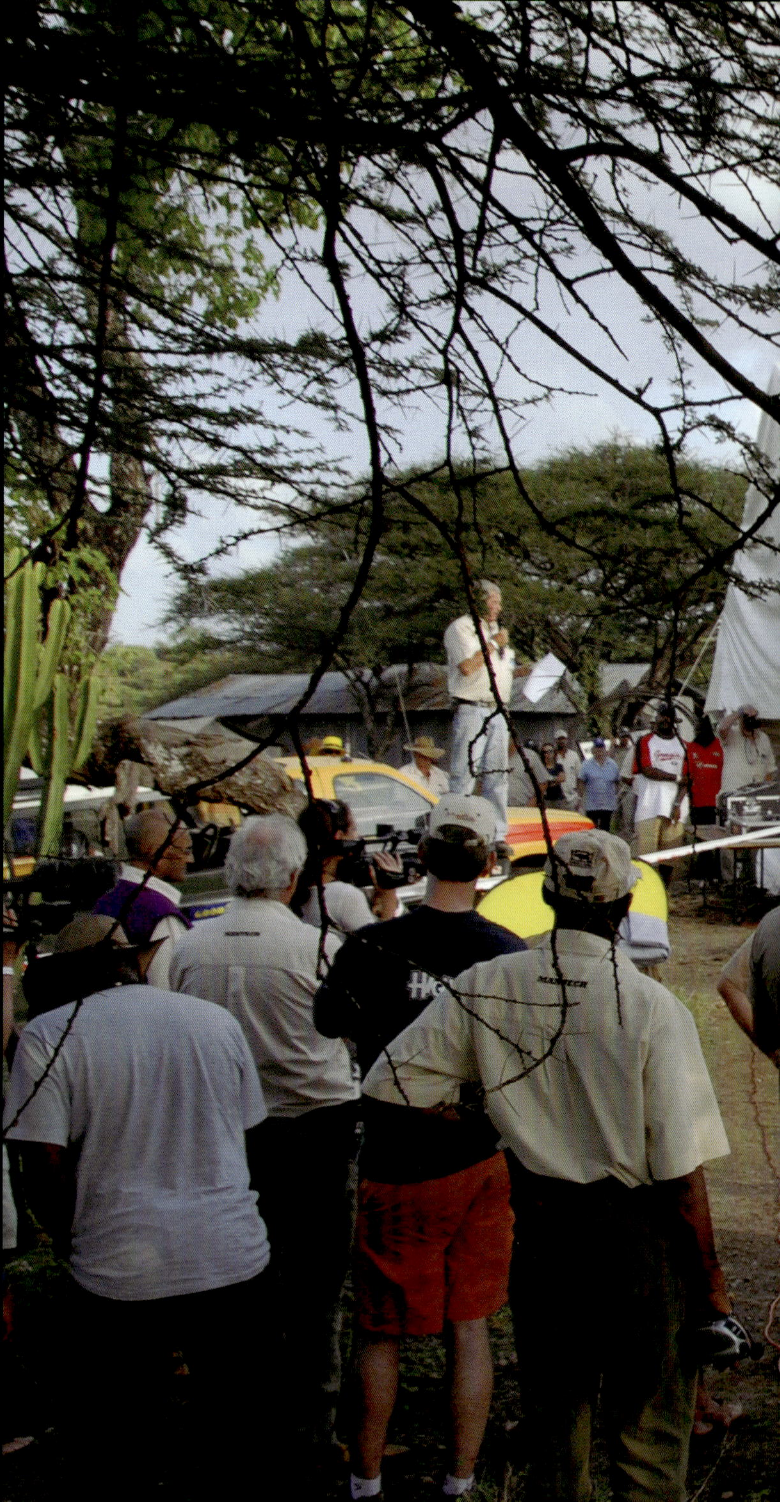

CHARGE

MENU
RHINO CHARGE
Competitor's camp cars 3, 13 & 46
FRIDAY 29 MAY 2009

LUNCH *(28 pax)*
Terrine on a Bed of Lettuce *(gherkins & pickled onions)*
Fish Salad with Capers
*(boil, drain & add lots of lime juice, add salt, pepper,
capers, parsley, a little mayo & a drop of olive.
Nile Perch 100 g × 28 pax = 2.8 kg =3.5 kg)*
Russian Salad *(80 g × 28 pax = 2 kg potatoes)*
Cucumber Salad with plain Yoghurt
Cheese Platter
Bread & Butter
Fresh Fruits
Tea & Coffee

SUNDOWNERS
Banana Crisps & Cream Cheese Dip
Green Olives
Vegetable Samosas with Limes

DINNER *(33 pax)*
Pumpkin & Carrot Soup & Croutons
(3 butternuts + 1 fresh cream)
Chicken Curry
*(300 g × 33 pax = 9.9 kg = ± 5 chickens of ± 2.2 kg each
+ lots of dania & parsley)*
Vegetarian Curry
Rice *(50 g × 33 pax = 1.65 kg)*
Lentils
Chapattis
Condiments *(chopped tomatoes; bananas; onions;
green peppers; mango chutney; fresh chillies, grated coconut)*

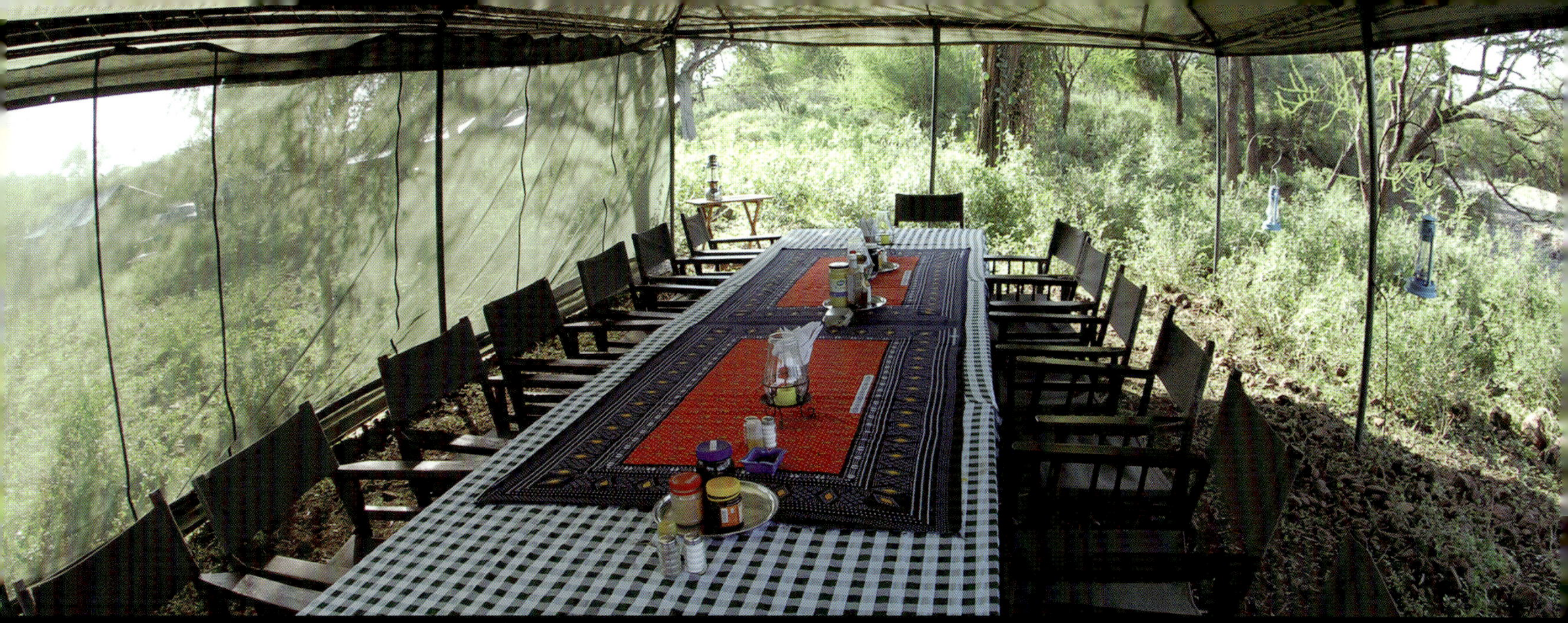

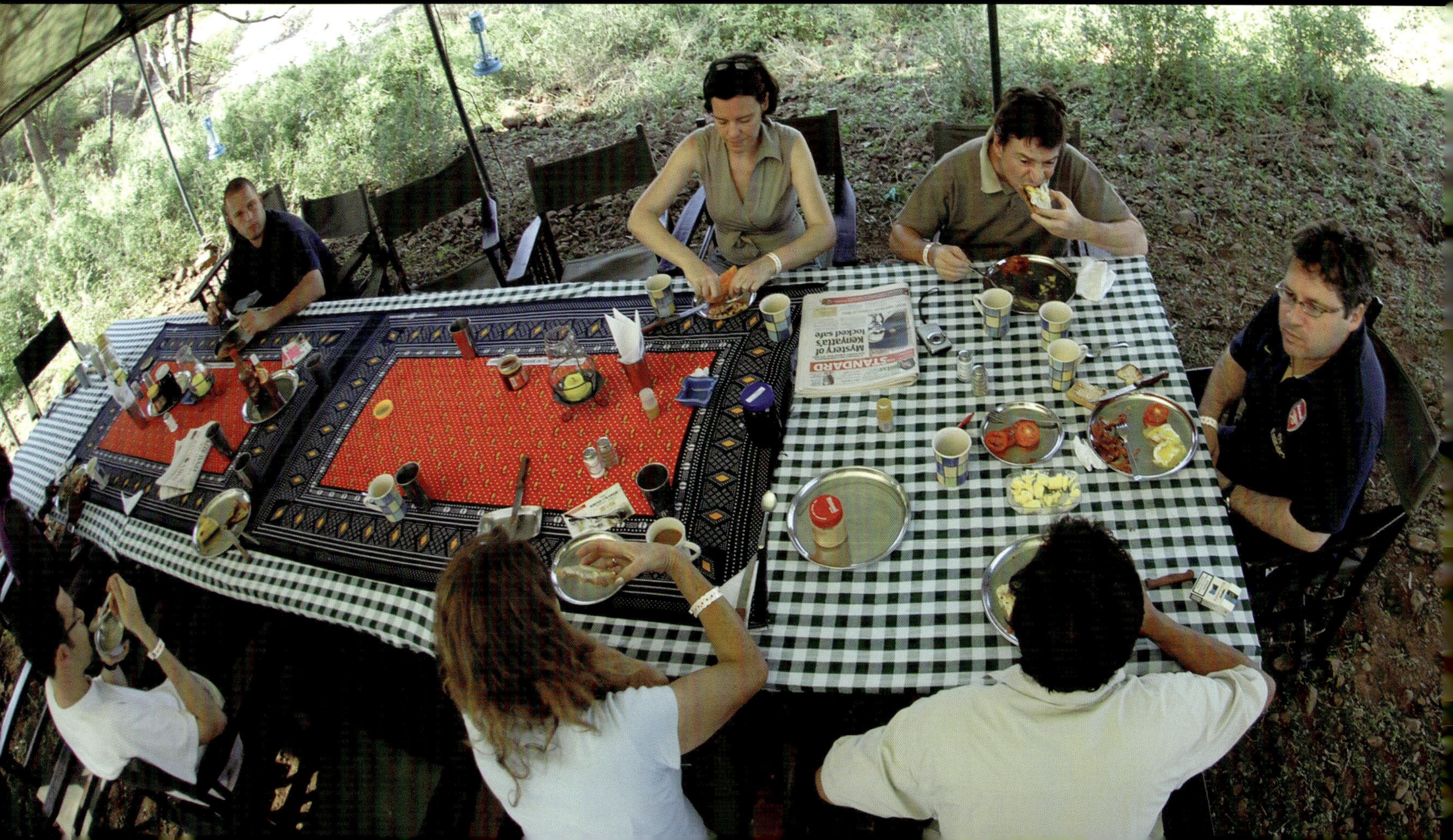
STANDARD
Mystery of Kenyatta's locked safe

Black forest ham with grilled asparagus, quail eggs and paprika hollandaise

RECIPE

Serves 4 people

Ingredients

- Paprika hollandaise sauce *(see recipe)*
- 1 bunch asparagus
- 1 dozen quail eggs
- 1 packet black forest ham

Method

1. Cut the woody stems from the asparagus. Place over some hot coals on a grill. Cook until slightly charred.
2. Place the quail eggs in boiling water for 2 minutes and 15 seconds (for perfectly soft boiled eggs).
3. Remove and place immediately in cold water for 1 minute.
4. Plate the ham with the asparagus. Spoon a generous portion of the hollandaise over the asparagus and serve.

'Bush' Hollandaise sauce

(Makes 1 Cup)

Ingredients

- 4 egg yolks
- Juice of 1 large lemon
- 4 tbsp melted butter
- Pinch of paprika
- Seasoning

Method

1. Vigorously whisk the egg yolks and the lemon juice in a stainless steel bowl until the mixture thickens and doubles in volume.
2. Place the metal bowl over the saucepan of boiling water so the eggs cooks during whisking.
3. Slowly add the hot melted butter into the eggs, whisking until all the butter is absorbed.
4. Add the paprika and the seasoning, and keep covered at room temperature.

Tips/Pointers

The texture of the hollandaise sauce should be like that of fresh mayonnaise. If the texture is too thick, either add more lemon juice, or – if lemony enough already – adding some tepid water will do the trick.

Rhino Charge 2009

RHINO CHARGE

SCRUTINEERING DAY

Saturday 30 May

BREAKFAST *(33 pax)*
Selection of Cut Fresh Fruits
(pawpaw, mango, banana, pineapple),
Fruit Juice, Toast & Butter
(Strawberry Jam, Raspberry Jam, Honey),
Tea & Coffee

ACTIVE STATION
Pancakes/Eggs of your choice,
Garnishes for omelettes *(green pepper, grated cheese, tomatoes, chilies, onions)*,
Bacon, Beef Sausage, Grilled Tomato,
Baked Beans *(50g x 33 pax = 1.65 kg = 6 tins)*
& Fried Bread

LUNCH *(+/− 38 pax)*
Jubilee Chicken Salad *(250 g x38 pax = 9.5 kg = 5 chickens)*, Rice Salad *(50 g x 38 pax = 1.9 kg)*,
Carrot and Mango Salad with Raisins,
Three-bean Salad, Mixed Salad,
Cheese Platter, Bread & Butter,
Fruit Salad, Tea & Coffee

SUNDOWNERS
Dates wrapped in Bacon / Green Olives
Chevda Fish Fingers *(1.8 kg Nile Perch)*
with Tartar Sauce

DINNER *(38 pax)*
Avocado *(20 pcs)* & Tuna *(5 tins)*
(Serve on a bed of lettuce; make a fan with the avocado)
Grilled Fillet of Beef with Pepper Sauce *(Fillets, 250 g x 38 pax = 9.5 kg)*
Ratatouille *(onions, garlic, courgettes, tomatoes, carrots, rosemary leaves)*
Roast Potatoes *(100 g x 38 pax = 3.8 kg potatoes)*
Spinach with Cream *(1 litre cream)*
Crêpes stuffed with Pineapple with Cinnamon
Tea & Coffee

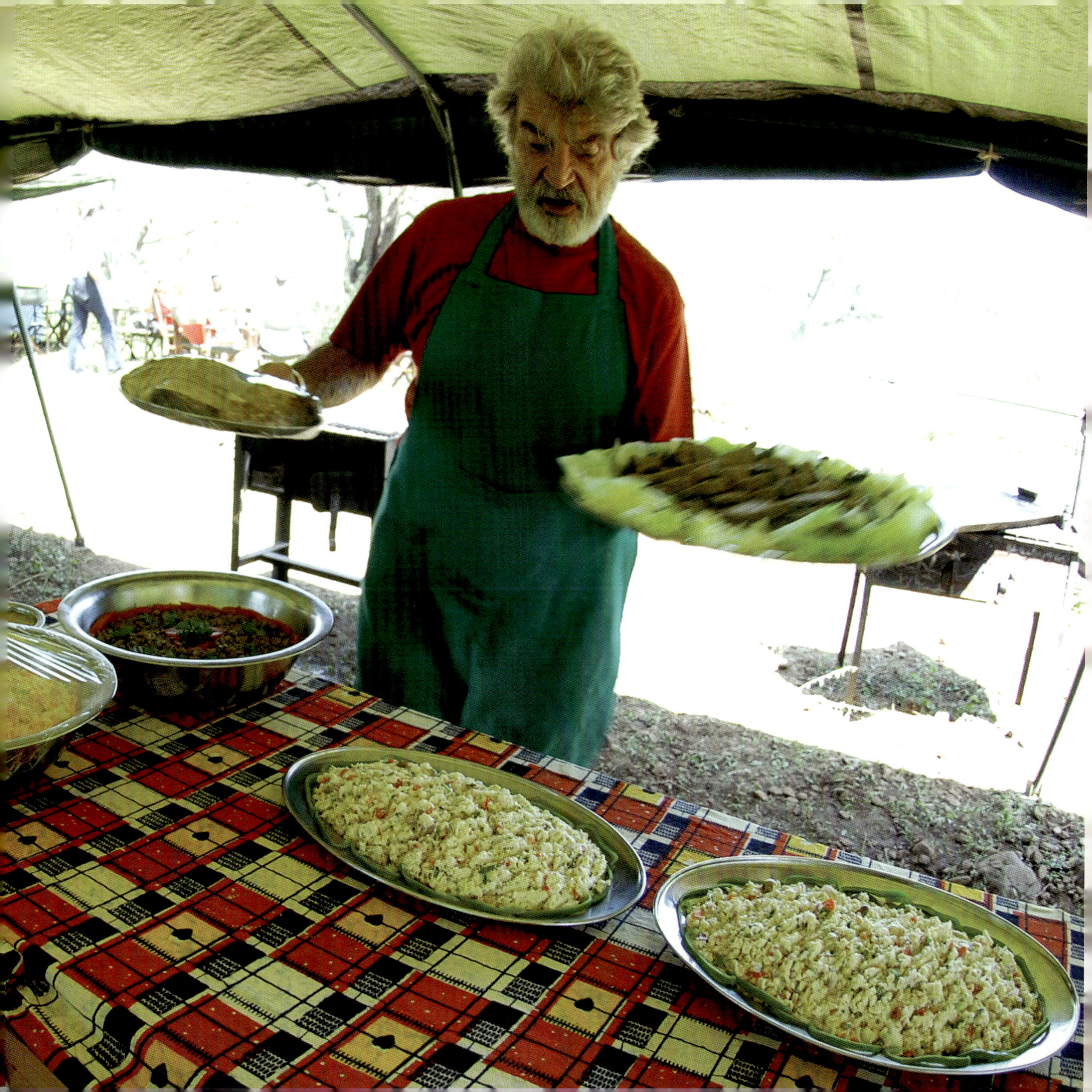

Slow-roasted rib of beef with roast onion and garlic purée

RECIPE

Serves 10 people

Ingredients

- 4 kg rib eye of beef on the bone
- 1 tbsp black pepper
- 1 tbsp coarse salt
- 1 tbsp brown sugar
- 1 tbsp chopped rosemary
- 1 large white onion, peeled and quartered
- 3 bulbs garlic
- 2 large potatoes
- ½ cup cream
- 1 tbsp Dijon mustard

Method

1. Mix the salt, pepper, sugar and rosemary in a bowl. Rub this mixture liberally over the beef.
2. Put the beef in a very hot oven for about half an hour. Cook until it starts to get some colour.
3. Reduce the heat to about 140°C, and cook the beef for about 5 hours. Remove and allow to rest for 15 minutes.
4. Meanwhile, peel, boil and mash the potatoes. Add the cream and the dijon mustard and set aside.
5. Place the whole bulbs of garlic and the onions in the oven, and slow roast with the beef until they start to caramelise.
6. Remove from the oven. Discard the skins of the garlic, and the purée.
7. Stir this mixture into the potatoes, and taste for seasoning.
8. Remove the rested beef from the bone and serve with the onion purée.
9. Serve up a rich gravy to complement the dish.

Tips/Pointers

If bone in rib-eye is not available, then bone in sirloin can be used instead. It is important to cook the meat on the bone, as this adds so much to the flavour of the dish as a whole.

RHINO CHARGE

Rhino Charge Day

Sunday 31 May

BREAKFAST *(38 pax)* 05:15 a.m.
Selection of Cut Fresh Fruits: Pawpaw, Mango,
Banana, Pineapple
Fruit Juice
Toast & Butter
Strawberry Jam, Raspberry Jam, Honey
Tea & Coffee
Hot Oatmeal with Cinnamon & Raisins

ACTIVE STATION
Pancakes/Eggs of your choice
Garnishes for Omelettes *(green pepper, grated cheese, tomatoes, chilies, onions)*
with
Bacon, Beef Sausage, Grilled Tomato
Baked Beans *(50g X 38 pax = 1.9 kg = 7 tins)*,
& Fried Bread

PICNIC LUNCH *(+ 22 pax)*
Cold Chicken Cuts
(30 g x 22 pax = 6.6 kg = 3 chickens of 2.2 kg apiece)
Boiled Eggs
Whole Tomatoes
Topside Sandwiches
Fresh Fruits

SUNDOWNERS
Crisps with Cottage Cheese Dip
Liver *(50 g x 38 pax = 1.9 kg = 2.1 kg; on a board with salt, pepper, mustard, waiters to go around serving)*
Fried Peanuts

DINNER *(38 pax)*
Black Forest Ham with Grilled Asparagus,
Quail Eggs & Paprika Hollandaise
Slow-roast Rib of Beef with Roasted Onion
and Garlic Purée
Pineapple-upside-down Cake with
Vanilla Ice-Cream

Tea & Coffee

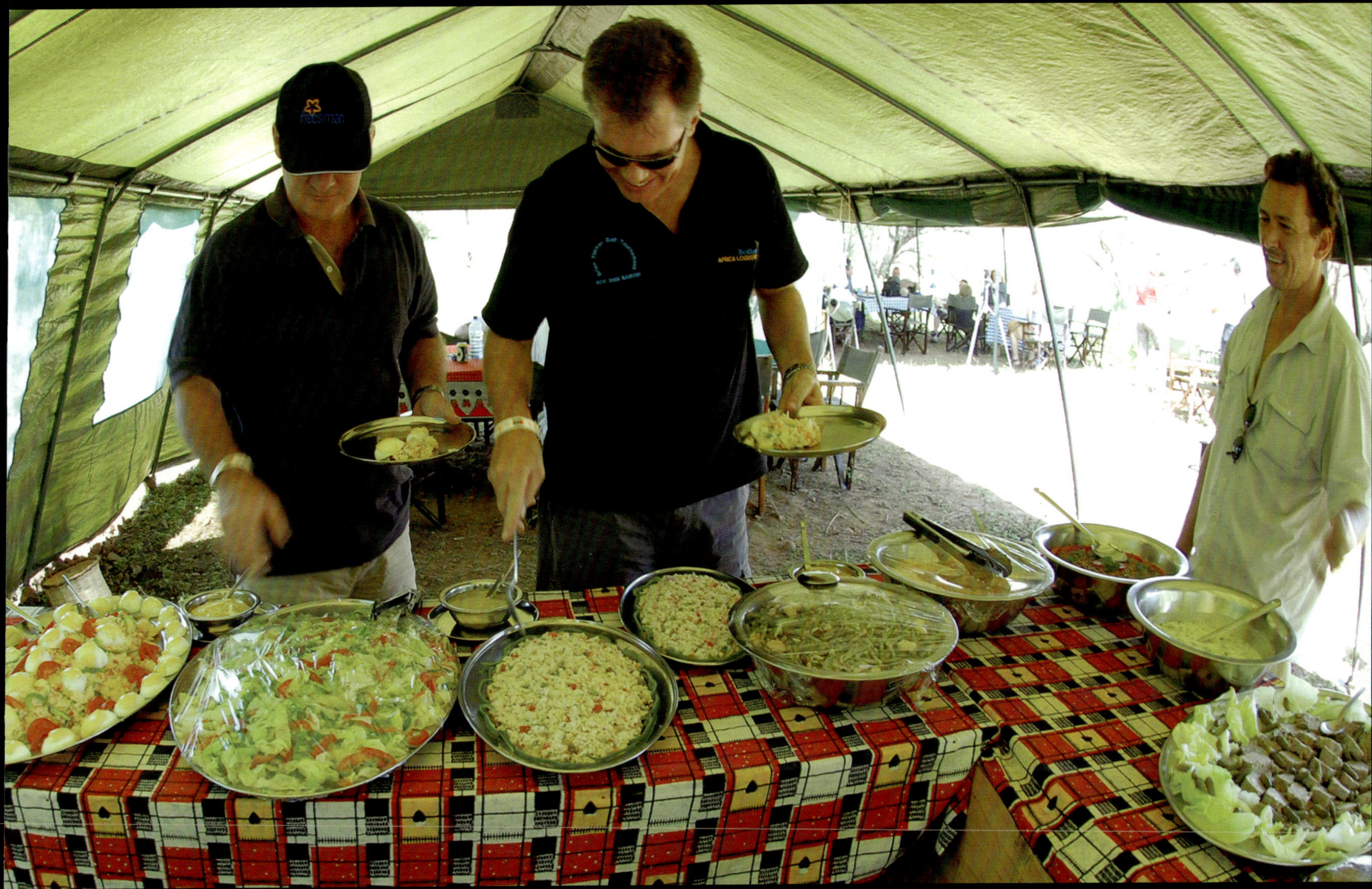

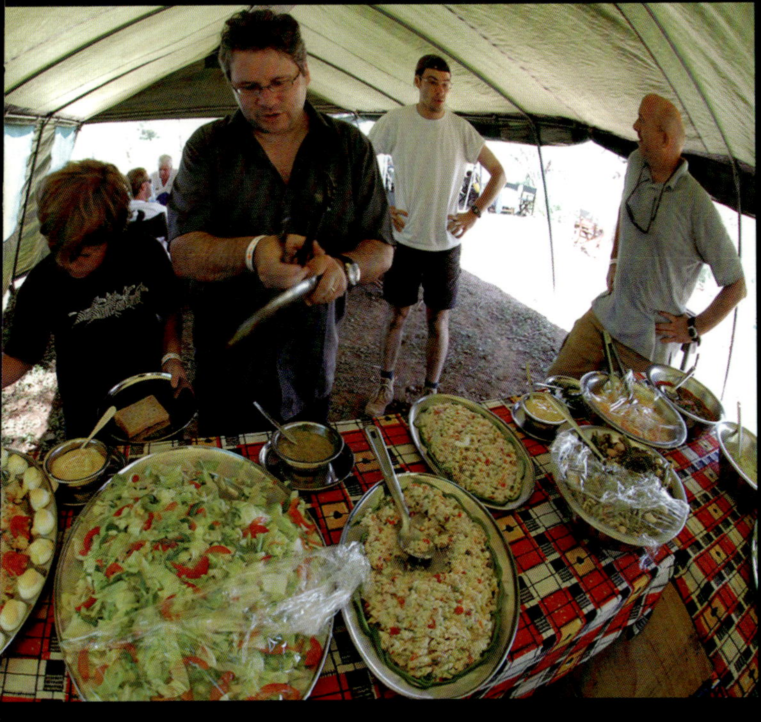

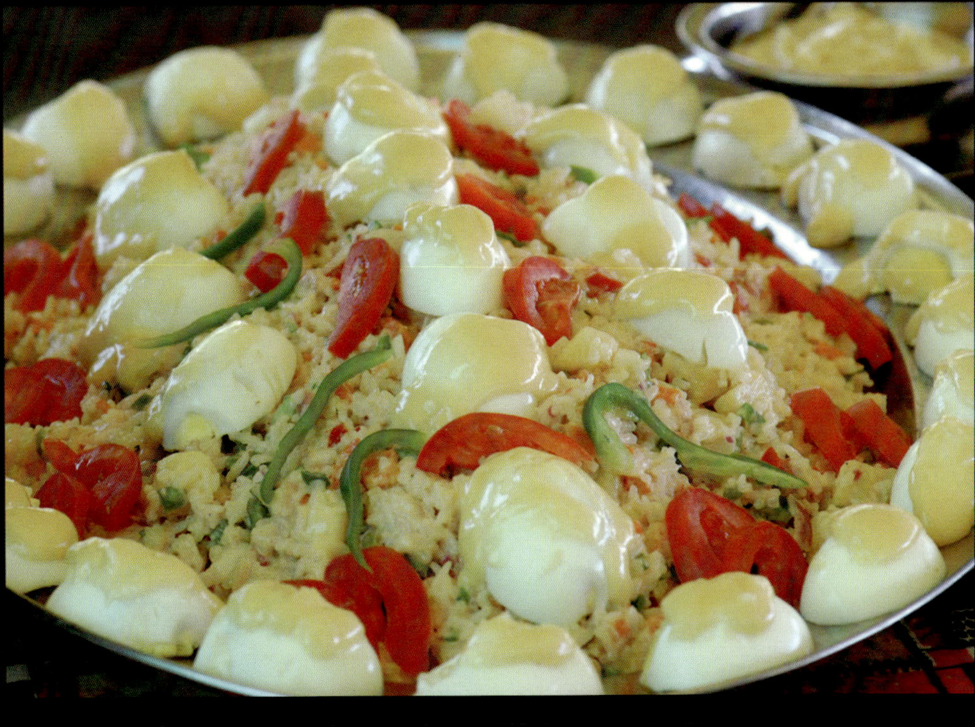

Pineapple upside-down cake with vanilla ice-cream

RECIPE

Serves 8 people

Ingredients

- 1½ cups softened butter
- 1 cup castor sugar
- 1 pineapple, sliced and cored
- 3 eggs, lightly beaten
- 2 tsp brandy
- 2 cups self-raising flour
- 1 tsp ground ginger
- 1 tbsp milk
- 2 tbsp unrefined sugar

Method

1. In a heated saucepan, place the unrefined sugar with a tablespoonful of water. Boil the sugar until you have a deep golden brown caramel. Pour this into the flan dish and immediately add the pineapple rings, so these cover the base of the dish.
2. Cream the butter and the castor sugar until they are white and fluffy, then add the eggs slowly. Beat constantly until you have a smooth mixture.
3. Fold in the flour and the ginger, then mix in the milk and the brandy.
4. Pour the mixture over the pineapple and place in the oven for 40 minutes at 180°C.
5. Remove from the oven, and turn on to a plate while still hot.
6. Slice up and serve warm with a good quality vanilla ice cream.

Tips/Pointers

It is important to turn the cake out while it is still hot. Otherwise the caramel that was poured into the flan dish will stick and cause the cake to break up.

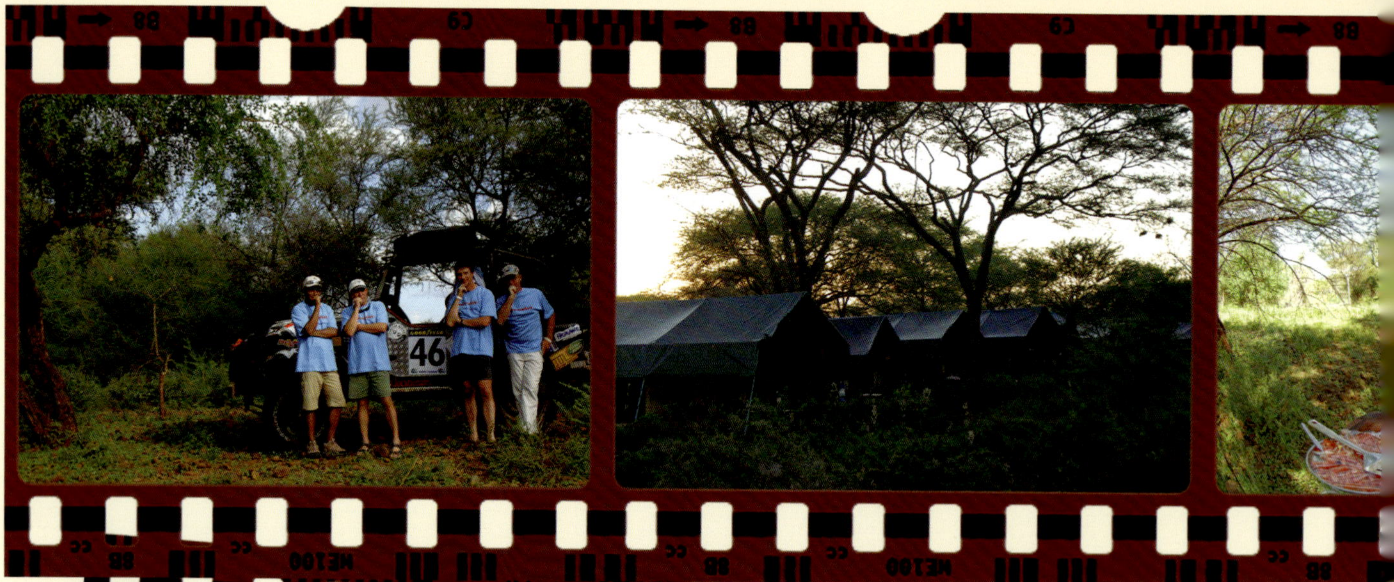

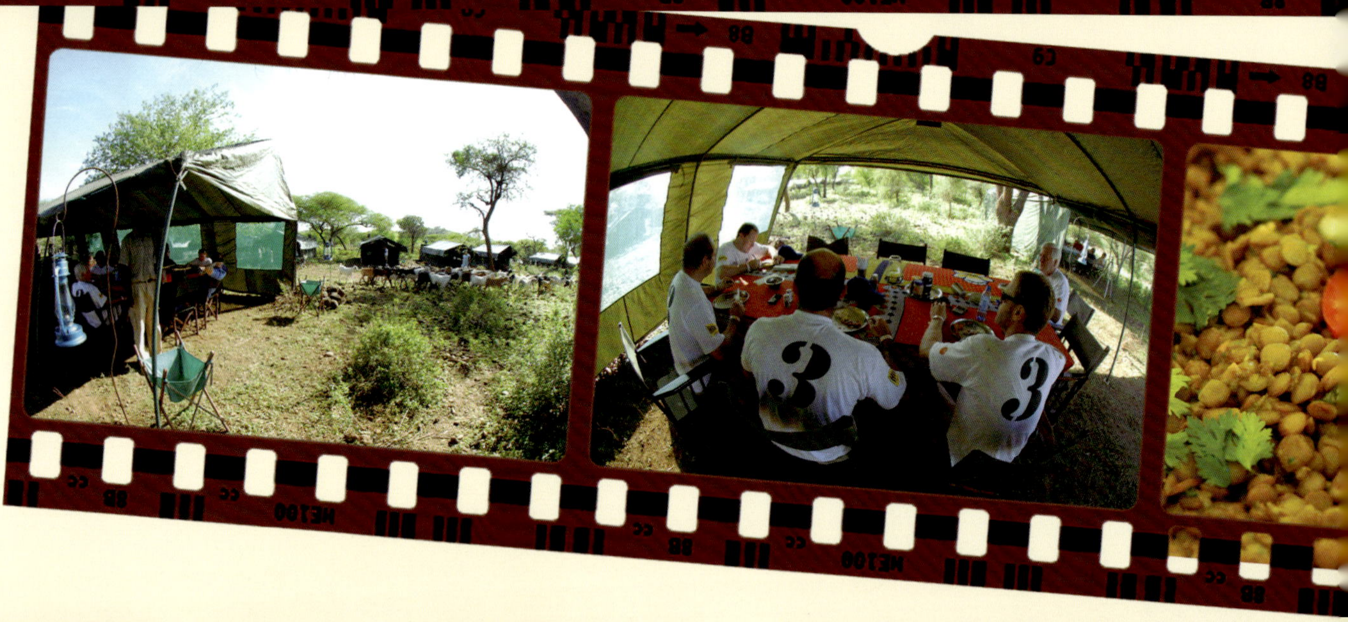

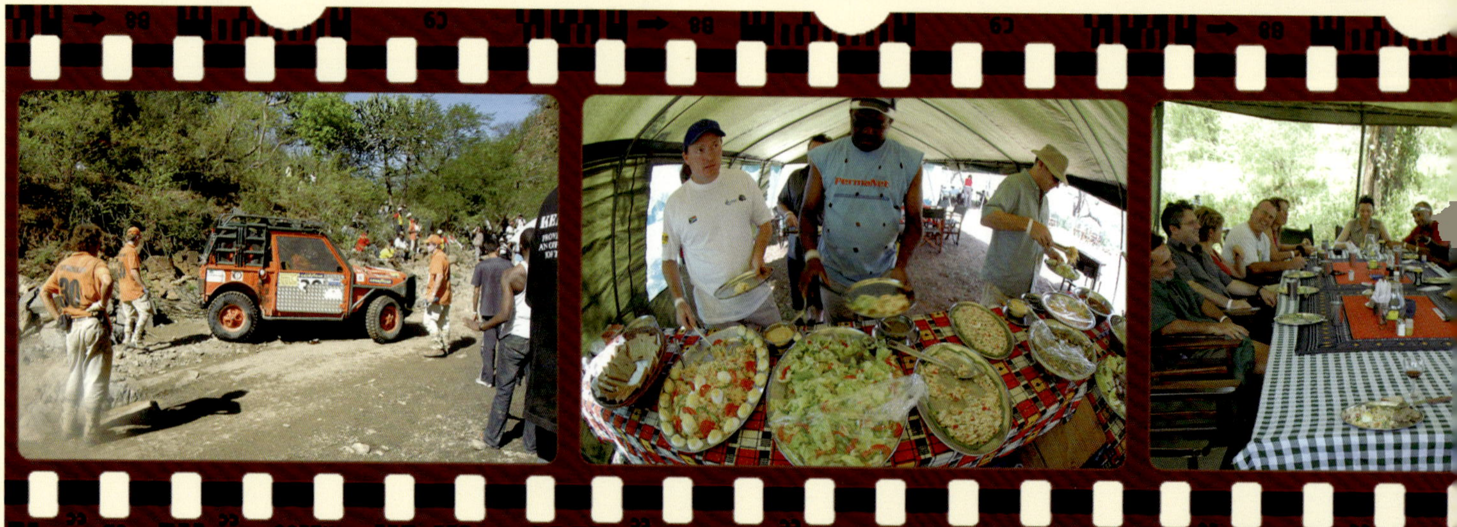

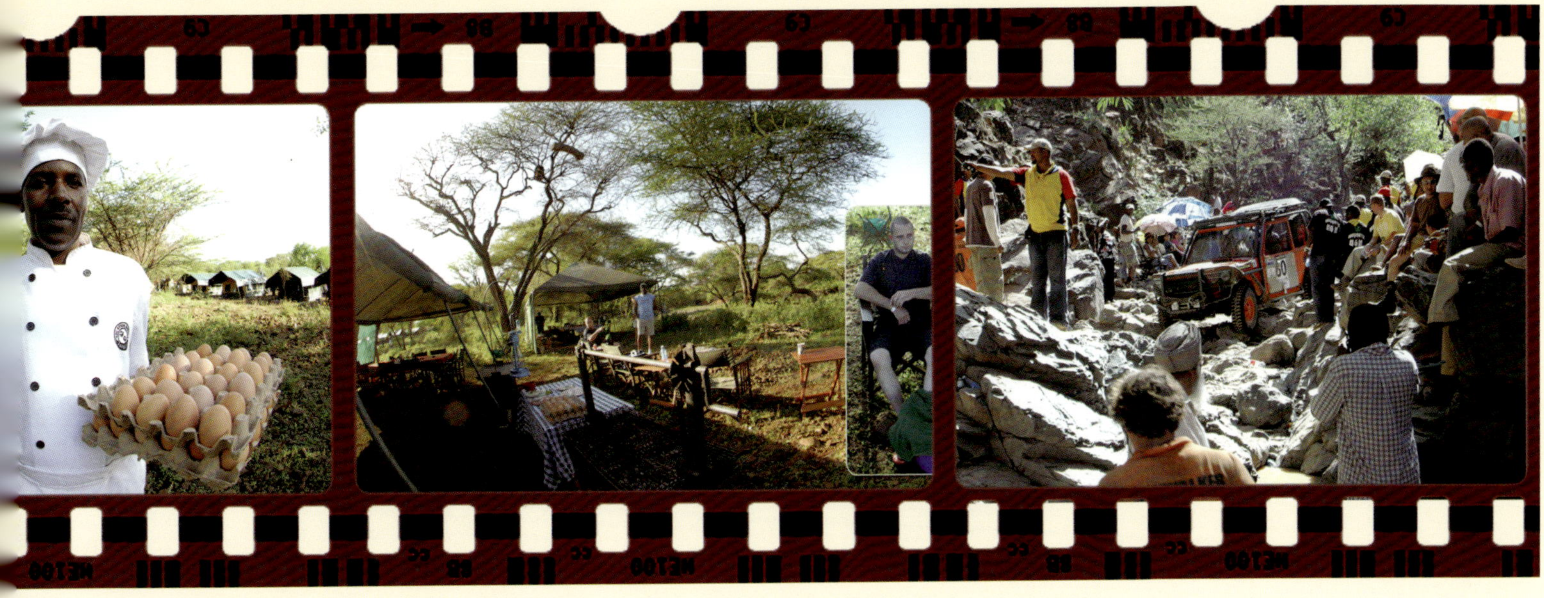

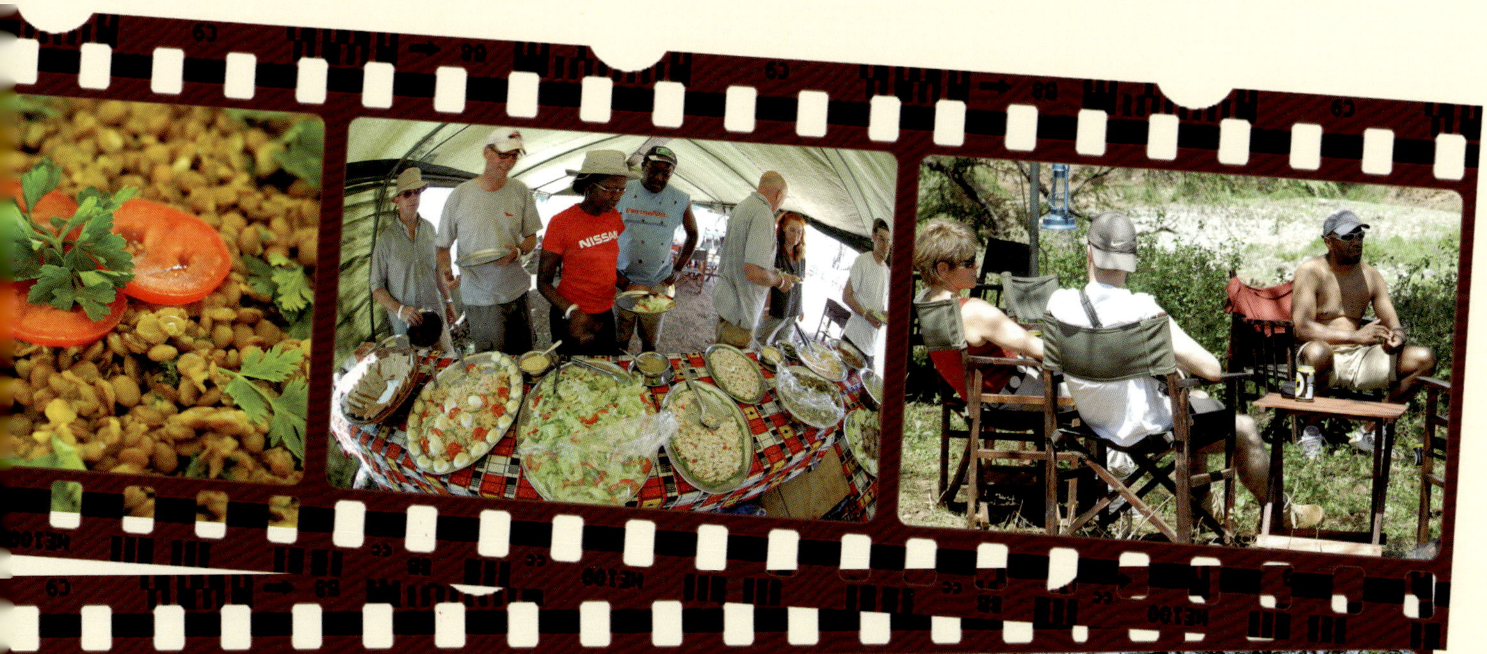
NISSAN

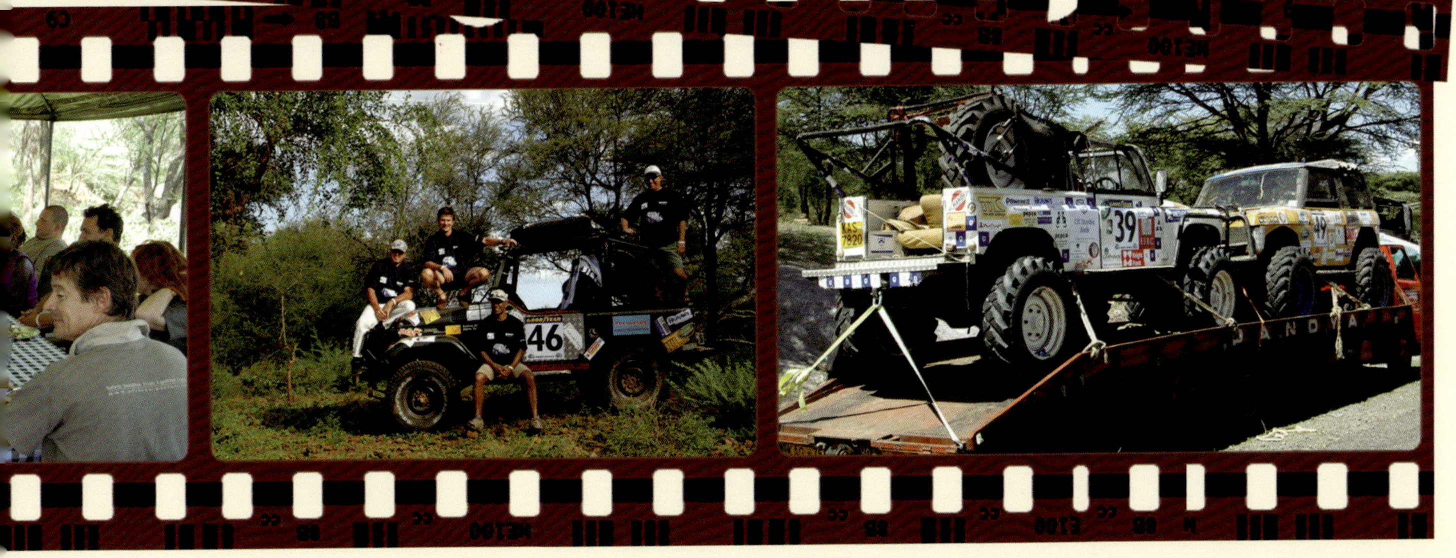
46
39

MARA

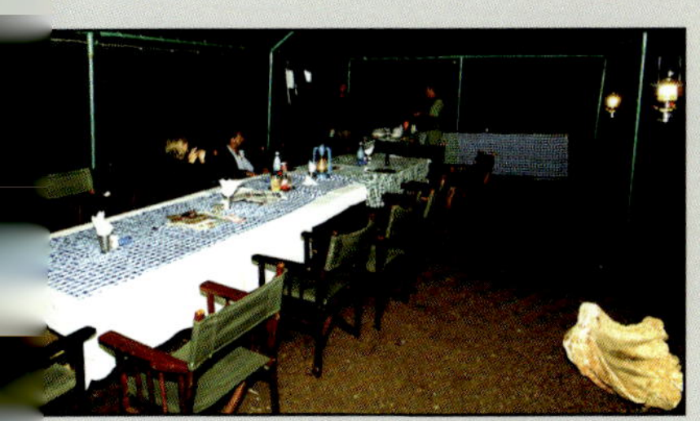

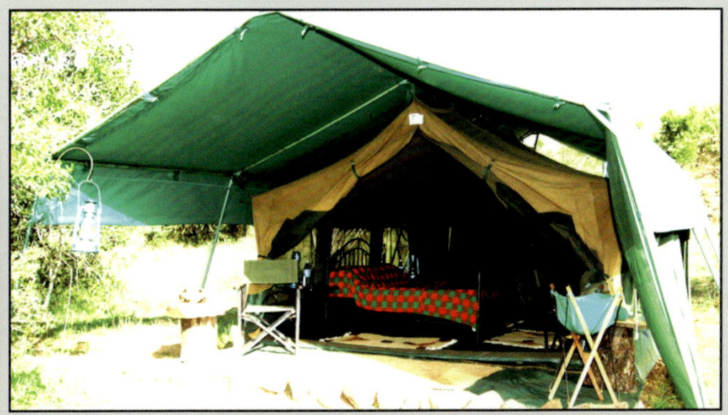

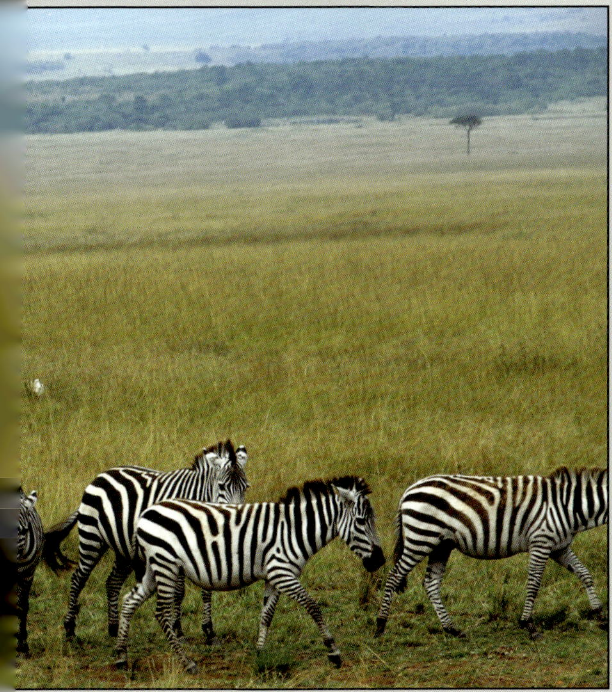

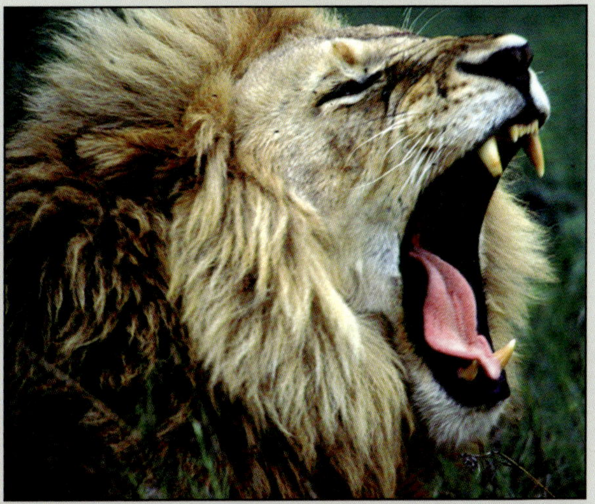

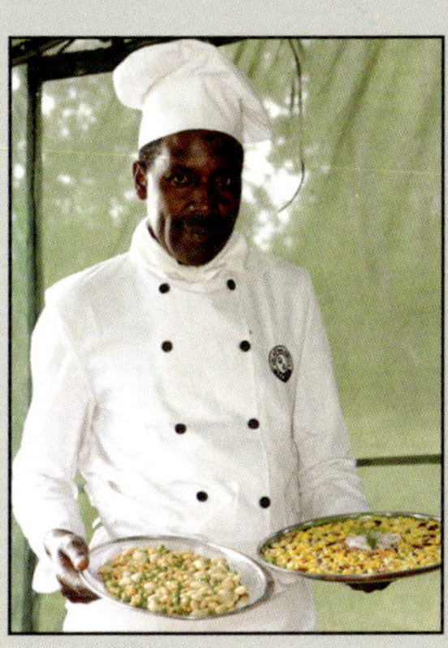

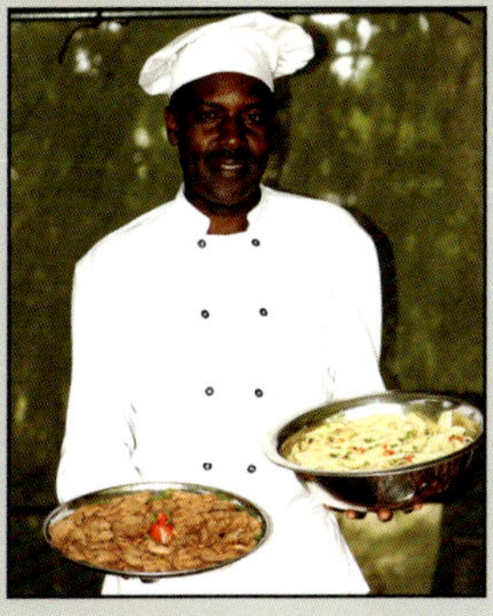

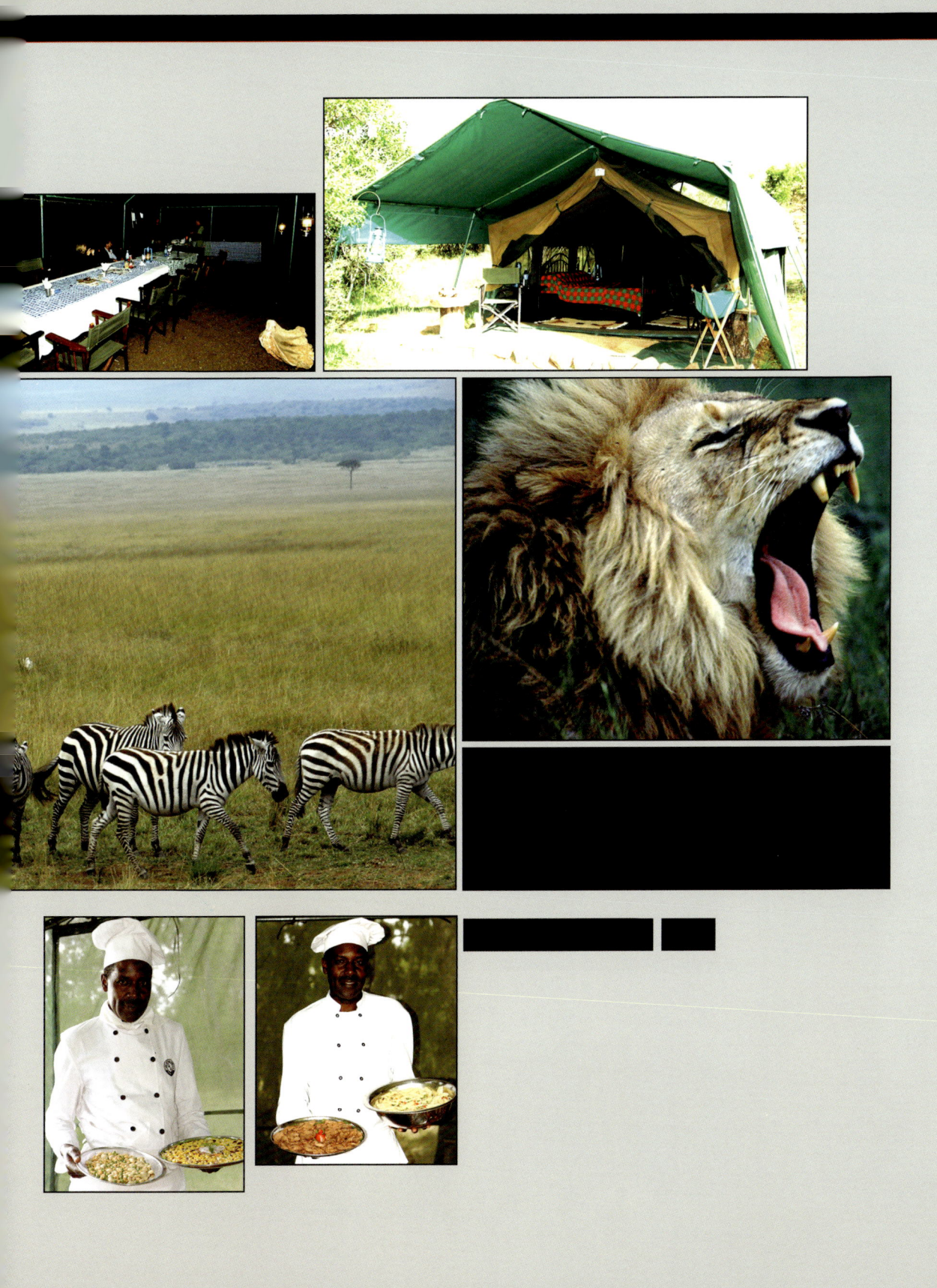

MENU
Masai Mara

Fresh beetroot and asparagus salad with cumin-crusted haloumi and balsamic syrup

Fillet of beef with bubble and squeak, fine beans and gorgonzola cream jus

Gooseberry crumble with oat and cinnamon crust and ginger custard

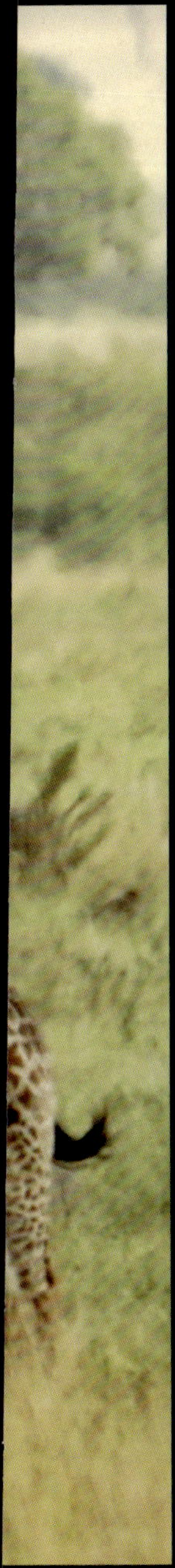
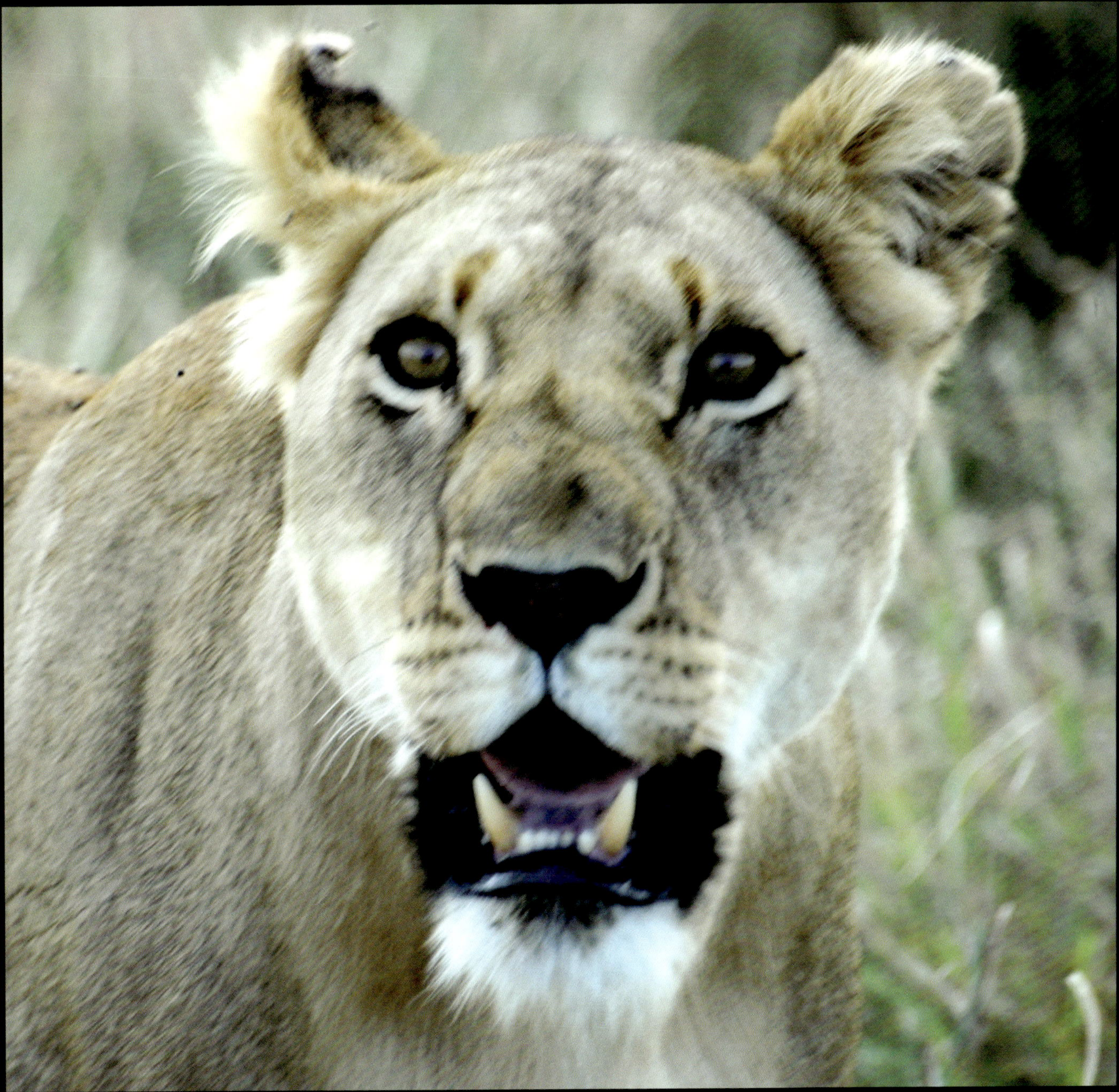
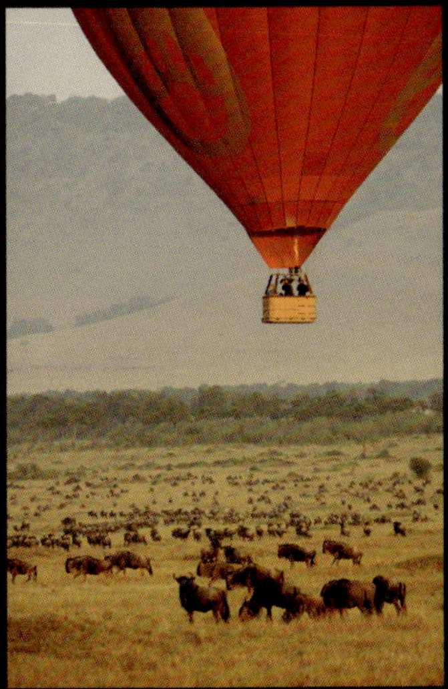
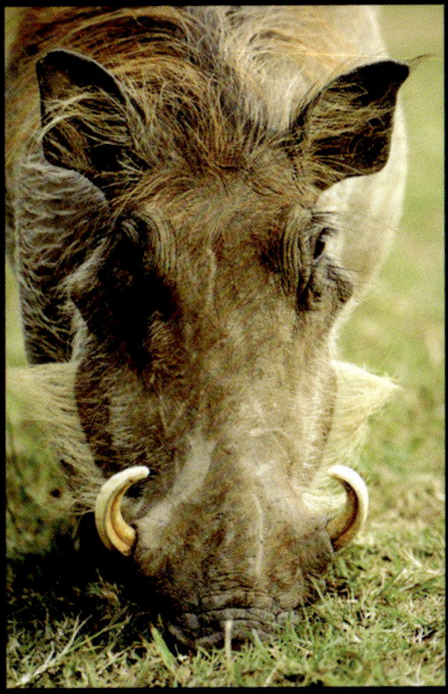
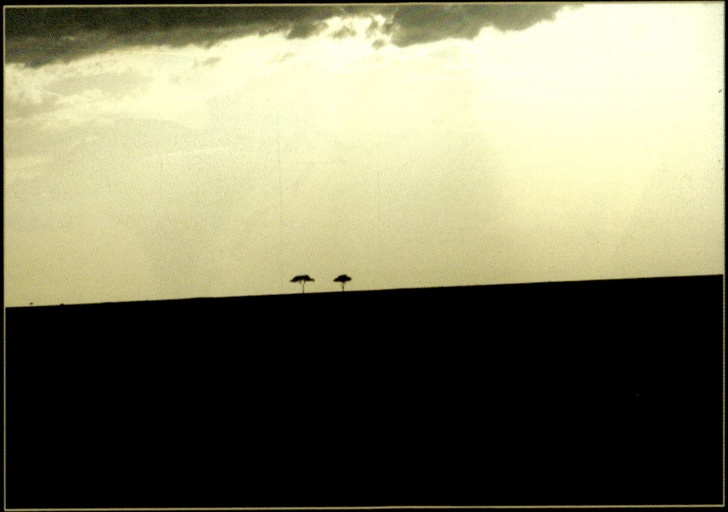
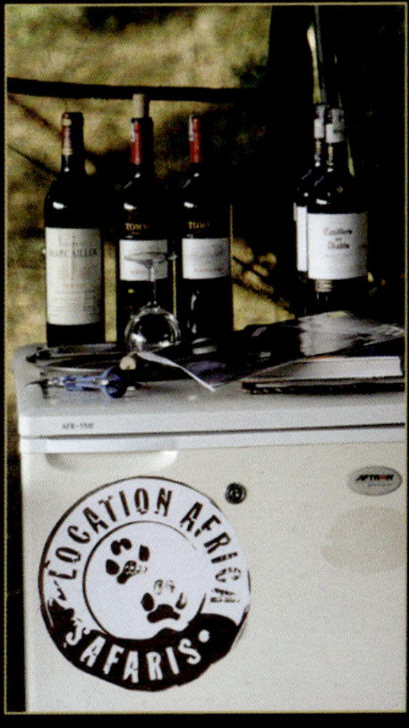
LOCATION AFRICA
SAFARIS

Fresh beetroot and asparagus salad with cumin-crusted haloumi and balsamic syrup

RECIPE

Serves 4 people

Ingredients

- 3 medium-sized fresh beetroots, peeled and cooked
- 1 bunch of asparagus
- 2 blocks of haloumi
- 2 tsp whole cumin seeds
- Olive oil
- Drizzle of balsamic syrup *(see recipe)*

Method

1. Cook the asparagus in hot water until it is al dente. Remove and set aside.
2. In a frying pan, heat some olive oil and sprinkle the cumin seeds into it.
3. When the seeds begin to fry and are giving off their aroma, add the sliced haloumi, and go on frying until golden brown.
4. Flip over and fry briefly on the other side.
5. Plate the dish, layering the beetroot, and the haloumi, with the asparagus over it.
6. Finish with a drizzle of balsamic syrup, and serve.

Balsamic syrup

Method

1. Pour 200 ml of balsamic vinegar into a saucepan, and heat until it is simmering.
2. Reduce the liquid by ¾ and allow to cool. This will leave you with a thick, rich syrup.

Tips/Pointers

Be sure to fry the cumin seeds until they smell almost roasted. This will give them a crunchy texture, as well as a deep flavour.

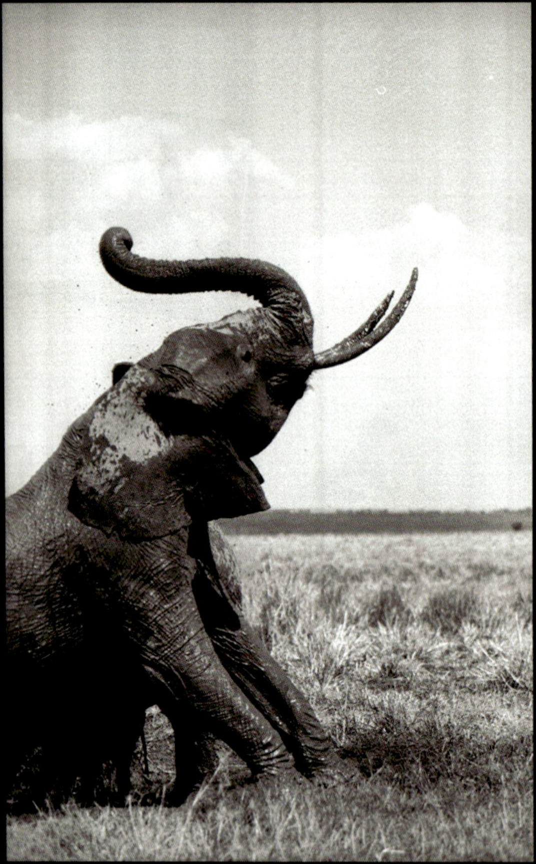
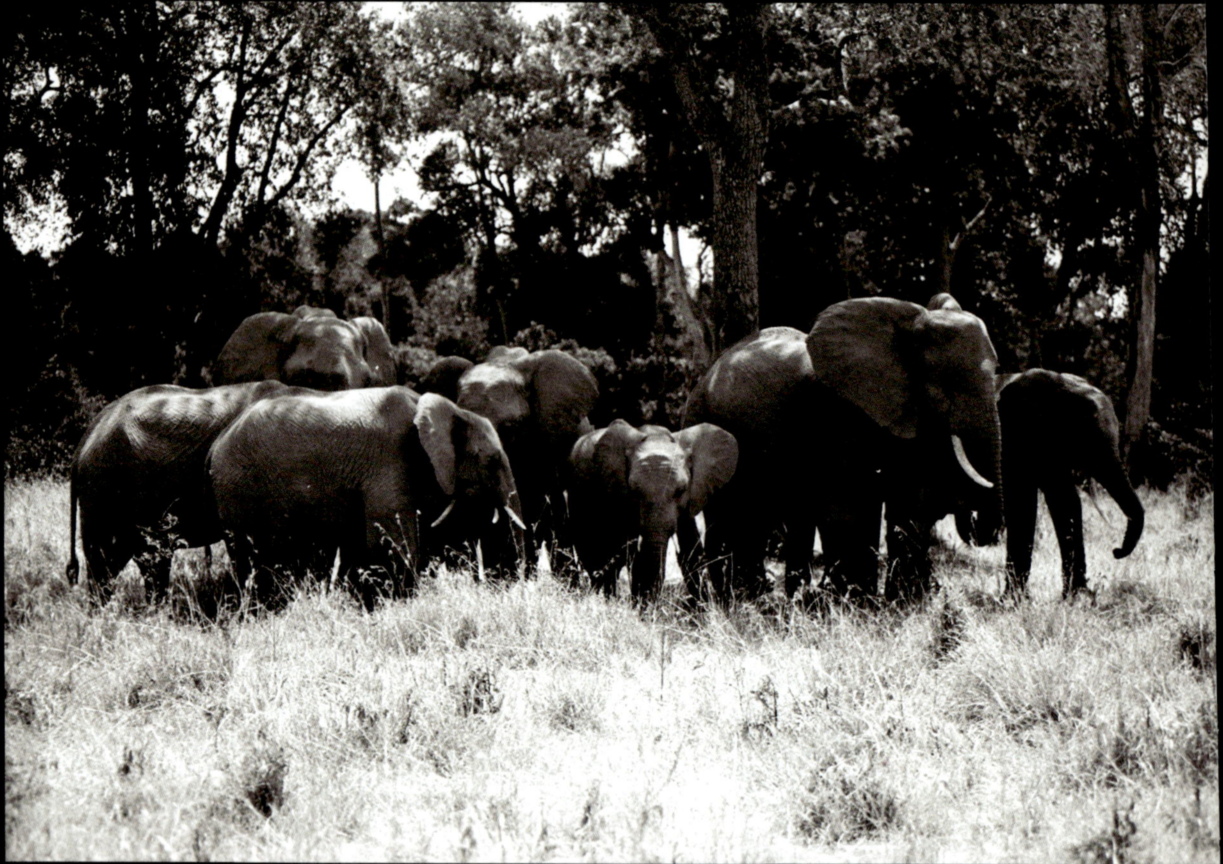
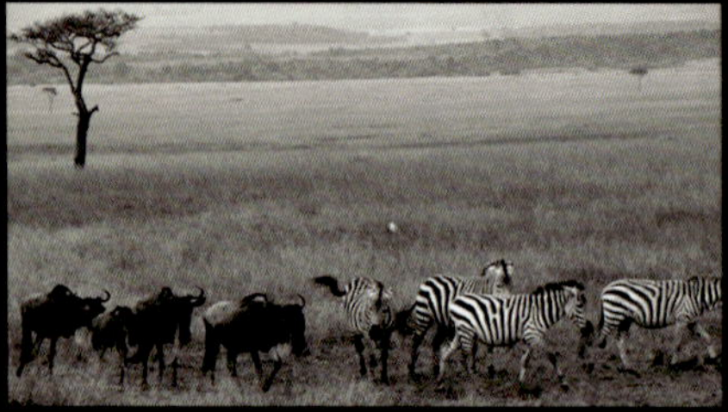
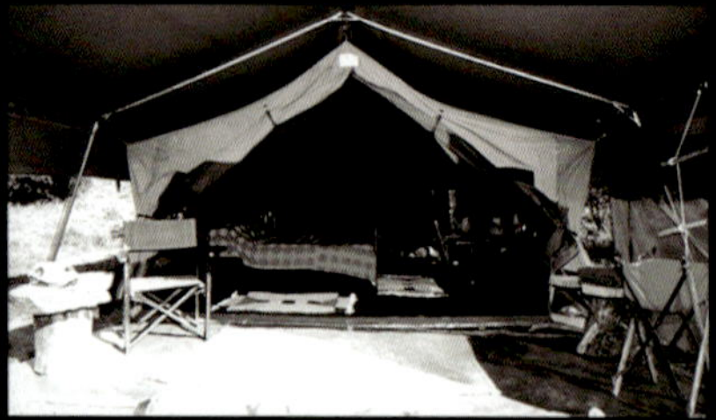
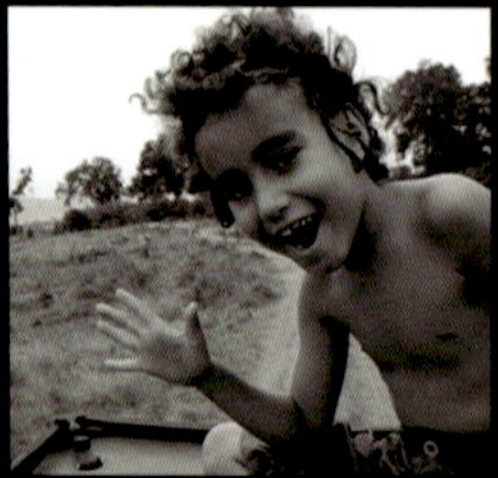
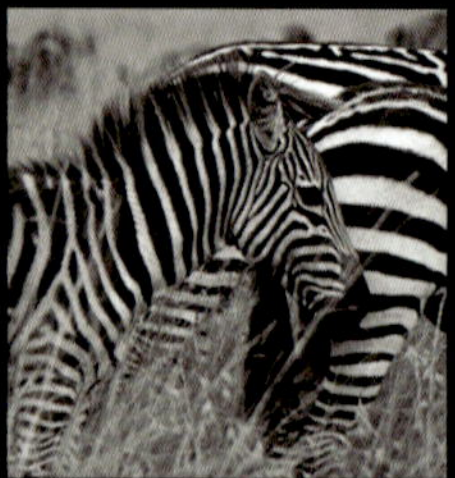
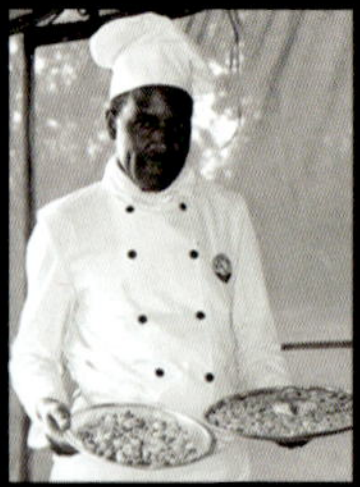
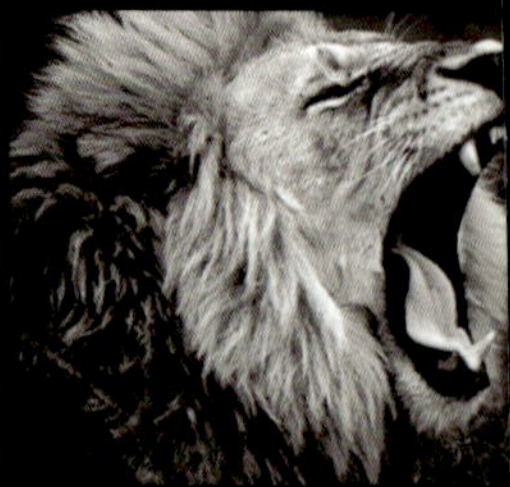

MARA

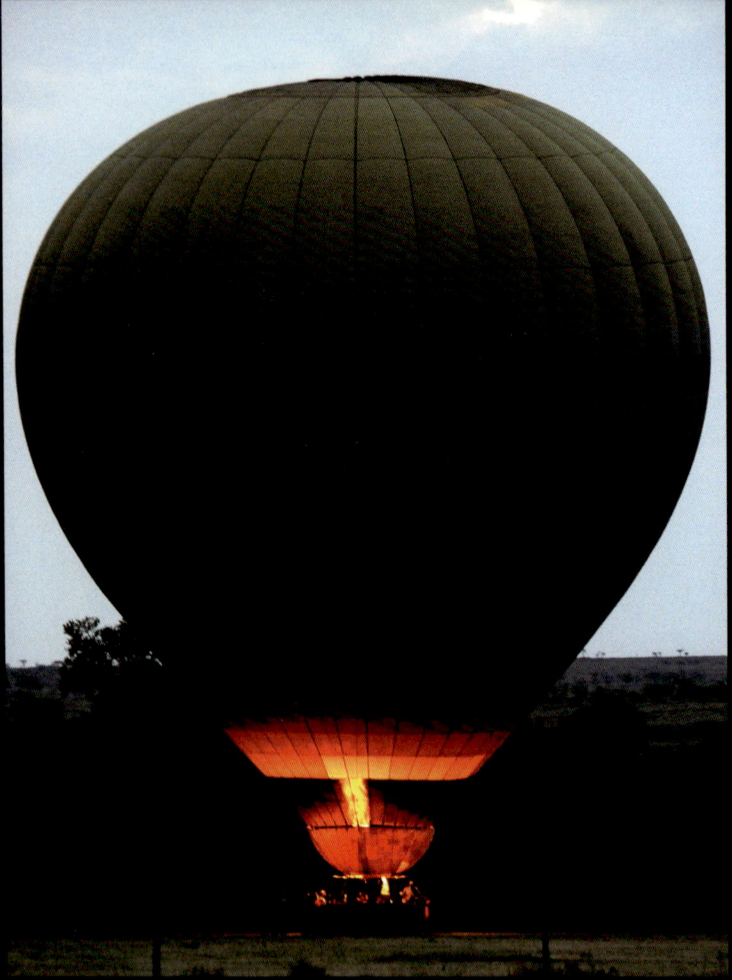
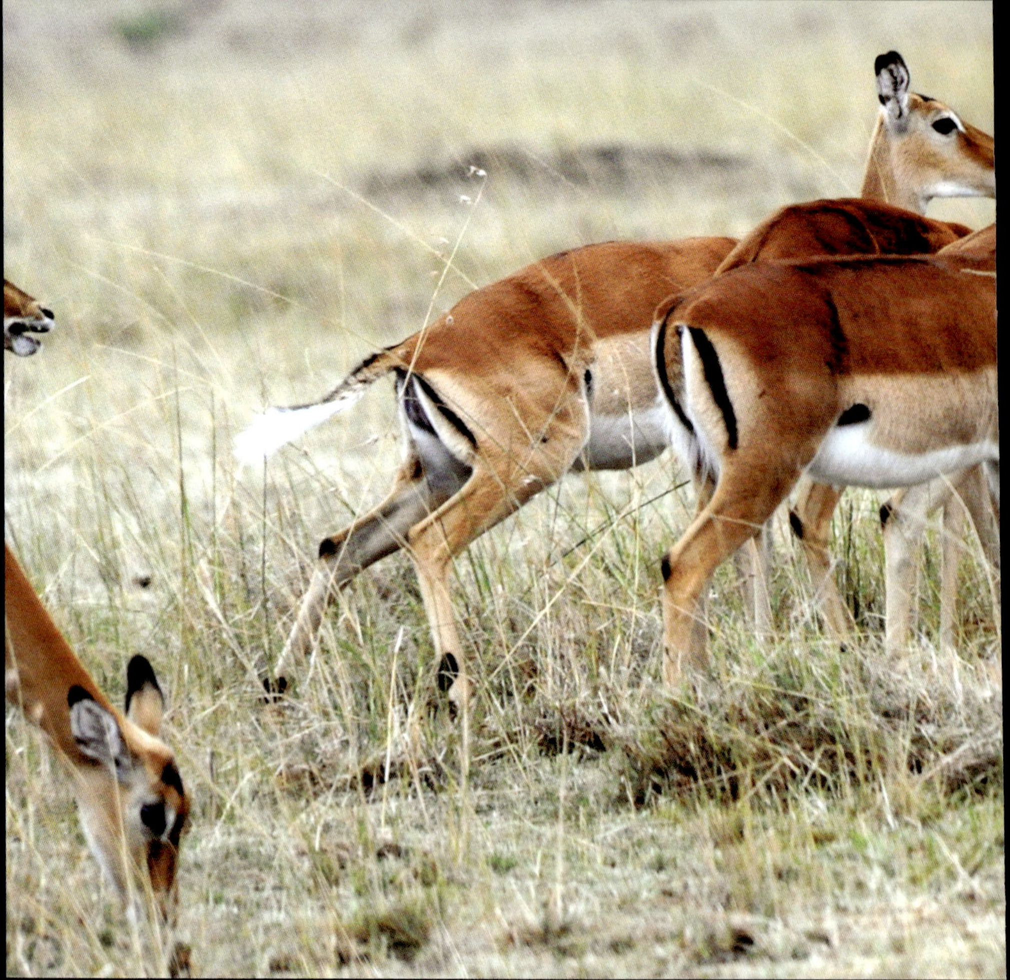
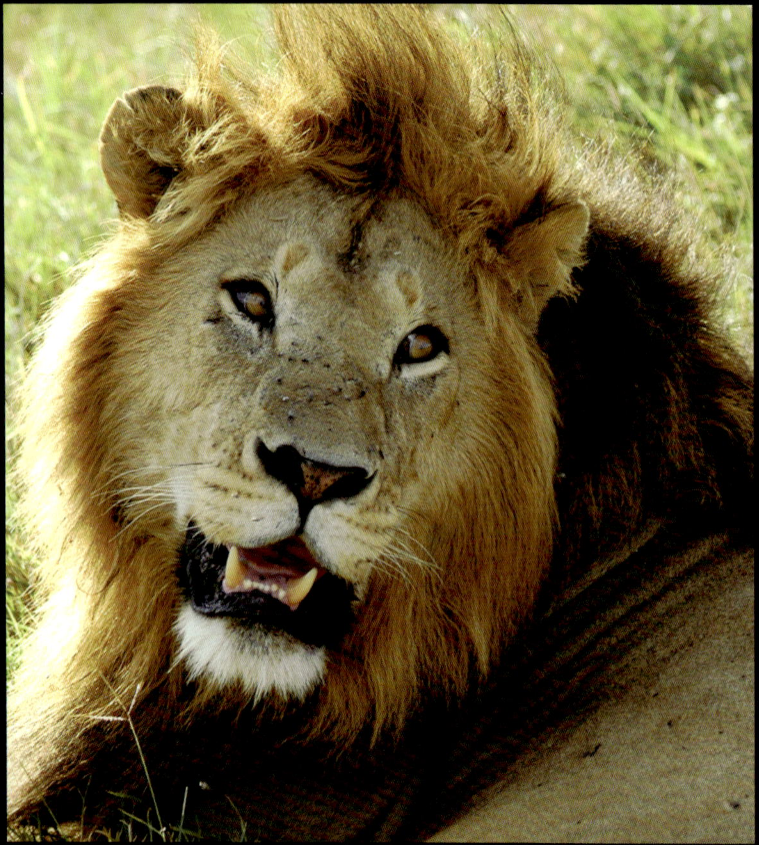
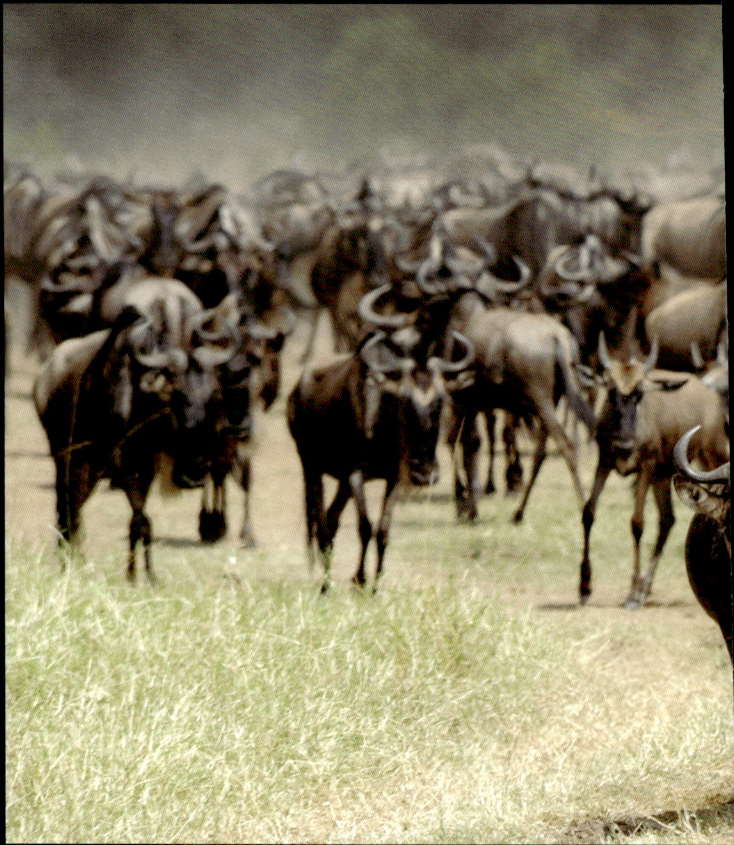

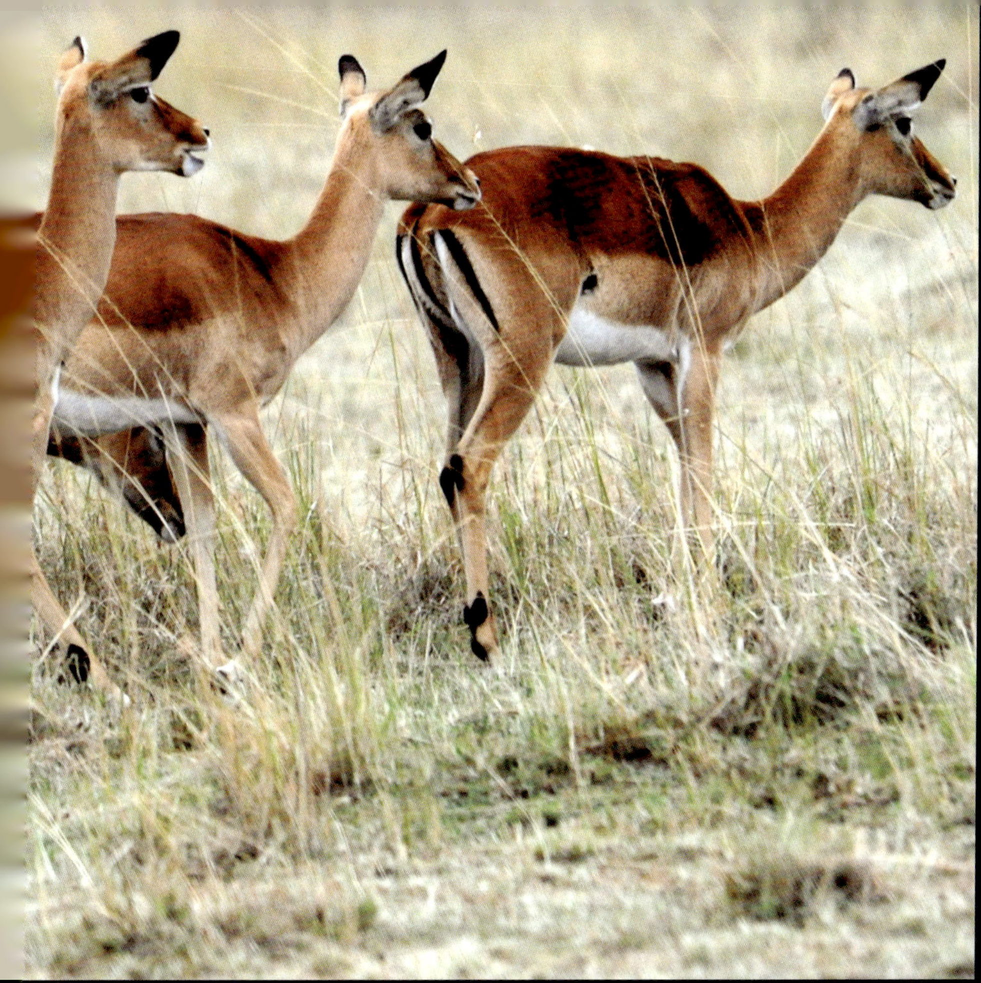
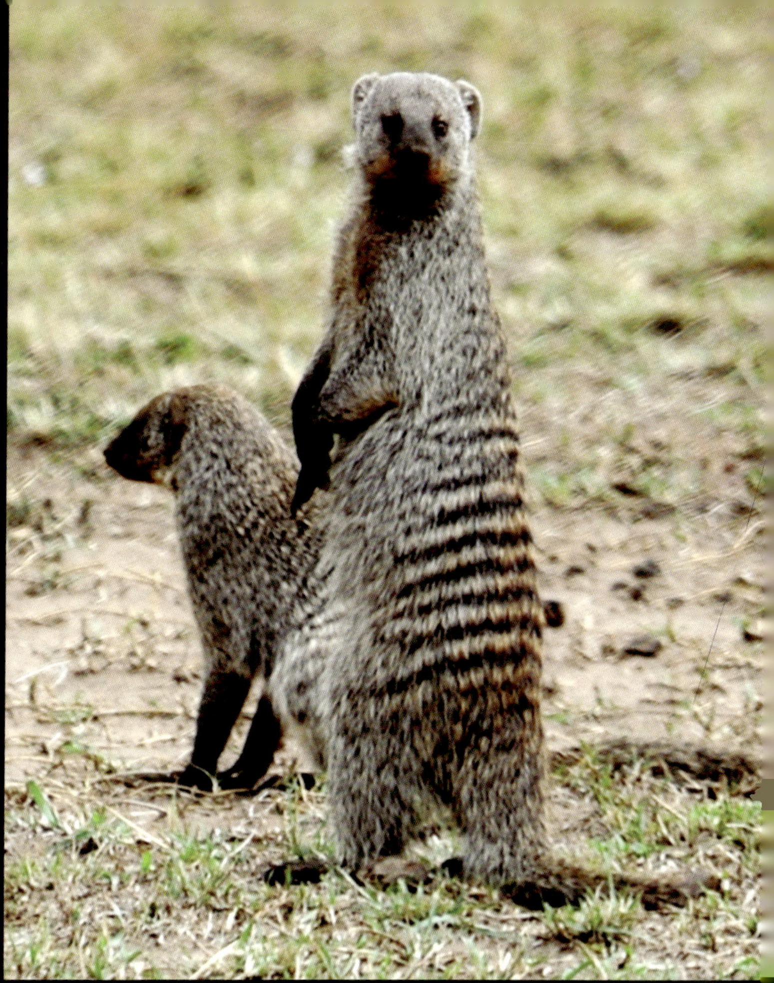
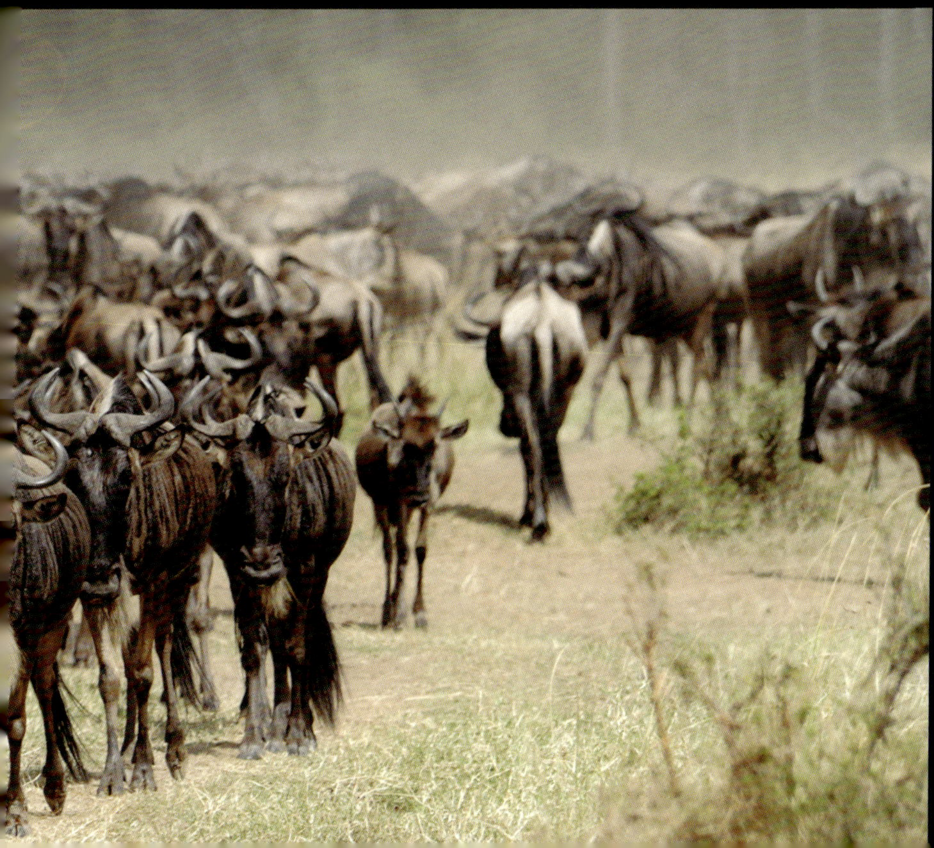
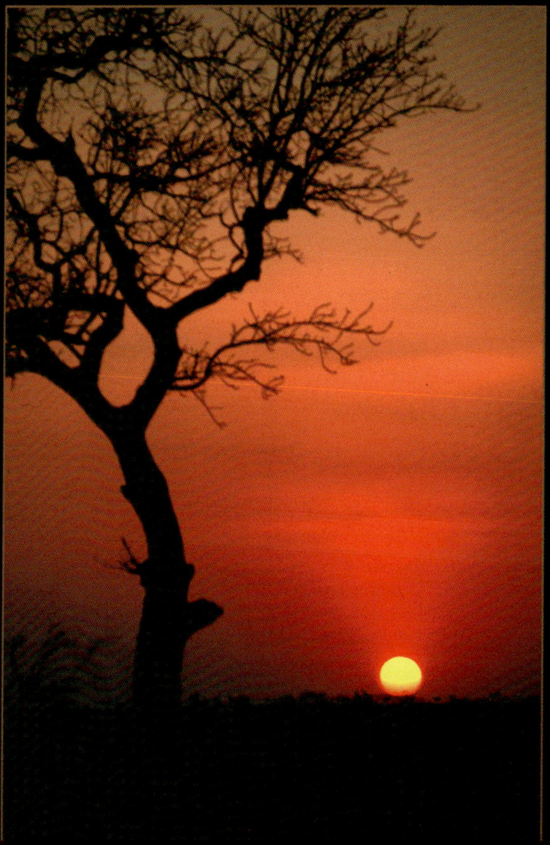

MARA

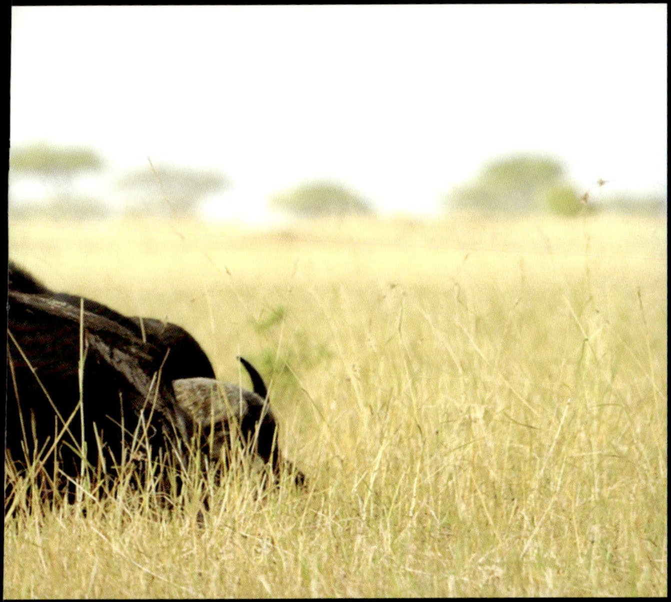
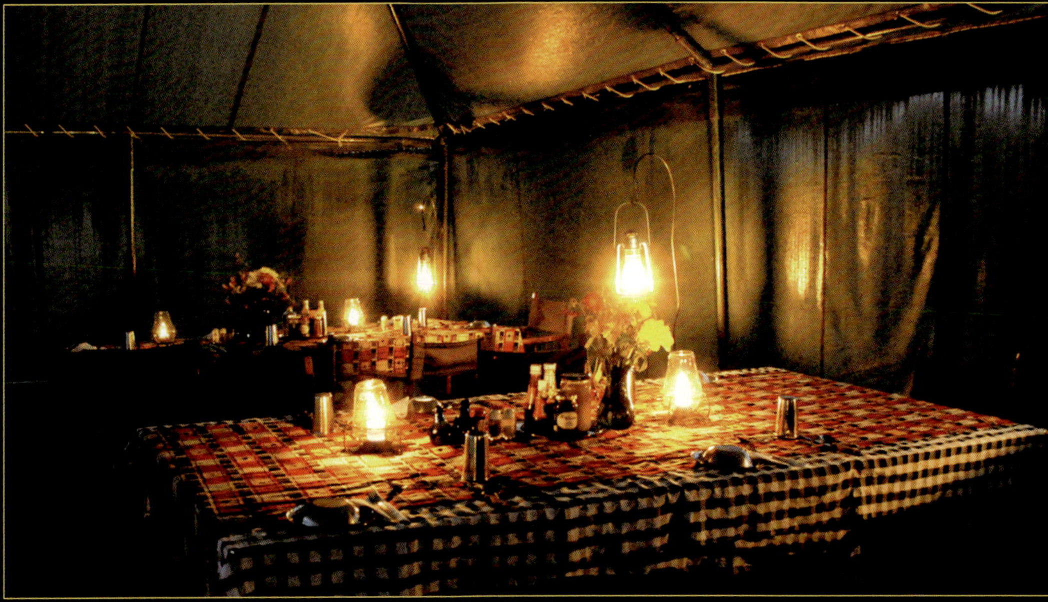
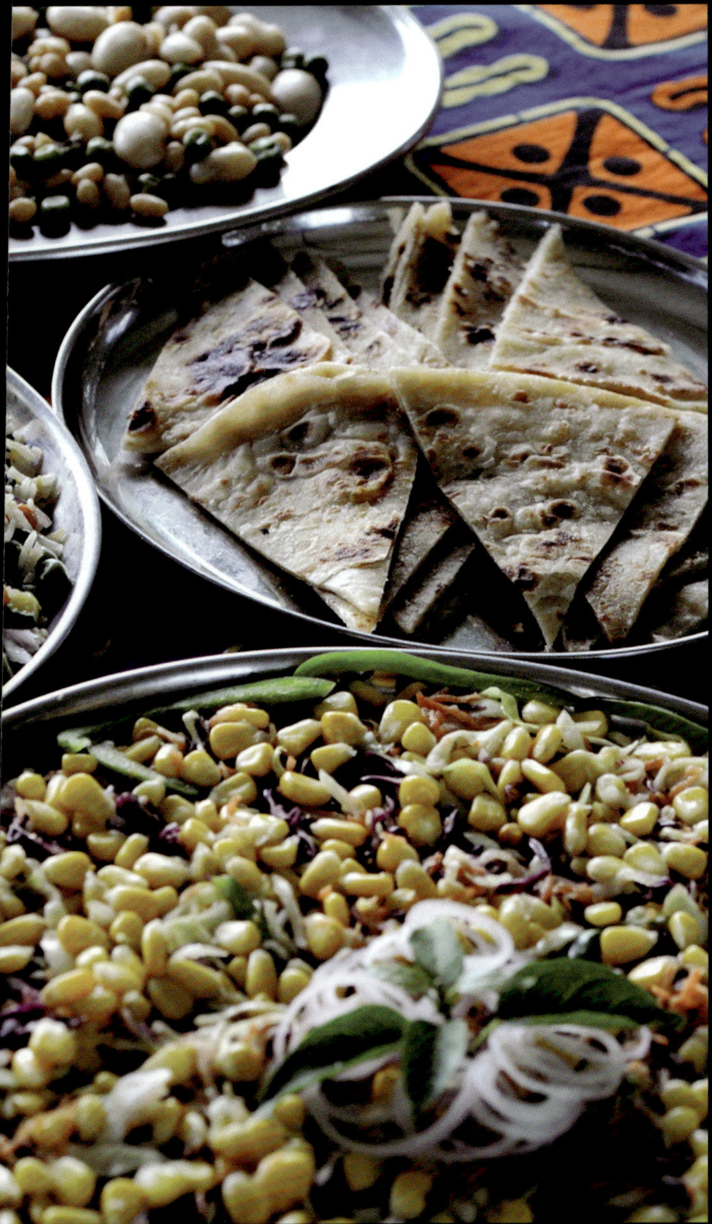
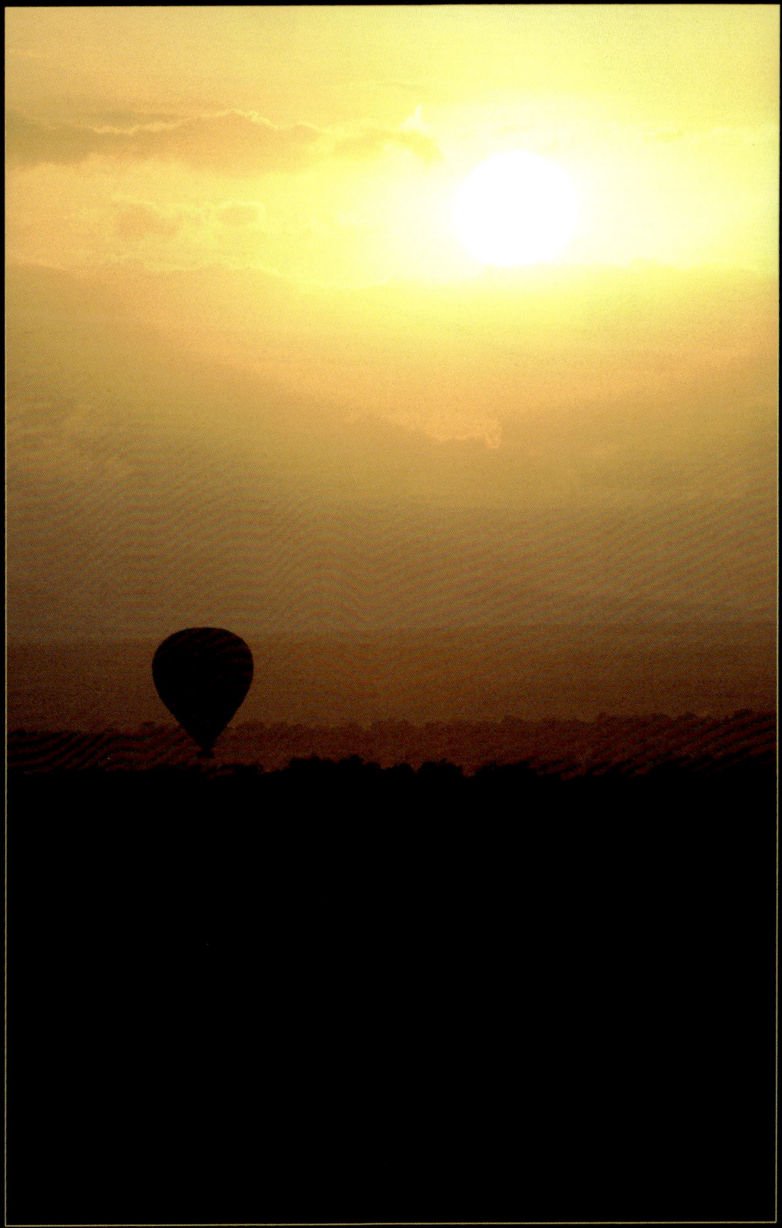

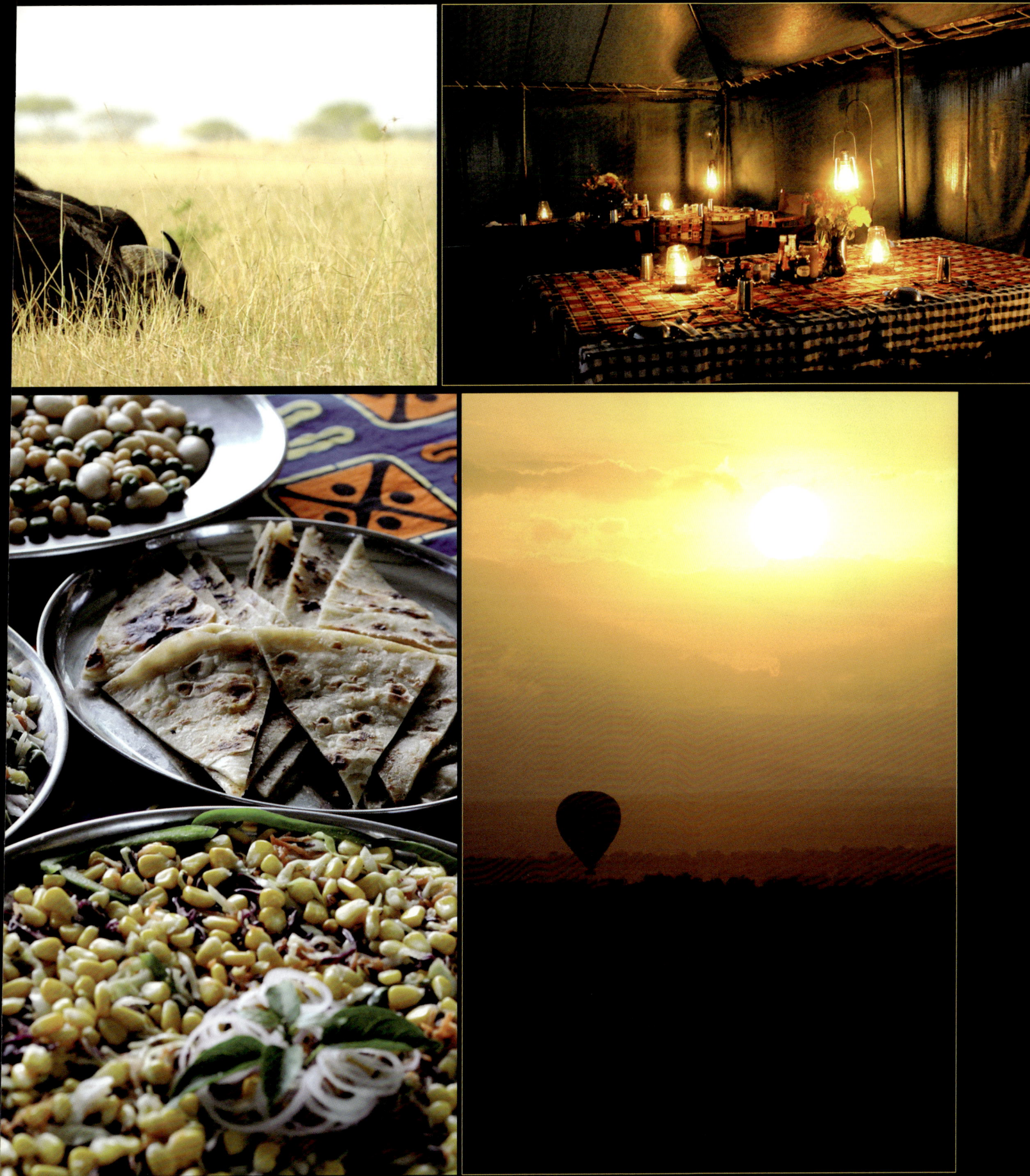

Fillet of beef with bubble and squeak, fine beans and gorgonzola cream jus

RECIPE

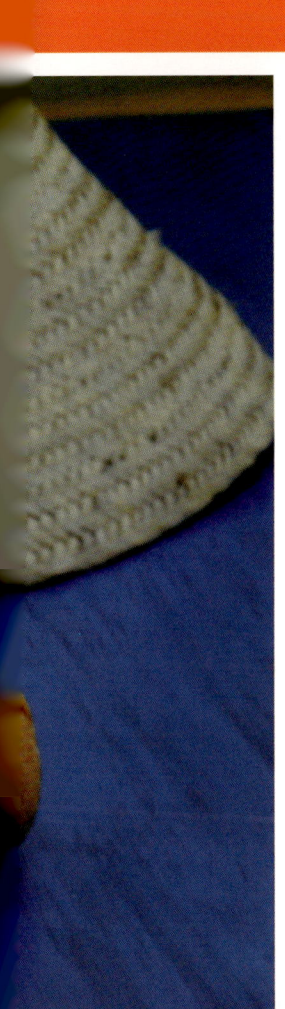

Serves 4 people

Ingredients

- 1 kg beef fillet, in 4 equal portions
- 1 tbsp gorgonzola cheese
- 1 cup cream
- 2 cups gravy *(see recipe)*
- 1 pkt green beans
- ½ shredded cabbage
- 4 potatoes, peeled
- 3 cloves roasted garlic
- 1 tbsp butter
- Sea salt
- Cracked black pepper

Method

1. Boil the potatoes and mash when cooked. While still hot, add the butter, and the crushed roasted garlic, with some cracked black pepper and some sea salt.
2. Blanch the shredded cabbage in water, then stir into the mashed potato and set aside.
3. Meanwhile, season the fillets with black pepper and sea salt and sear in a hot pan on all sides until caramelised. Place in the oven and cook as desired. Keep all the juices for the sauce.
4. Make patties out of the mash and cabbage.
5. Fry these in hot butter until caramelised on both sides and place in oven to heat through.
6. For the sauce: To 2 cups of gravy *(separate recipe)*, add half a cup of cream and the gorgonzola. Do not let all the cheese dissolve, as small chunks of cheese lend character to the sauce.
7. Remove the fillet and the bubble and squeak from the oven. Plate with green beans and with the sauce.

For the Gravy

1. Place all the juices and fat from the fillet on the heat and begin to fry with the chopped garlic. Deglaze with a touch of red wine.
2. Add 2 cups of water in which a stock cube has been dissolved.
3. In a separate cup, dissolve 1 tsp of corn flour in about 100 ml of milk. Whisk into the boiling gravy until the desired thickness is achieved.
4. Stir in 2 tbsp of butter, and test for seasoning.

Tips/Pointers

Bubble and squeak is traditionally made with cabbage and potato. It can just as well be made with other vegetables, however, such as spinach, or small florets of broccoli or cauliflower. Some fried chopped bacon will impart added character.

Masai Mara

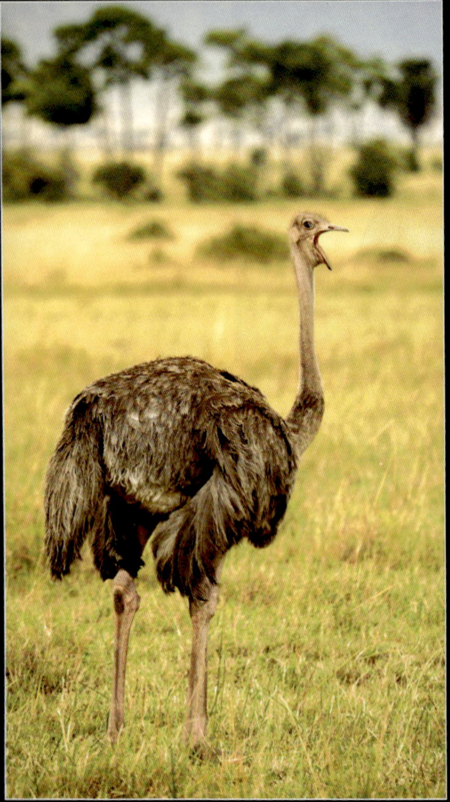
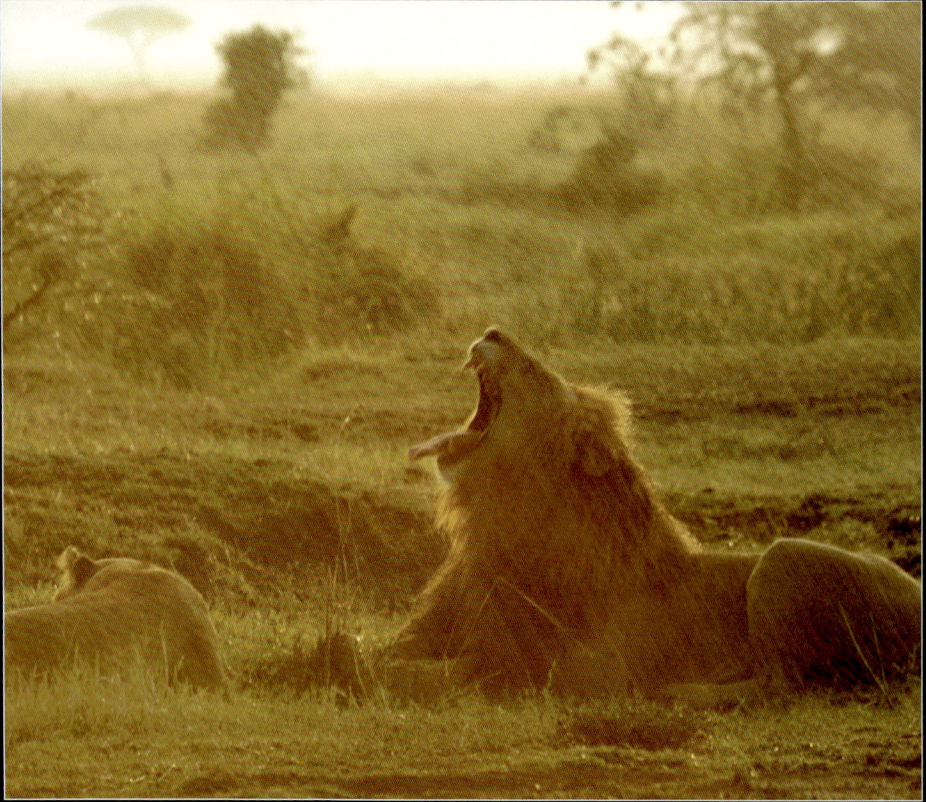
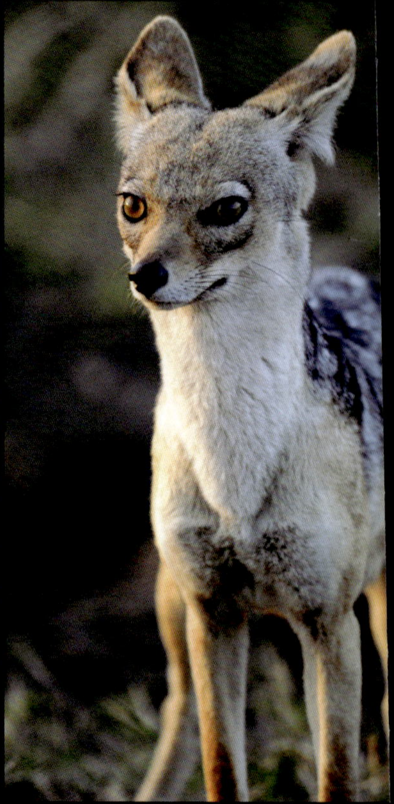
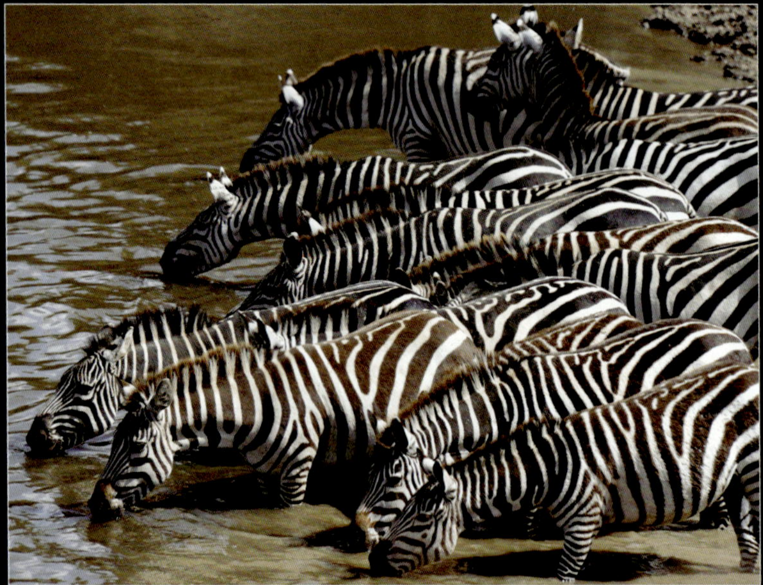
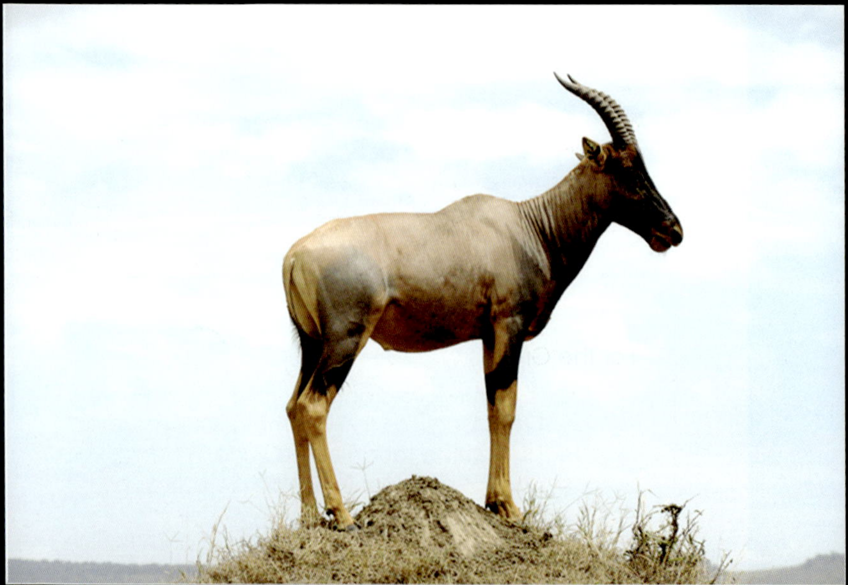

MARA

Gooseberry crumble with oat and cinnamon crust and ginger custard

RECIPE

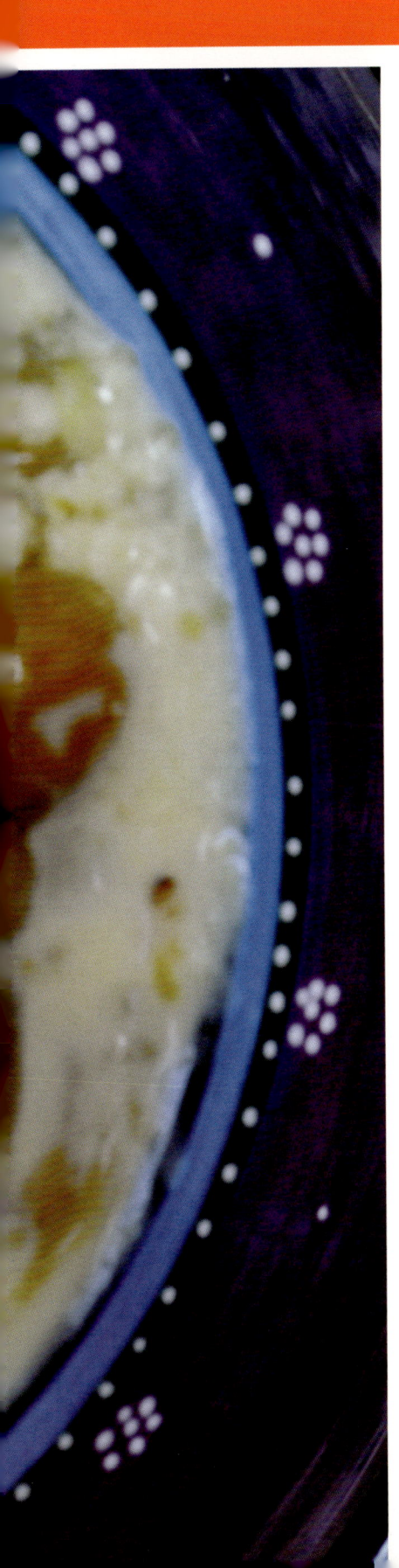

Serves 8 people

Ingredients

For the filling
- 4 cups gooseberries, cleaned
- 1¼ cups white sugar
- 1 tsp vanilla extract
- ¼ tsp ground cardamom

For the crumble topping
- 1 cup all-purpose flour
- ½ cup oats
- ½ tsp salt
- 1 cup light brown sugar
- ½ cup of butter, cut into cubes

For the ginger custard
- 1½ cup whipping cream
- 1 cup milk
- Seeds of 1 vanilla pod
- 4 egg yolks
- ½ cup castor sugar
- 2 tbsp corn flour
- 1 tsp ground ginger

Tips/Pointers

Crumble is as good cold as warm, so it can be made before a safari and taken with you. All you then need do is to make the fresh warm custard. The two complement each other beautifully.

Method

1. Pre-heat oven to 200°C. In a medium-sized bowl, mix the goose berries, the white sugar, the vanilla extract, and the ground cardamom. Spoon into a 9- x 13-inch baking dish.
2. Mix 1 cup of flour with the salt and the brown sugar. Add the butter and rub until the mixture is crumbly. Stir in the oats. Spread topping mixture over the gooseberry mixture.
3. Place in the oven and cook for 35–45 minutes until the filling is bubbly and the topping is lightly browned.
4. Meanwhile, to make the custard, pour the cream and milk into a saucepan and begin to warm. Add the vanilla seeds and bring to the boil. Set aside.
5. Whisk the egg yolks, the sugar and the corn flour together in a large bowl.
6. Re-heat the cream to boiling point, then pour it on to the egg mixture, whisking constantly.
7. Return to the heat and cook gently until the mixture is thick enough to coat the back of a spoon. Stir in the ginger, and allow to cool.
8. Serve the warm crumble with the custard.

Masai Mara

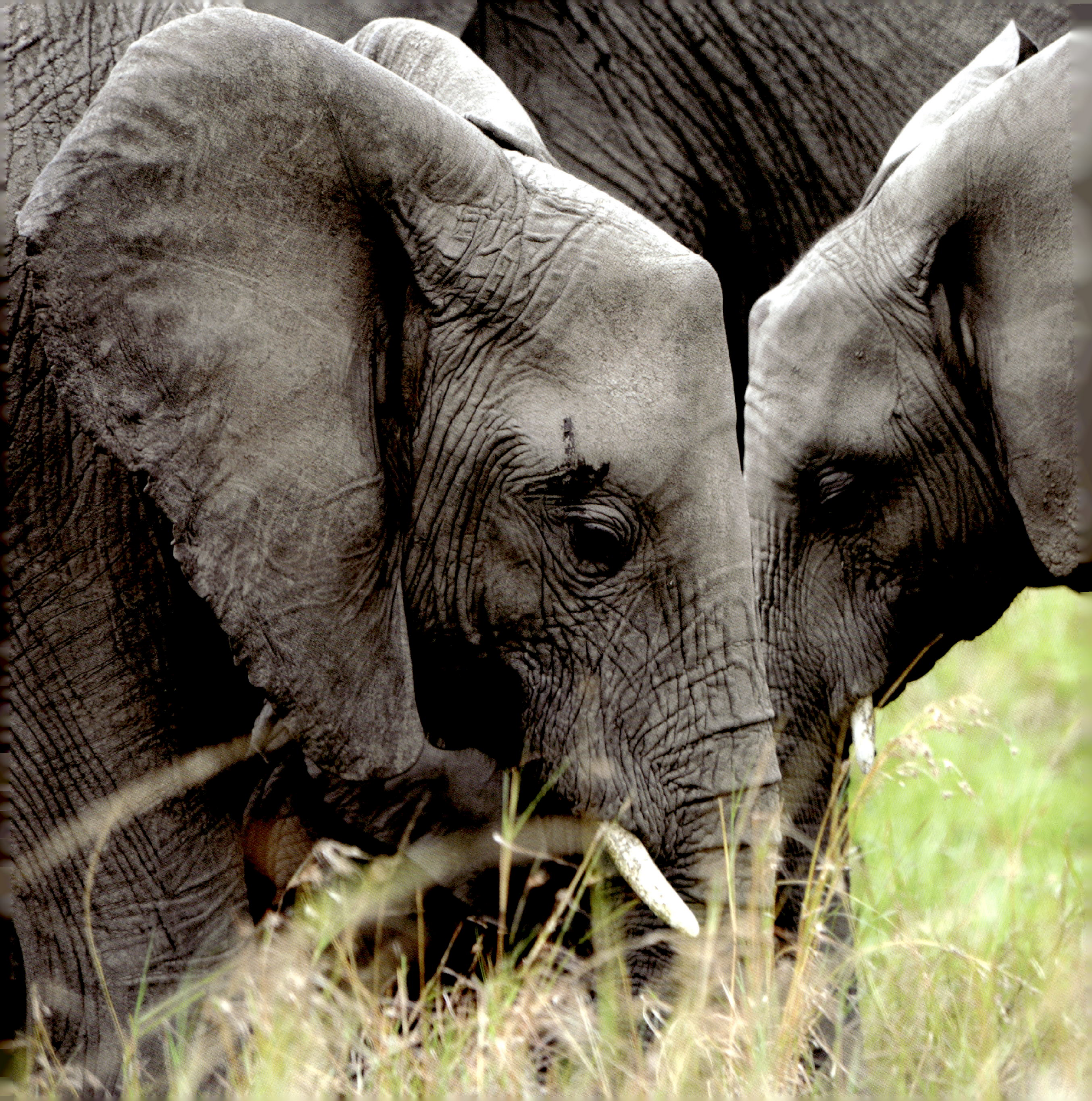

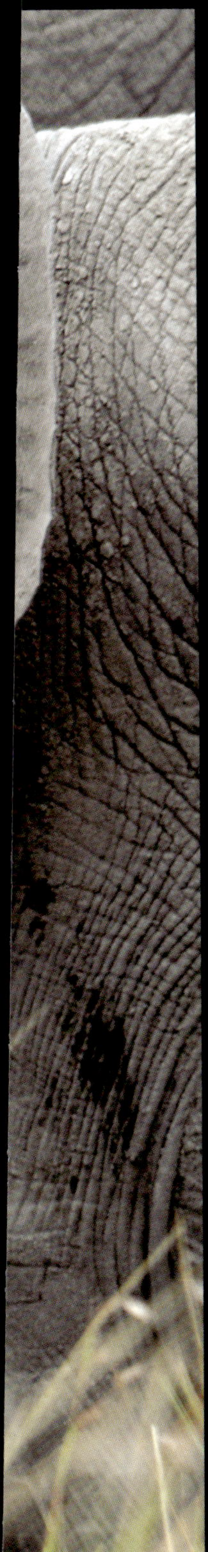
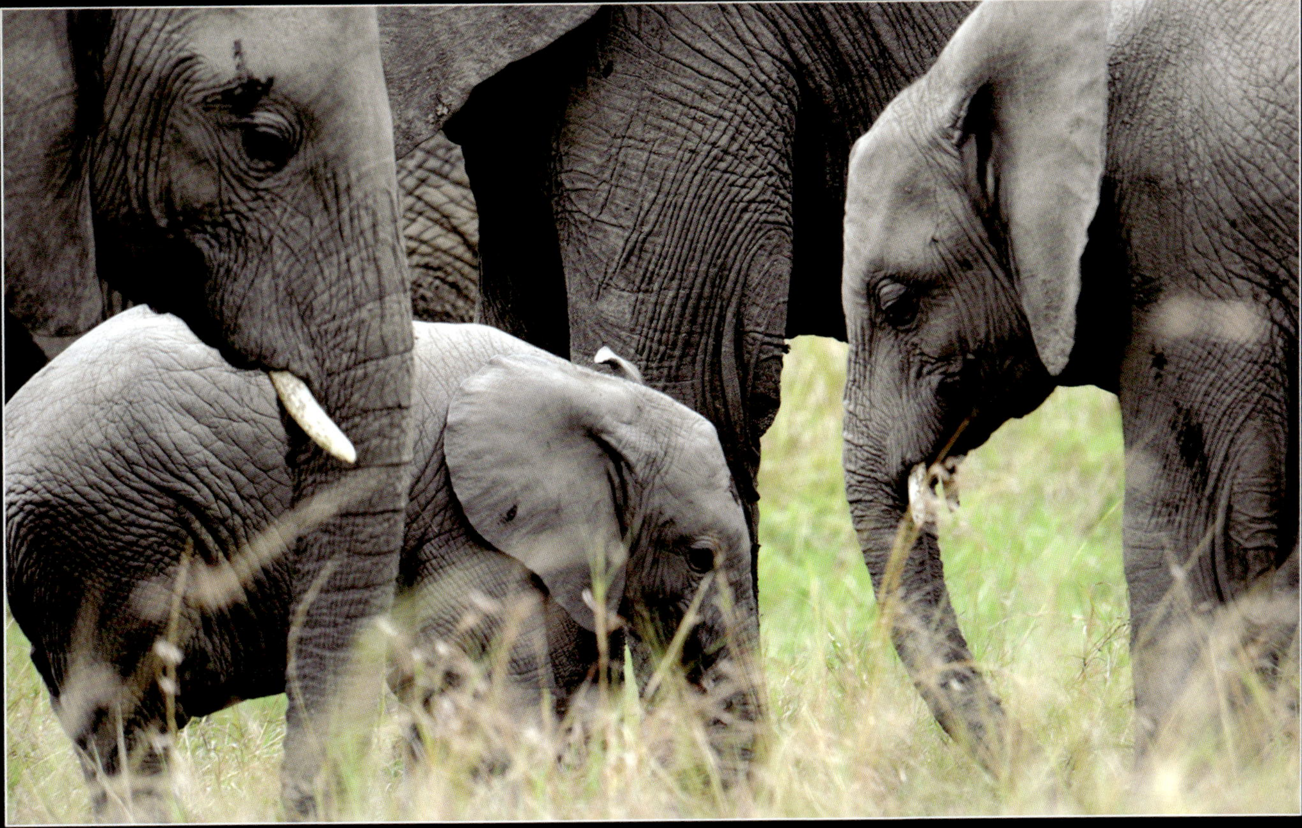
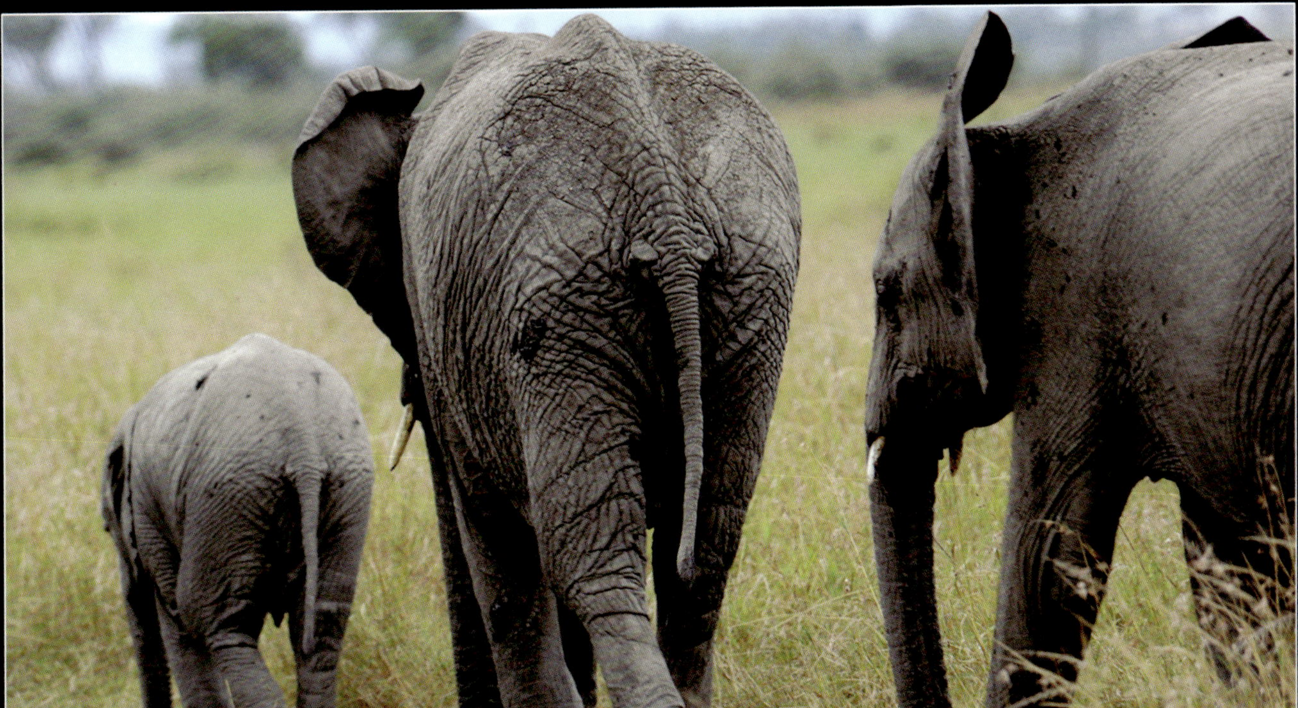

SOUTH

COAST

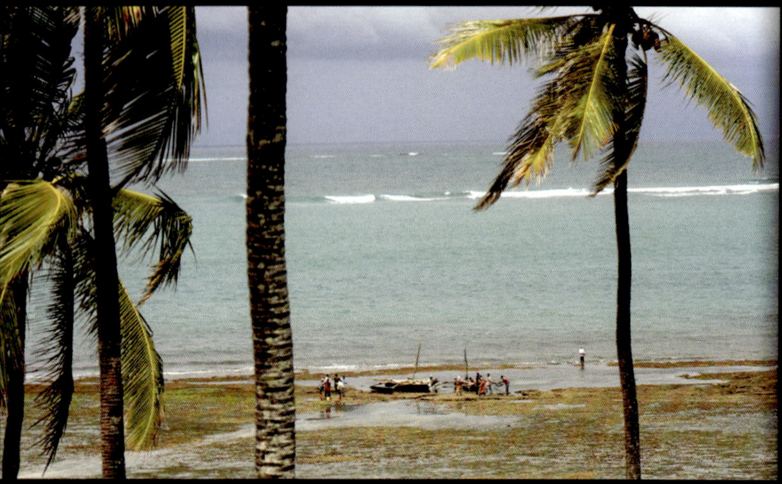
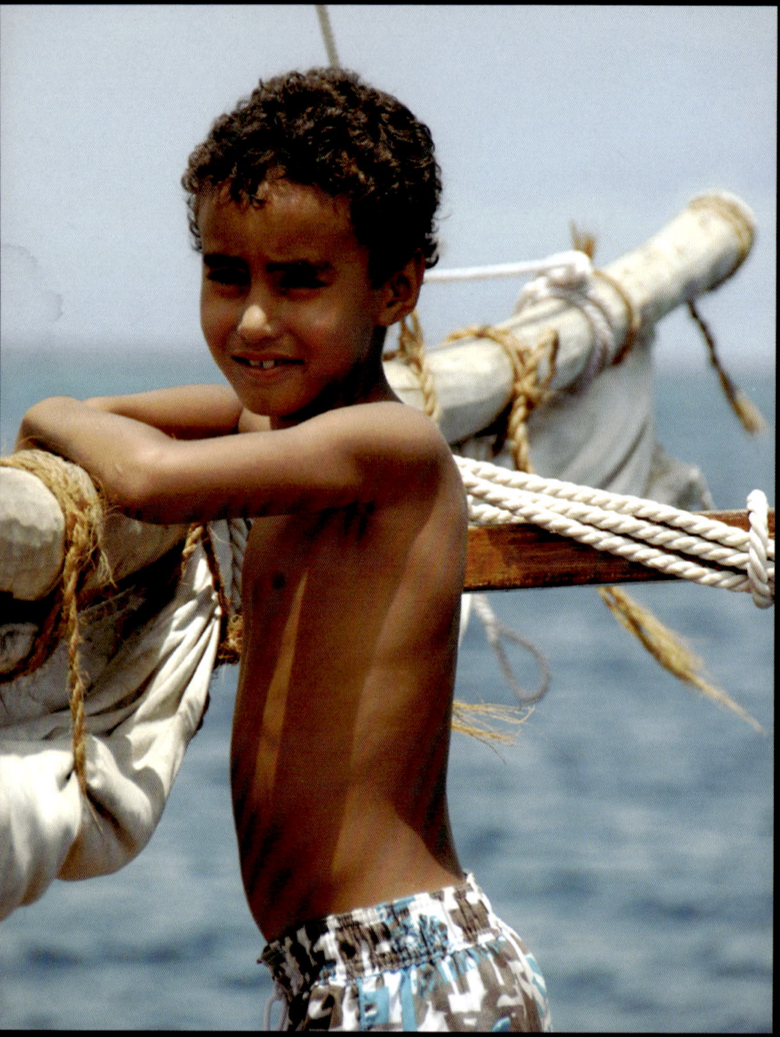
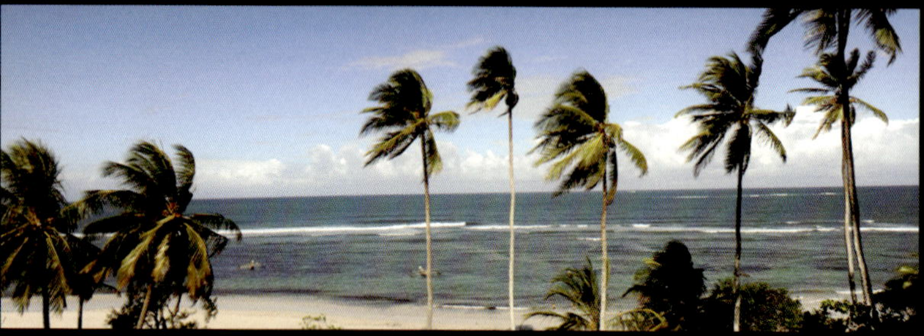
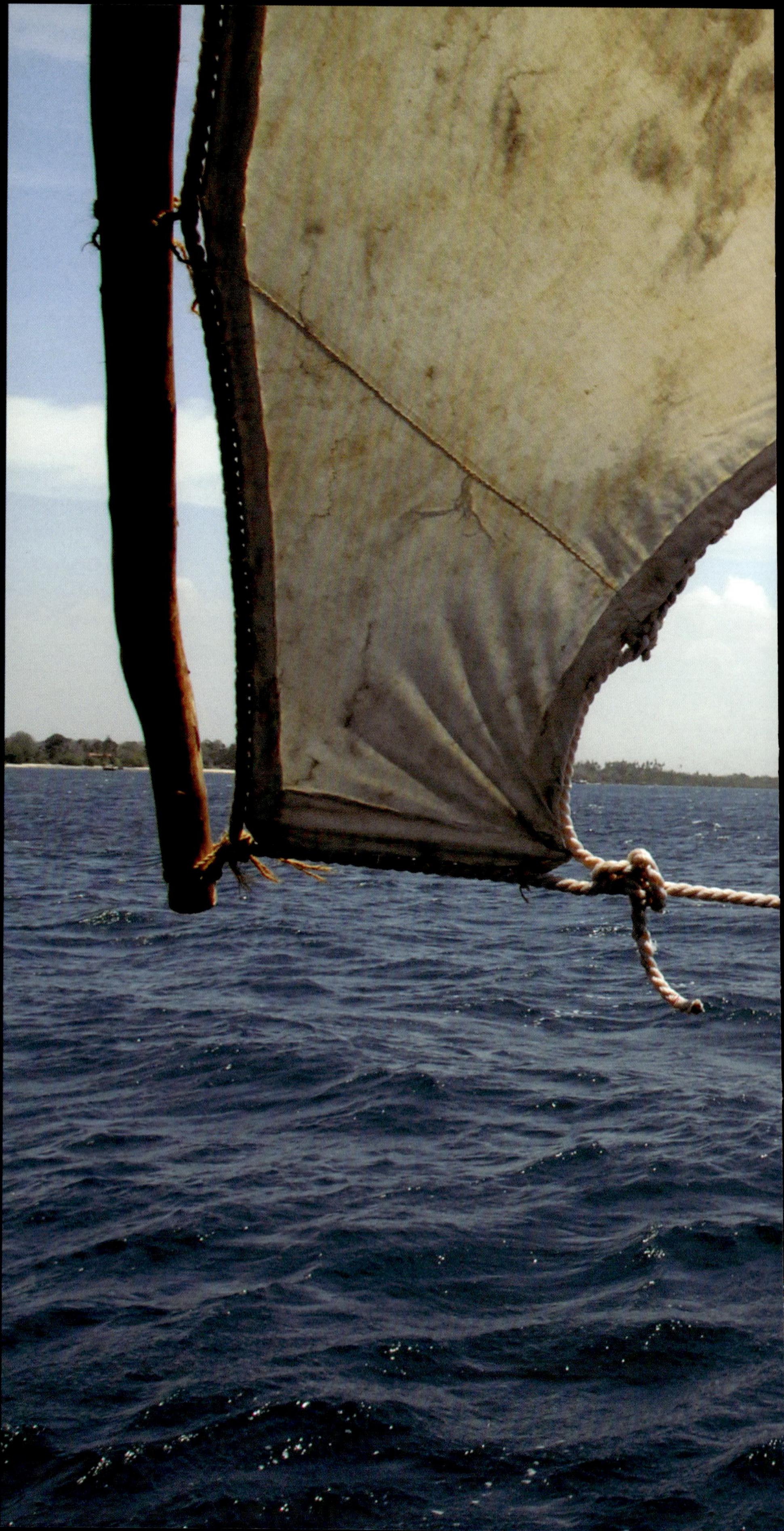

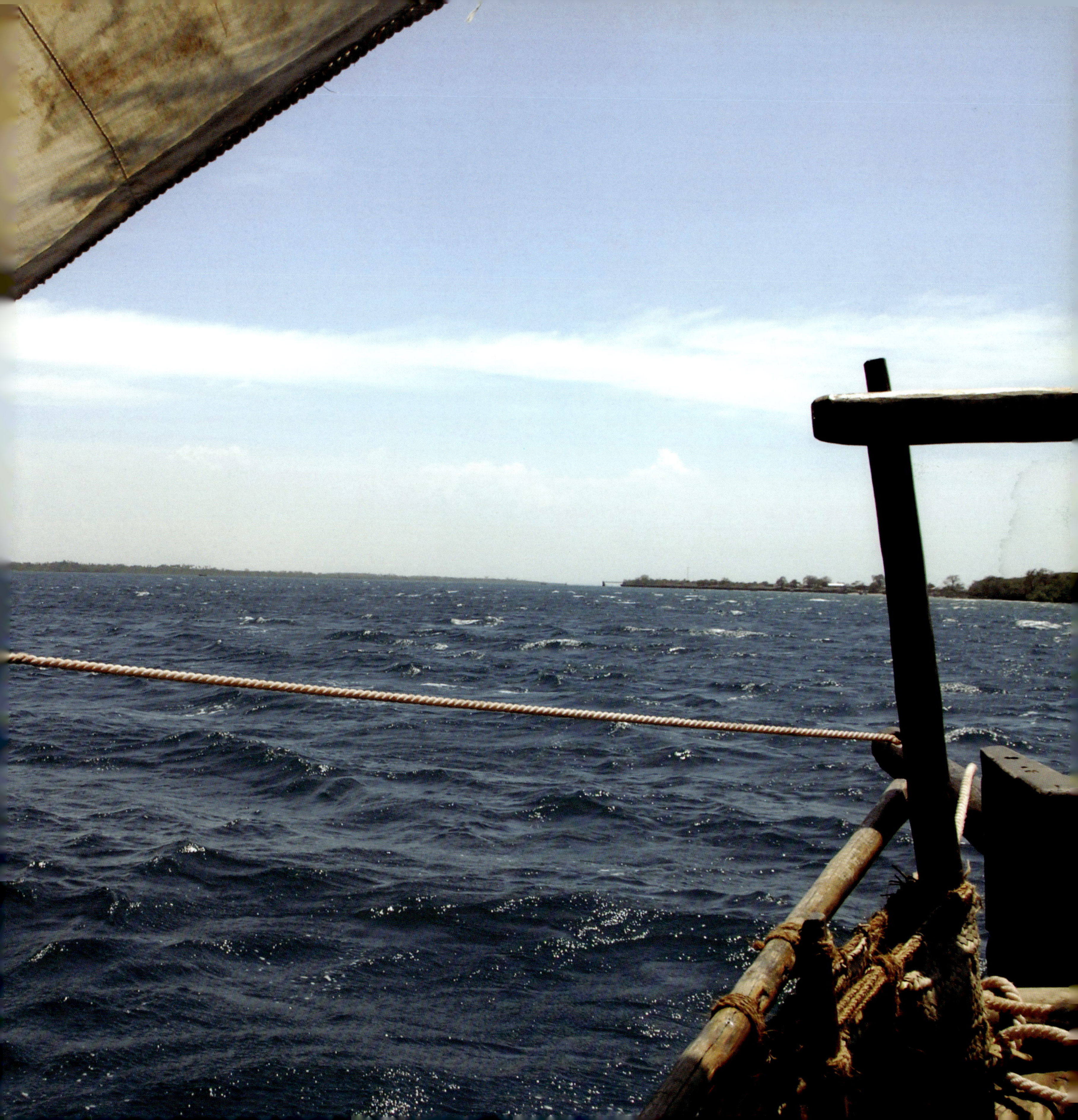

Artichoke vol au vent with smoked aubergine lemon and parsley

RECIPE

Serves 10 people

Ingredients

- 4 large aubergines
- Juice of 3 lemons
- 1 bunch flat-leaf parsley, chopped
- 3 tbsp olive oil
- 2 tsp chopped capers
- 1 tbsp chopped calamata olives
- 2 anchovy fillets
- 4 cloves roasted garlic
- 1 large jar of artichoke hearts
- 1 roll of frozen puff pastry
- 1 egg beaten

Method

1. Place whole aubergines on a grill over a hot, smoky fire. Cook until soft in middle. Do not worry if the skin becomes charred. This adds to the flavour.
2. Remove charred skin and chop the aubergines into a pulp.
3. Add the olive oil, the lemon juice and the parsley.
4. Then add the olives, the capers, the anchovy fillets and the roasted garlic. Stir in thoroughly and set aside.
5. For the vol au vent, unroll the frozen puff pastry and cut out 10 four-inch squares.
6. Press a round object (the rim of an inverted wine glass is perfect) into the middle of each pastry square.
7. Brush with egg and place in a hot oven.
8. Bake for about 15 minutes until the pastry squares have risen and are golden brown.
9. Pressing with the glass will have left circular indents. Scoop these out to create wells in the pastry. Keep the excised circular pastry discs for garnishing.
10. Place a good scoop of the aubergine into each of the pastry wells.
11. Over this, place a couple of artichoke hearts and serve

Tips/Pointers

The smoky flavour of the aubergines is what makes this dish special. Do not be afraid of charring them lightly on an open fire. An open fire will lend a much more interesting flavour to the dish as a whole.

South Coast

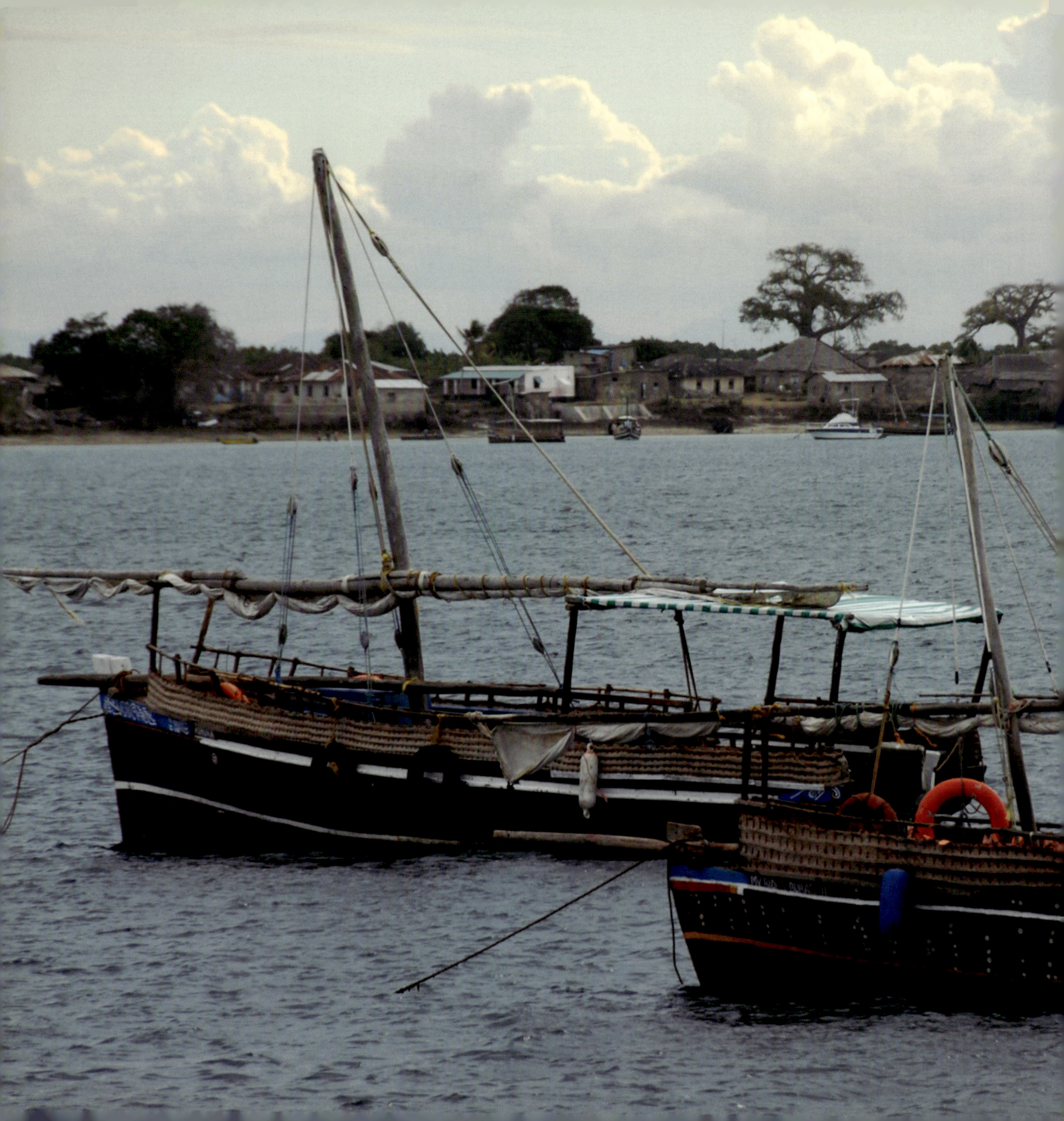

WASINI ISLAND
SOUTH COAST
MENU

Artichoke volauvons with smoked
aubergine lemon and parsley

Swahili seafood curry with roasted coconut
and cumin-steamed jasmine rice

English trifle with amarula cream
and raspberry cointreau jelly
and candied cashew nuts

Swahili seafood curry with roasted coconut and cumin-steamed jasmine rice

RECIPE

Serves 12 people

Ingredients

- 1 kg large tiger prawns, shelled but with heads
- ½ kg calamari, cleaned and chopped into cubes (keep tentacles)
- 2 kg clams
- 3 fillets red snapper
- 1 large mangrove crab, cleaned and portioned
- 4 red onions, chopped
- 4 tsp cumin seeds
- 2 cinnamon sticks
- 1 tsp cardamom seeds
- ½ tsp cloves
- 1 tsp whole black pepper
- 2 large bulbs crushed garlic
- 2 large bulbs crushed ginger
- 2 tbsp crushed green chilies
- 2 tsp turmeric powder
- 2 tsp ground cumin
- 1 tsp ground coriander
- 1 tsp garam masala
- 5 chopped tomatoes
- 2 tins coconut cream
- 1 whole coconut
- 3 bunches chopped coriander
- 2 tsp brown sugar
- Juice of 2 limes
- 12 handfuls of basmati rice

Method

1. In a large saucepan, add enough oil to cover the bottom. Heat, then add the cinnamon, cloves, cardamoms, black pepper and half of the cumin seeds. Fry this until the spices start emitting a rich aroma.
2. Add the chopped onions. Cover and reduce the heat. Cook for about 5 minutes until the onions are soft and translucent.
3. Add the ginger, the garlic and the chilies and fry for a further 5 minutes.
4. Add the tomatoes and the remaining spices. Cook until the tomatoes have broken down to form a thick sauce.
5. Now add the coconut cream, the clams and the crab, and boil again intil you have a thick consistency.
6. In the pan, arrange all the remaining seafood, so it is covered by the sauce. Bring back to the boil for 2 minutes. Remove from the heat and allow to stand for 2–4 minutes. It is important not to stir the dish too much, as this might break up the seafood.
7. Crack open the whole coconut and scoop out the flesh. Slice thinly and fry until golden brown and fragrant.
8. In a separate pan, heat some more oil and fry the remaining cumin seeds.
9. To this, add the rice and fry for a couple of minutes. Then add 1.5 times the amount of water in volume as you have rice.
10. Boil until the water level has been reduced to that of the rice. Cover with a tight-fitting lid. Turn the heat to low, and steam for 15 minutes. Watch closely, to make sure no sticking occurs.
11. Just before serving, heat the seafood curry and add all the chopped fresh coriander, the deep fried coconut and the lime juice.

Tips/Pointers

It is important to keep the heads on the prawns when making this dish. While the thought of eating prawn heads may not appeal to some, the flavour they impart is significant. If you feel the heads may be offensive, discard them before serving.

South Coast

Vela-Rossa

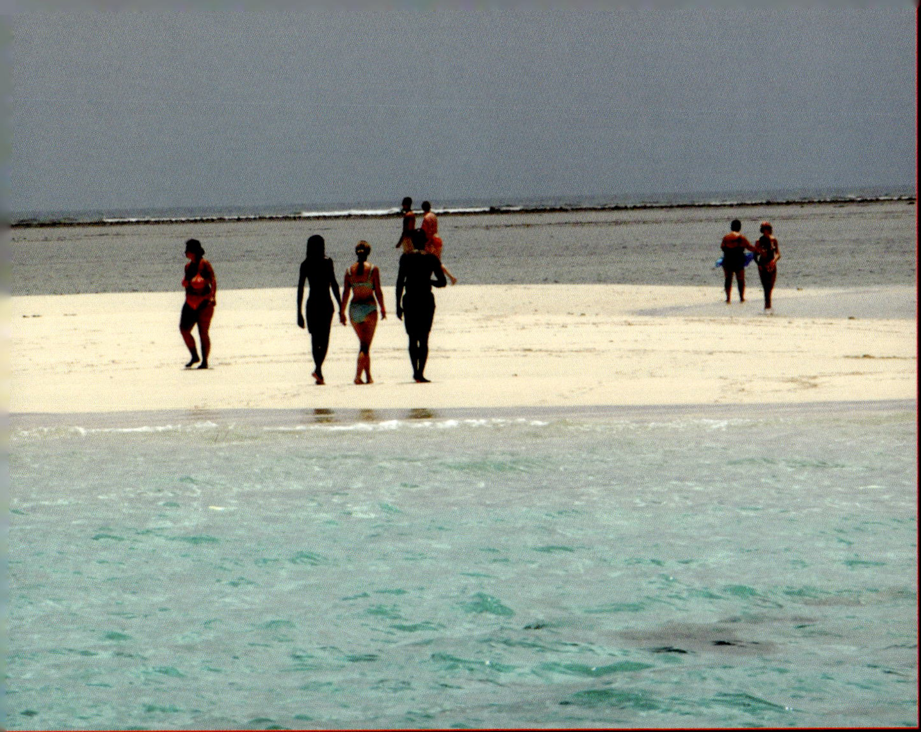

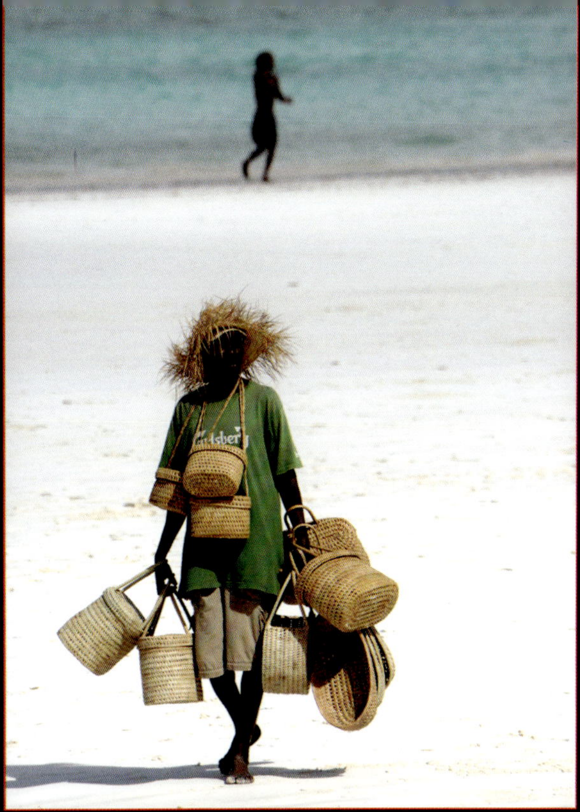

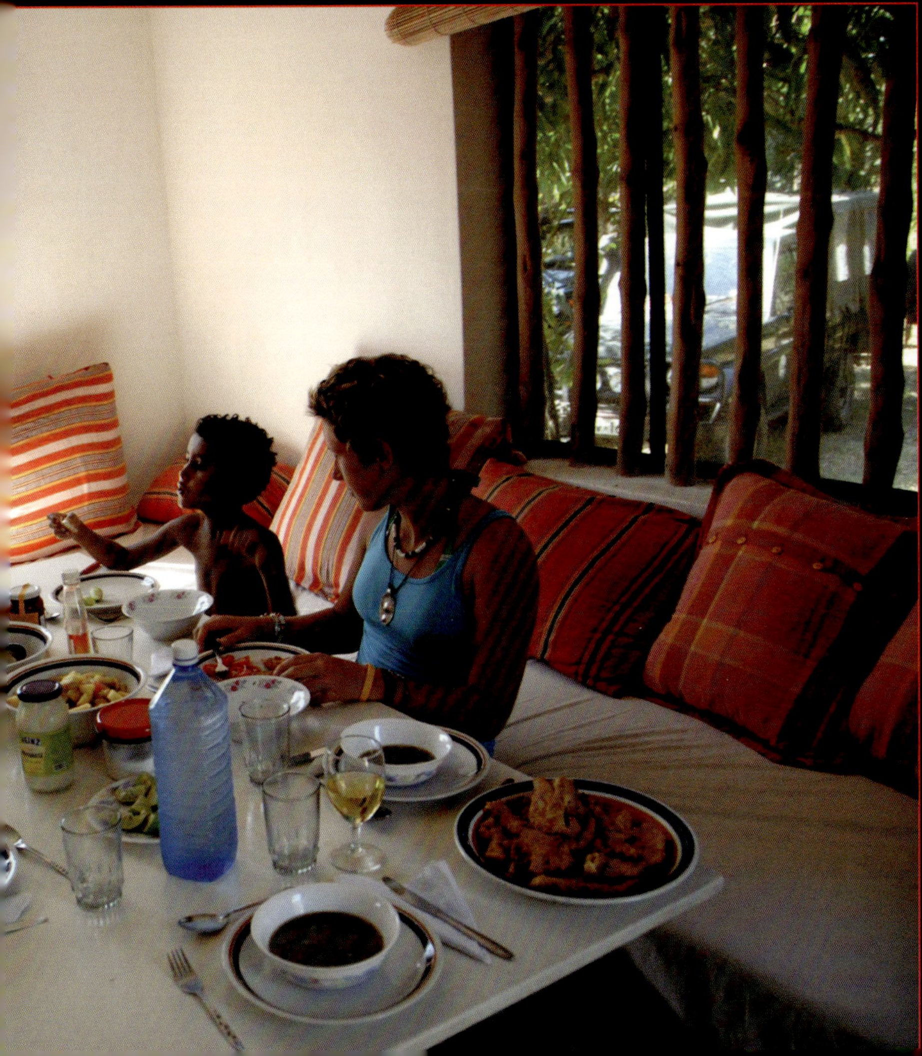

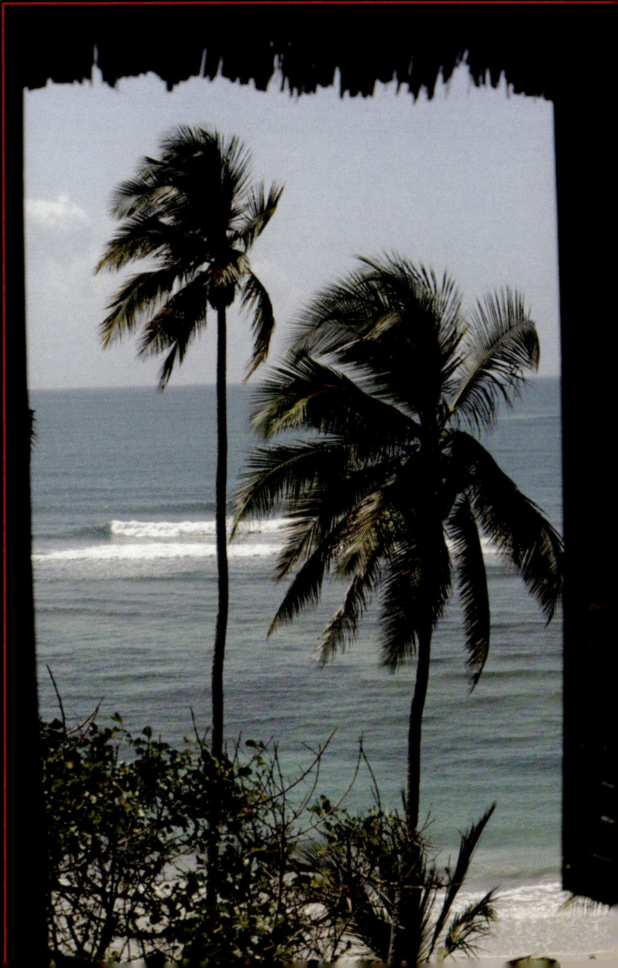

186 Safari Cuisine

English trifle with amarula cream and raspberry cointreau jelly and candied cashew nuts

RECIPE

Serves 6 people

Ingredients

For the candied cashew nuts
- 1 cup cashew nuts
- 3 tbsp castor sugar
- 4 tbsp gran marnier

For the sponge
- 3 eggs
- 4 tbsp castor sugar
- ½ cup flour
- 1 tbsp corn flour
- 2 tbsp melted butter

For the raspberry cointreau jelly
- 2 punnet raspberries
- 100ml water
- 2 tbsp sugar
- 4 gelatin leaves
- 150ml sparkling water
- 2 tbsp cointreau

For the amarula custard
- 1½ cups whipping cream
- 1 cup milk
- Seeds of 1 vanilla pod
- 4 egg yolks
- ½ cup castor sugar
- 2 tbsp corn flour

Other ingredients
- 6 tbsp medium sherry
- 1 cup whipping cream

Method

1. For the candied nuts, place the ingredients in a heavy-based saucepan over a medium heat. Heat until the sugar begins to caramelise. Turn the nuts out on to a tray and allow to cool.
2. To make the sponge, whisk the eggs and the sugar until they become light and fluffy, and almost double in volume.
3. Fold in half the flour, then add the butter and fold in the rest of the flour.
4. Grease a cake tin. Pour in the mixture, and bake at 180°C for 20–30 minutes.
5. For the jelly, gently heat the raspberries in 100 ml of sugar syrup. Poach until soft. Pass through a fine sieve to remove the seeds.
6. Place the gelatin leaves in warm water until soft. Remove and squeeze off excess liquid, then stir into the warm raspberry mixture until dissolved.
7. Add the cointreau when the mixture has cooled slightly. Then slowly add the sparkling water, being careful retain as many bubbles as possible.
8. Place in the fridge and allow to cool for 3–4 hours, or until set.
9. To make the custard, pour the cream and milk into a saucepan and begin to warm. Add the vanilla seeds and bring to the boil. Set aside.
10. Whisk the egg yolks, the sugar and the corn flour in a large bowl.
11. Reheat the cream to boiling point, then pour on to the egg mixture, whisking constantly.
12. Return to the heat and cook gently until the mixture is thick enough to coat the back of a spoon. Stir in the amarula and allow to cool and thicken further.
13. To assemble the trifle, divide the sponge into six equal portions, and press each portion into the bottom of a tall glass each one. Sprinkle 1 tbsp of sherry over each of the sponges.
14. Break up the jelly and spoon this over the soaked sponge. Sprinkle some of the candied nuts over the jelly
15. Spoon some custard over the jelly, and smooth the remaining whipped cream over this. Garnish with the remaining candied cashew nuts and serve.

Tips/Pointers

The jelly, the custard and the sponge can all be made beforehand, and the trifle assembled when needed. Given the time it takes for the custard and the jelly to set, this is probably advisable.

South Coast 187

KISITE

MPUNGUTI

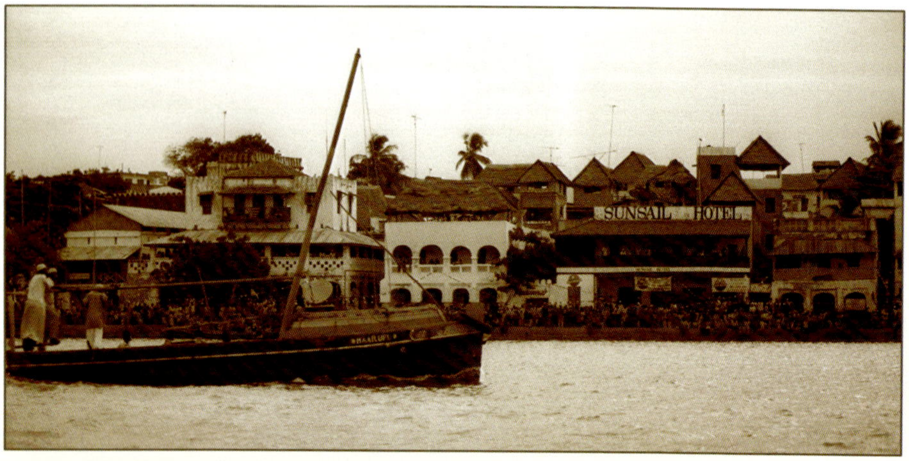
SUNSAIL HOTEL

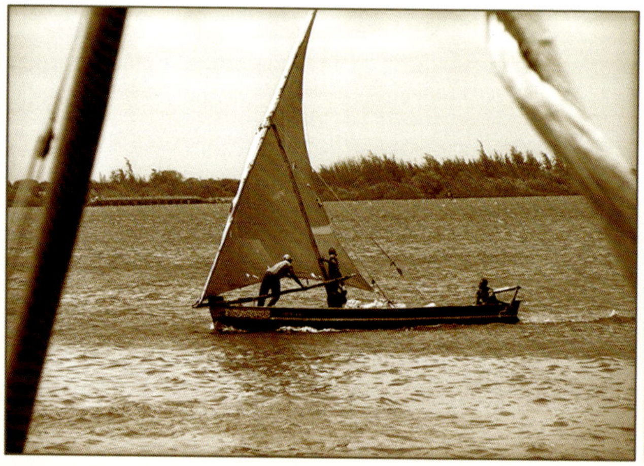

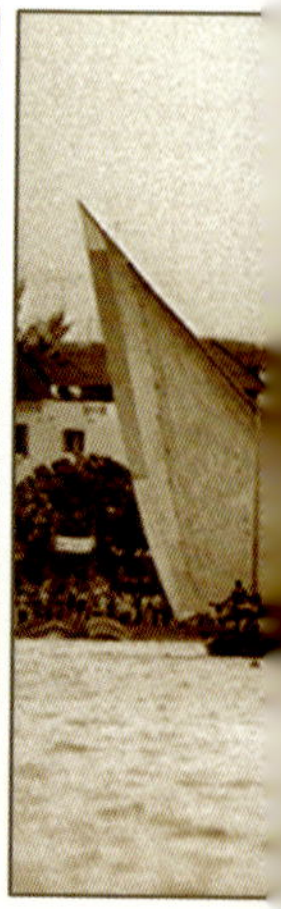

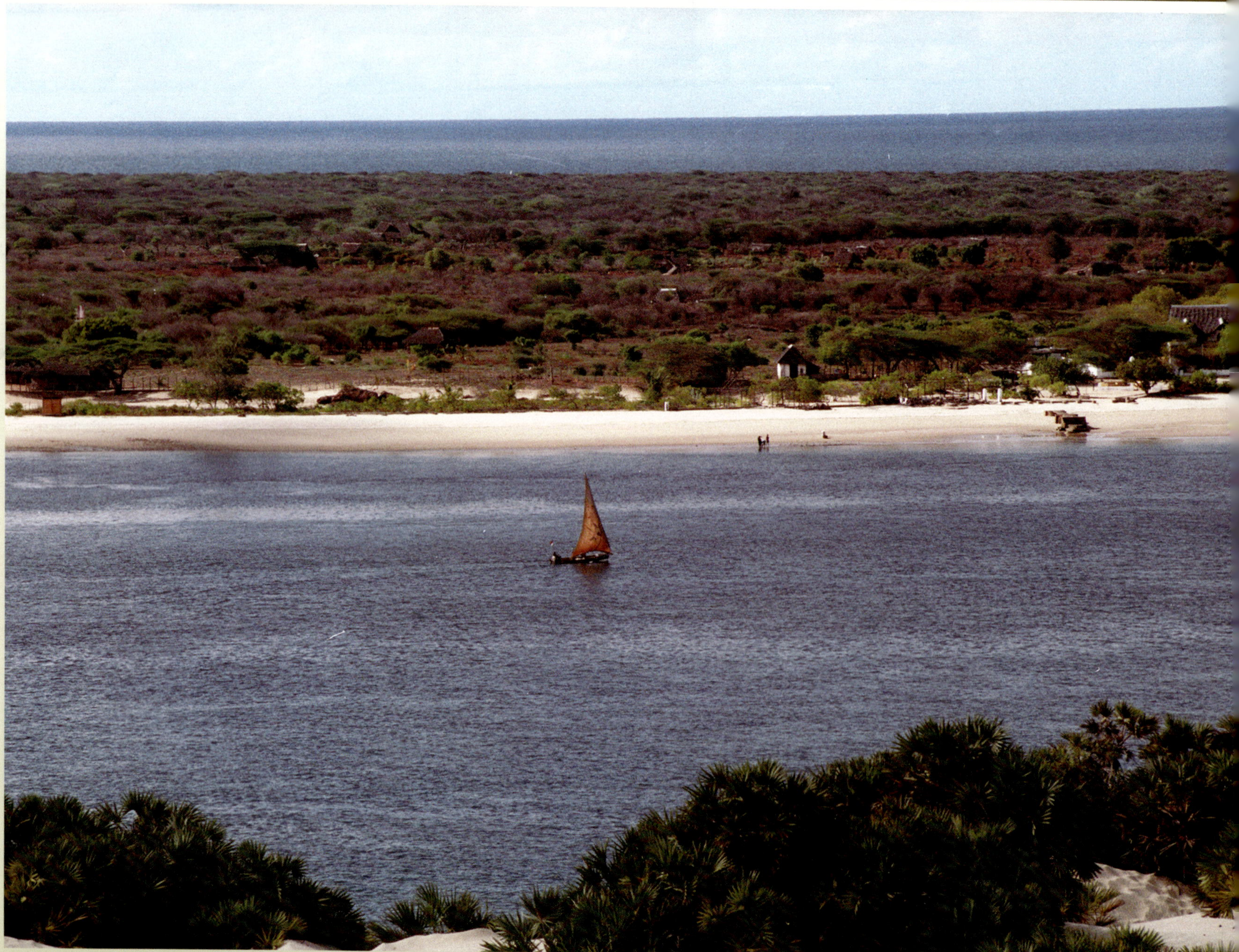

LAMU

LAMU

Chana-stuffed sweet peppers with a fresh tomato and coriander chutney

BBQ'd lobster with a smoked sweet pepper and chili marinade, a lemon and basil beurre blanc and polenta chips

Pear and frangipane tart with clotted cream

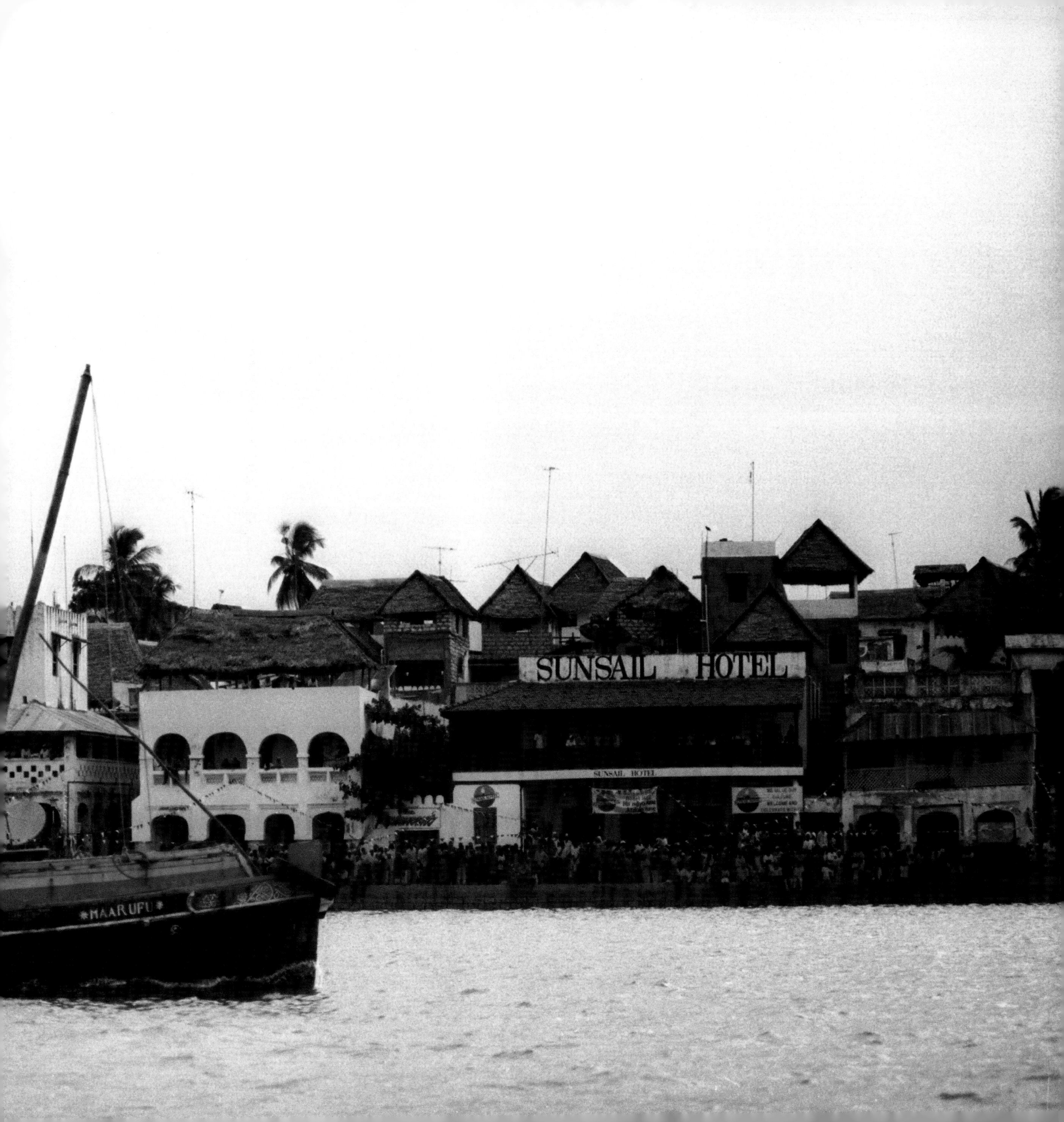
SUNSAIL HOTEL
SUNSAIL HOTEL
MAARUFU

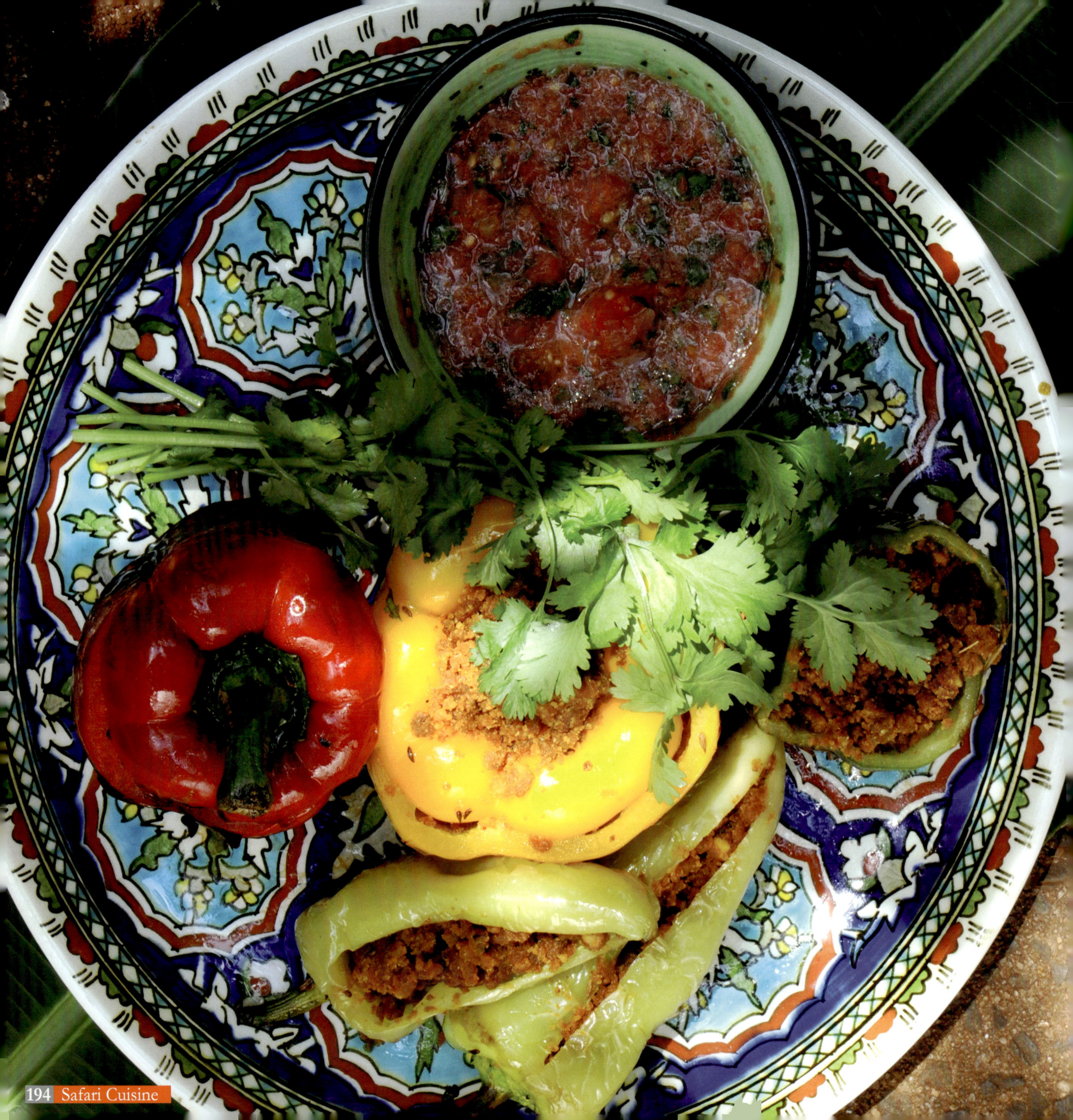

Chana-stuffed sweet peppers with a fresh tomato and coriander chutney

RECIPE

Serves 5 people

Ingredients

- 200 g chickpea flour (chana atta)
- 3 tbsp vegetable oil
- 1 kg mixed peppers (yellow, red and green)
- 2 tsp ground cumin
- 2 tsp ground coriander
- 1 tsp ground turmeric
- 2 tsp sugar
- 2 tsp whole cumin
- Juice of 2 lemons
- 1 bunch fresh coriander chopped
- Tomato salsa *(see recipe)*

Method

1. Roast the chickpea flour thoroughly in a hot saucepan. The flour should brown slightly, become smoky and give off a strong aroma.
2. Add the vegetable oil to form a paste.
3. Return to a low heat and add the cumin, the turmeric and the coriander powder.
4. Allow to cool slightly, then add the sugar, the chopped fresh coriander and the lemon juice.
5. The lemon juice will react with the paste to form a crumbly stuffing. Taste and adjust seasoning.
6. Heat some more oil in a frying pan. Sprinkle the cumin seeds into the oil. When they start to fry, toss in the whole peppers and fry until their skins take on some colour.
7. Remove and allow to cool.
8. Cut off the stem sides of the peppers to reveal the insides. Scoop out and discard the seeds and the membranes.
9. Fill the peppers with the chickpea stuffing and place in an oven to heat.
10. Serve with tomato salsa *(Separate recipe)*.

The tomato salsa

Ingredients

- 1 kg tomatoes
- 1 bunch coriander
- 1 tsp salt
- Juice of 4 limes
- 1 chopped red onion
- 1 clove crushed garlic

Method

1. Drop the whole tomatoes into boiling water for 1 minute. This will make it easy to remove their skins. Once skinned, place on a board.
2. Roughly chop the tomatoes to the consistency of a chunky salsa.
3. Add the remaining ingredients, then taste for sea soning and serve.

Tips/Pointers

It is important to roast the chickpea flour properly before adding the other ingredients. Failure to do so may result in a bitter, floury texture and flavour. These peppers are delicious when served cold, so they can be made before a trip and eaten with the minimum amount of fuss.

Lamu 195

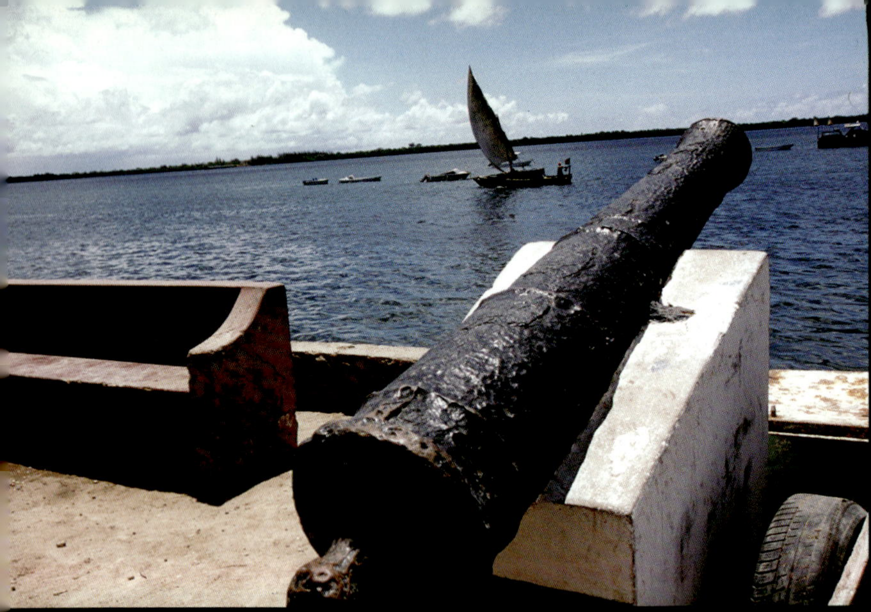

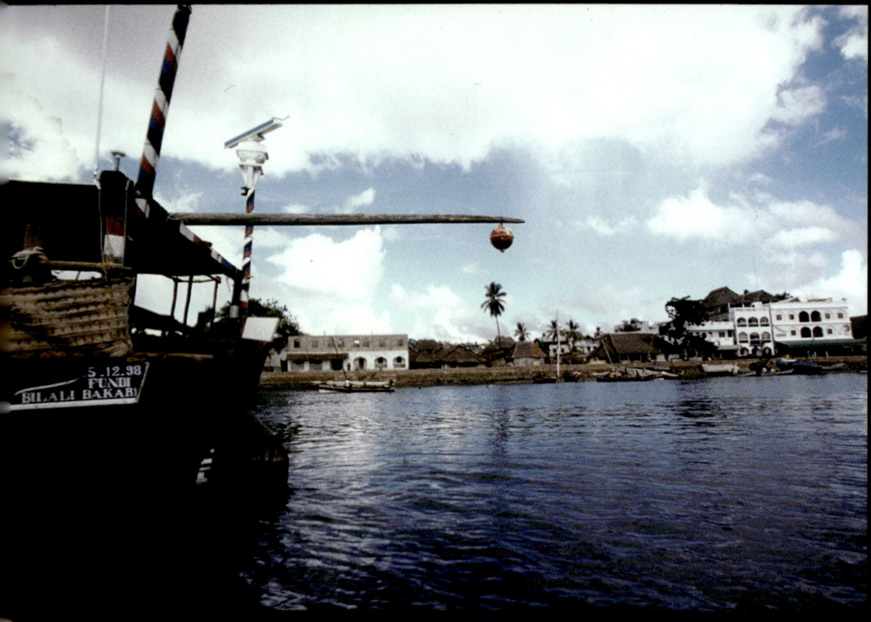
5.12.98
FUNDI
BILALI BAKARI

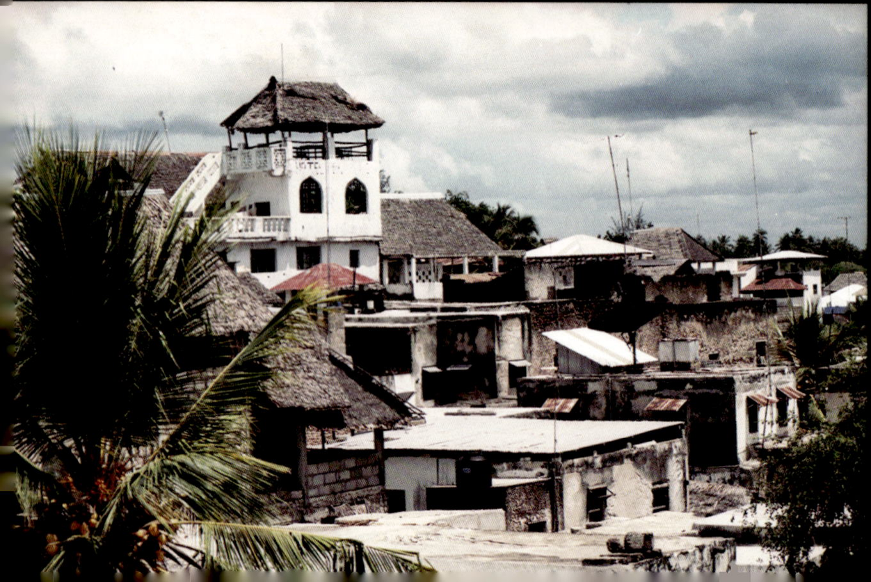

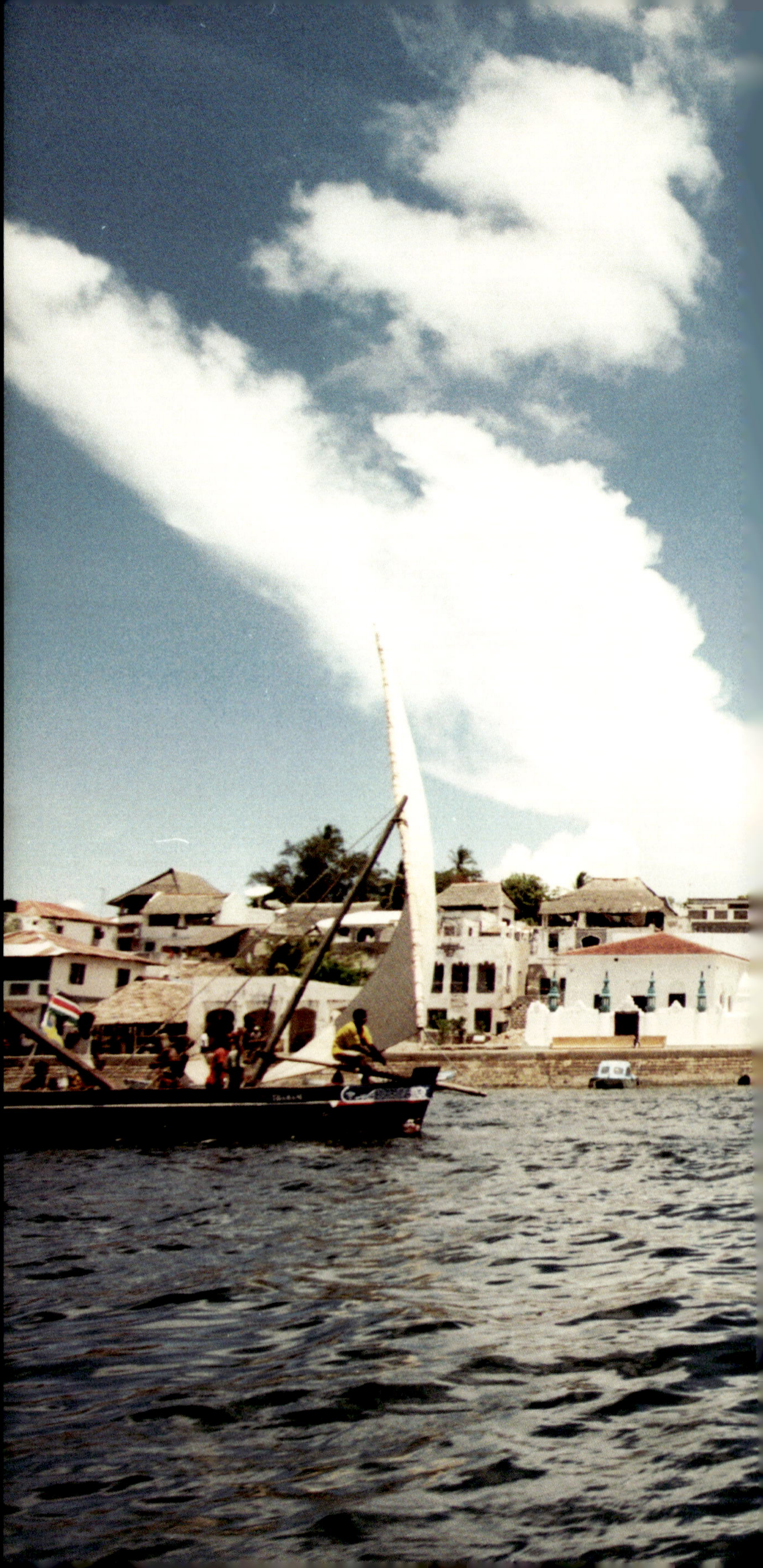

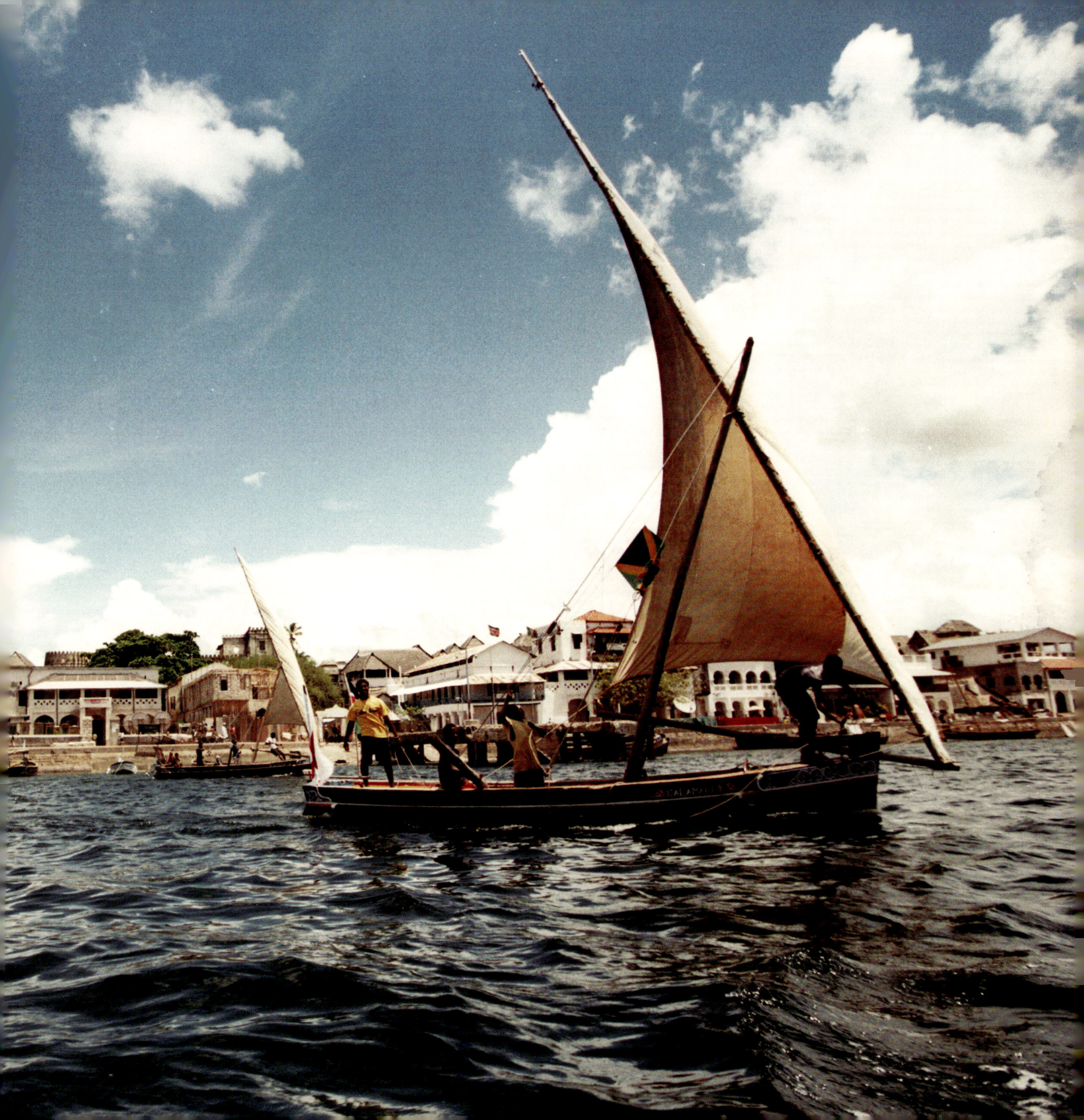

198 Safari Cuisine

BBQ'd lobster with a smoked sweet pepper and chili marinade, a lemon and basil beurre blanc and polenta chips

RECIPE

Serves 4 people

Ingredients

- 2 large lobsters
- 2 red peppers
- 4 red bullet chilies
- ½ cup olive oil
- ¼ cup red wine vinegar
- 1 tbsp brown sugar
- 2 cloves garlic
- 1 rosemary sprig
- 5 tbsp butter
- Juice of 1 lemon
- ½ cup cream
- 1 cup polenta
- ½ litre water
- 1 cup milk
- ½ cup grated parmesan
- Seasoning

Method

1. Prepare the lobster by cutting it in half down the middle and washing out the head section. Place in the fridge until needed.
2. For the marinade: Place the red peppers and the bullet chilies over an open fire and char the skins completely. Then remove them, and place in a plastic bag to steam in their own heat.
3. Meanwhile, boil the water and add the milk. Then add 2 tbsp of butter. When boiling slowly, whisk in the polenta until the mixture begins to thicken.
4. Cook this out for 5 minutes until thick, and add the parmesan cheese.
5. Spread the polenta out a tray, so it is about 1-inch thick, and allow to cool.
6. Return to the peppers and bullet chilies. Wash off the charred skins and extract the seeds. Chop finely.
7. Put the peppers and chilies into a blender with the olive oil, the vinegar, the brown sugar and the garlic.
8. Blend until a sauce-like consistency is achieved. Then add the rosemary and allow to sit.
9. For the beurre blanc: Melt the remaining butter and whisk the cream into it. Then whisk in the lemon juice gradually to make sure it does not split. Set aside.
10. Cut the cooled polenta into chips and deep fry until golden brown.
11. Place the lobsters on the grill in their shells. Apply a good basting of the marinade. Turn the lobsters, from shell-side to flesh-side, at least 4 times, basting the flesh each time. They will take 5–7 minutes to cook.
12. Season to taste and serve with the beurre blanc and polenta chips.

Tips/Pointers

Preparing the lobsters with marinade in advance will allow the flavour to infuse, making the final dish much tastier. Use of an open coal fire will further enhance the flavour of the dish.

Lamu 199

L A M U

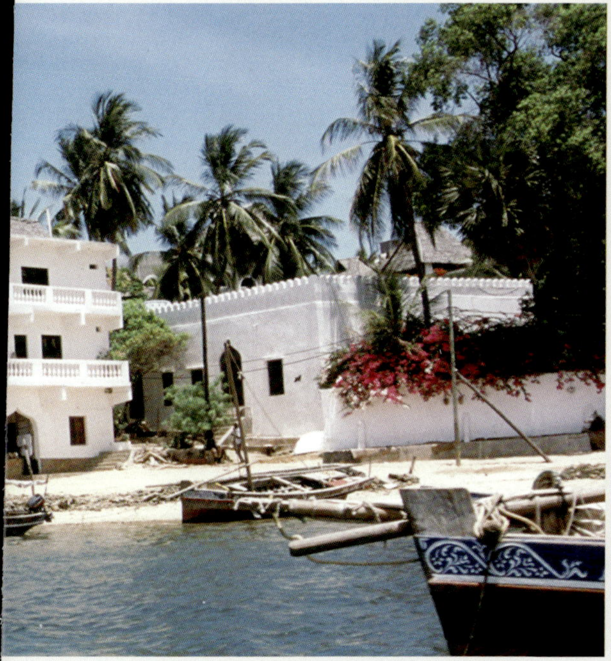
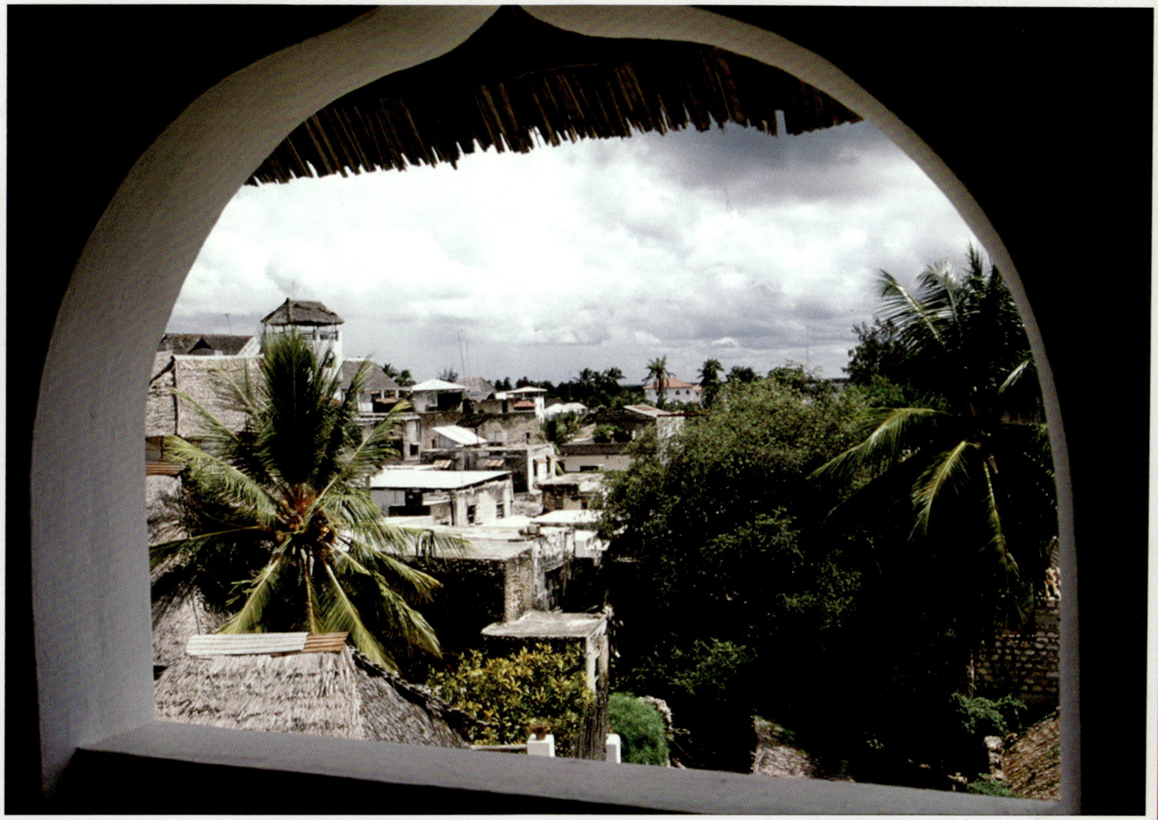
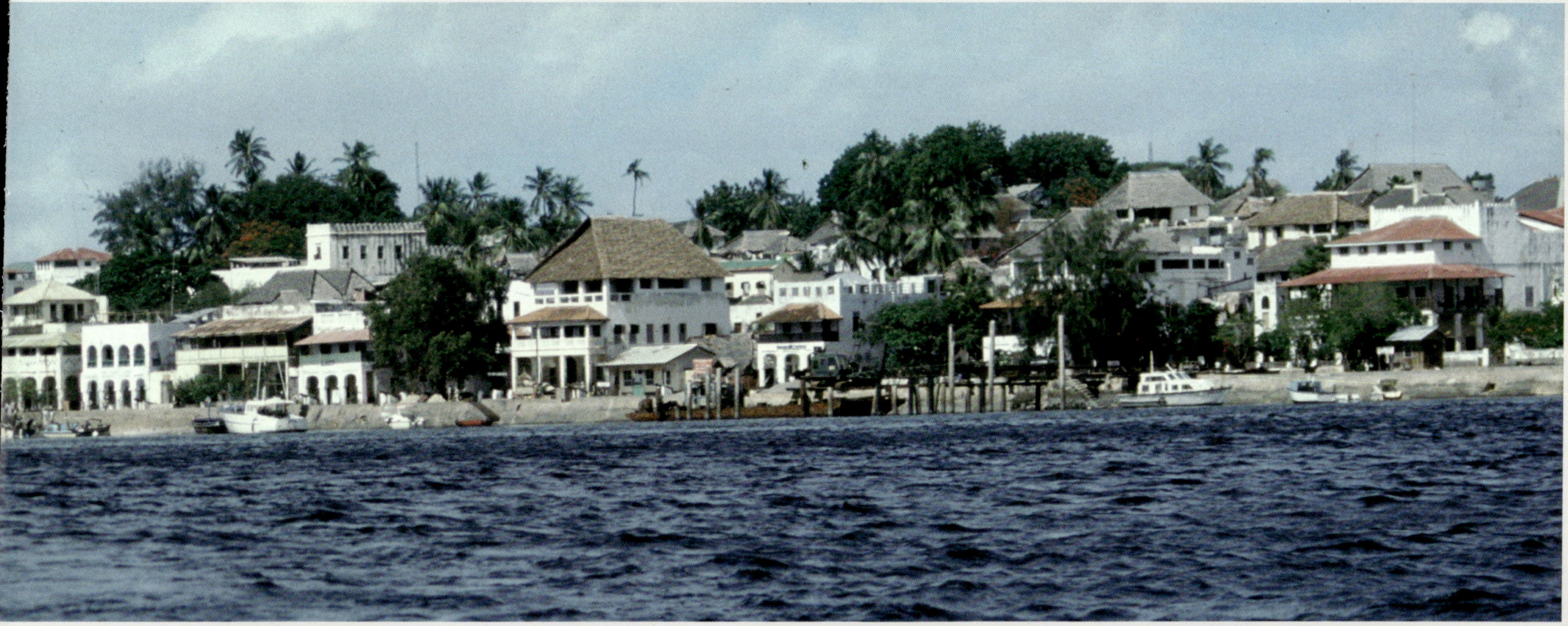

Safari Cuisine

Pear and frangipane tart with clotted cream

RECIPE

Serves 4 people

Ingredients

- 300 g ready-made puff pastry
- 1 egg yolk to glaze
- 3 ripe pears
- 2 tbsp castor sugar
- 3 tbsp water
- 1 cinnamon stick
- Juice of 1 lemon

For the frangipane

- 3 tbsp soft butter
- 3 tbsp icing sugar
- 1 egg beaten
- 3 tbsp ground almonds
- 2 tbsp flour
- 1 tsp amaretto

Method

1. Roll out the pastry and cut a circle of diameter 20 cm for the tart. Score a 2-cm border around the edge and glaze with egg wash.
2. Make a sugar syrup, with the sugar, the lemon juice and the cinnamon.
3. For the frangipane: Beat the butter and the sugar together. Slowly add the egg until it is incorporated, then add the almonds, the flour and the amaretto.
4. Peel and core the pears. Slice thinly, and place in the sugar syrup.
5. Spread a thin layer of frangipane over the pastry and arrange the pears. Place in an oven and bake until the pears are soft
6. Brush the pears with remaining the sugar syrup and serve with clotted cream.

Tips/Pointers

Be careful not to use too much frangipane on the tart. If you do, it may run when it expands, spoiling the appearance of the tart.

Lamu